Cambridge English

EMPOWER

COMBO A
STUDENT'S BOOK

B1+

Adrian Doff, Craig Thaine
Herbert Puchta, Jeff Stranks, Peter Lewis-Jones
with Rachel Godfrey and Gareth Davies

This page is intentionally left blank

Contents

STUDENT'S BOOK

Map of Student's Book	4
Unit 1 Talk	7
Unit 2 Modern life	19
Unit 3 Relationships	31
Unit 4 Personality	43
Unit 5 The natural world	55
Communication Plus	127
Grammar Focus	132
Vocabulary Focus	152
Audioscripts	162
Phonemic symbols and Irregular verbs	174

WORKBOOK

Map of Workbook	2
Unit 1 Talk	4
Unit 2 Modern life	10
Unit 3 Relationships	16
Unit 4 Personality	22
Unit 5 The natural world	28
Vox pop video	64
Audioscripts	72
Answer key	77

Contents

Lesson and objective	Grammar	Vocabulary	Pronunciation	Everyday English
Unit 1 Talk				
Getting started Talk about communication				
1A Talk about different forms of communication	Subject and object questions	Communication	Sound and spelling: /ɪ/ and /iː/	
1B Describe experiences in the present	Present simple and present continuous	Gradable and extreme adjectives	Sentence stress: gradable and extreme adjectives	
1C Give and respond to opinions			Word groups	Giving and responding to opinions
1D Write a guide				
Review and extension More practice		WORDPOWER *yourself*		
Unit 2 Modern life				
Getting started Talk about the workplace				
2A Talk about experiences of work and training	Present perfect simple and past simple	Work	Present perfect and past simple: *I've worked / I worked*	
2B Talk about technology	Present perfect simple and present perfect continuous	Technology	Sentence stress: main verb / auxiliary verb	
2C Make and respond to suggestions			Sentence stress	Making and responding to suggestions
2D Write an email giving news				
Review and extension More practice		WORDPOWER *look*		
Unit 3 Relationships				
Getting started Talk about relationships				
3A Talk about a friendship	Narrative tenses	Relationships	Linking sounds	
3B Talk about families	*used to, usually*	Family; Multi-word verbs	Sentence stress: multi-word verbs	
3C Tell a story			Stress in word groups	Telling a story
3D Write about someone's life				
Review and extension More practice		WORDPOWER *have*		
Unit 4 Personality				
Getting started Talk about people				
4A Describe people and their abilities	Modals and phrases of ability	Ability	Stress in modal verbs	
4B Describe feelings	Articles	*-ed / -ing* adjectives; Personality adjectives	Sound and spelling: final *-ed* in adjectives	
4C Offer and ask for help			Intonation in question tags	Offering and asking for help
4D Write an informal online advert				
Review and extension More practice		WORDPOWER *so* and *such*		
Unit 5 The natural world				
Getting started Talk about endangered animals				
5A Talk about the future	Future forms	Environmental issues	Sound and spelling: *a*	
5B Talk about *if* and *when*	Zero conditional and first conditional	The natural world	Consonant clusters	
5C Give reasons, results and examples			Voiced and unvoiced consonants	Giving reasons, results and examples
5D Write a discussion essay				
Review and extension More practice		WORDPOWER *problem*		

Communication Plus   p.127   Grammar Focus   p.132   Vocabulary Focus   p.152

Listening and Video	Reading	Speaking	Writing
A talk: communicating across the generations	Article: *How do you communicate?*	Things you have done recently	
	Article: *Can you really learn a language in 22 hours?*	Learning a foreign language	
At the flower shop		Giving and responding to opinions; Using *me too, me neither*	Unit Progress Test
Conversation: learning vocabulary	Article: *What kind of learner are you?*	Ways of learning vocabulary	A guide Introducing a purpose; Referring pronouns
Radio report: likeability	Article: *Not the best interview I've ever had!*	Work-related experiences	
	Article: *What's your favourite app?*	Interviewing classmates about technology	
A problem		Making and responding to suggestions; Sounding sympathetic or pleased	Unit Progress Test
Conversation: life changes	An email about a new job	Life changes	An informal email Adding new information
	Film review: '*Untouchable*' – the true story of an unlikely friendship	The story of a friendship	
Two monologues: being a twin		Family traditions	
A mistake		Reacting to what people say; Telling a story	Unit Progress Test
Conversation: grandparents	An email about how grandparents met	A member of your family	A biography Describing time
Radio programme: successful people	Article: *What happens to talented children when they grow up?*	Becoming successful at something	
	Article: *Why the world needs introverts*	A time when you experienced strong feelings	
Asking for help		Question tags; Offering and asking for help	Unit Progress Test
Three monologues: websites	Three online adverts	Using the internet to buy and sell things	An informal online advert The language of adverts
Conversation: an environmental project	Web page: *The Whitley Fund for Nature*	Predictions about the future	
Interview: inventions inspired by nature	Article: *Animals have adapted to survive everywhere*	The best place to experience natural beauty	
Talking about possible jobs		Reasons, results and examples; Giving yourself time to think	Unit Progress Test
Monologue: rescuing whales	An essay about water pollution	A quiz about whales	A discussion essay Organising an essay; Signposting language

Audioscripts   p.162   **Phonemic symbols and Irregular verbs**   p.174

This page is intentionally left blank

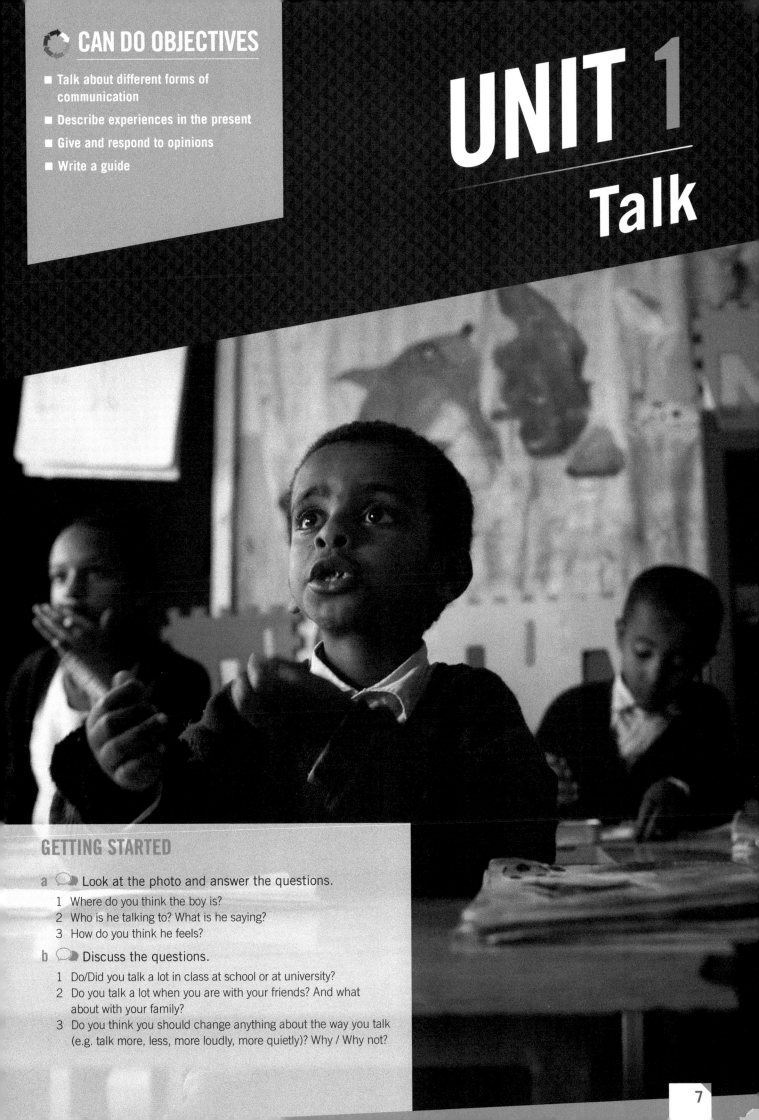

CAN DO OBJECTIVES

- Talk about different forms of communication
- Describe experiences in the present
- Give and respond to opinions
- Write a guide

UNIT 1
Talk

GETTING STARTED

a 💬 Look at the photo and answer the questions.

1 Where do you think the boy is?
2 Who is he talking to? What is he saying?
3 How do you think he feels?

b 💬 Discuss the questions.

1 Do/Did you talk a lot in class at school or at university?
2 Do you talk a lot when you are with your friends? And what about with your family?
3 Do you think you should change anything about the way you talk (e.g. talk more, less, more loudly, more quietly)? Why / Why not?

1A Keeping in touch

Learn to talk about different forms of communication

G Subject and object questions
V Communication

1 VOCABULARY Communication

a 💬 Look at photos a–e below and answer the questions using words from the box.

1 How are the people communicating?

> face to face   expressing feelings
> giving a presentation   interviewing
> telling a joke   keeping in touch
> speaking in public   giving opinions

2 When was the last time you were in a similar situation to each of the photos?

3 Which situations in the photos do you enjoy? Which don't you enjoy? Why?

b ▶1.2 **Pronunciation** Do the <u>underlined</u> vowels have a long or a short sound? Listen and check.

1 expressing f<u>ee</u>lings
2 interview<u>i</u>ng
3 sp<u>ea</u>king in publ<u>i</u>c
4 k<u>ee</u>ping in touch
5 g<u>i</u>ving op<u>i</u>nions

c ▶1.2 Listen again and repeat the phrases.

d ▶ Now go to Vocabulary Focus 1A on p.152

2 READING

a 💬 Read *How do <u>you</u> communicate?* on p.9 and answer the questions.

1 Which generation are you?
2 How many of these generations are there in your family?
3 Which generation are most of the people where you work or study?

b 💬 Read the article again and match quotes 1–4 with generations a–d.

1 ☐ 'Let's talk about this over lunch tomorrow.'
2 ☐ 'I had a lovely letter from Emma. I'll write a long letter back at the weekend.'
3 ☐ 'My Facebook status got 62 likes!'
4 ☐ 'Sorry, I haven't got time for this. Just tell me what you want.'

a Veterans
b Baby Boomers
c Generation X
d Millennials

c 💬 Think about yourself and people of different generations that you know. Do you agree with the descriptions?

HOW DO YOU COMMUNICATE?

What do we all want from life? As well as love and money, most of us want someone to understand us. But we don't communicate in the same way. People born at different times have very different styles of communication. Which generation are you?

VETERANS

Born before 1945, 'Veterans' are the oldest and most experienced members of society. They think that family life is important and prefer traditional forms of communication. 'Veterans' are the richest generation, possibly because they worked hard and were loyal employees.

BABY BOOMERS

A large number of babies were born after 1945. (In the USA, the peak of the baby boom was in 1957, when eight babies were born every minute!) This increase in births was called a 'boom', which gave the name to a generation. These people have money and good jobs. Many are in positions of power. They are optimists and like face-to-face communication.

GENERATION X

'Generation X' was born after 1965. They are independent thinkers and want to be different from their parents. They have seen the introduction of the home computer, video games, satellite TV and, of course, the internet, so they are good at adapting to changes. This generation is busy – they don't want to wait to hear what you say.

MILLENNIALS

'Millennials' were born after 1980. They are confident, they like computers, and work well in teams. Family and friends are more important than work, but they spend a lot of time online. In fact, 65% of Millennials say that losing their phone or computer would change their daily routine more than losing their car.

3 GRAMMAR
Subject and object questions

a Look at the questions and answers and underline the correct words in rules a–c.

1 Which of the generations **grew up** in the digital age?
   Millennials.
2 What do we **want** from life?
   Someone to understand us.

  a The answer to question 1 is the *subject / object* of the verb in **bold**.
  b The answer to question 2 is the *subject / object* of the verb in **bold**.
  c We use the auxiliary verbs *do*, *does*, *did* in *subject / object* questions.

b Are the questions below subject or object questions?

1 Who do I give this to?
2 What happened to your leg?
3 Which of these books do you want to borrow?
4 Who gave you the flowers?
5 Which car uses less petrol?
6 What did he say to you?

c ▶ Now go to Grammar Focus 1A on p.132

d Make questions with the words below.

1 Who / phone / you / yesterday?
   _____
2 Who / you / email / yesterday?
   _____
3 What / you and your friends / talk about?
   _____
4 What / make / you and your friends / laugh?
   _____
5 Which of your friends / you / see / every day?
   _____
6 Which of your friends / know / you / best?
   _____

e 💬 Discuss the questions from 3d. Ask follow-up questions.

Who phoned you yesterday?

My mum phoned me.

What did you talk about?

4 LISTENING

a 💬 Talk about family, friends or colleagues. What problems do you think different generations might have when they communicate?

> Older people sometimes think younger people are rude because they use more informal language.

b ▶1.7 Listen to someone talking about communication across the generations. Tick (✓) the things he mentions.

1 ☐ Millennials like connecting with people online.
2 ☐ Millennials and Veterans usually hate each other.
3 ☐ Generation Xers and Baby Boomers are similar because they both express how they feel.
4 ☐ Men and women have different ways of communicating.
5 ☐ We shouldn't get upset because other generations don't do what we expect.
6 ☐ It's important to use correct spelling when writing an email or text.
7 ☐ Different generations can learn a lot from each other.

c ▶1.7 Listen again and answer the questions.

1 Which generation is the speaker from?
2 What does Generation X believe communication is important for?
3 Which two generations don't want to talk about their personal goals?
4 What do Millennials expect other people to tell them?
5 What can younger generations offer to older generations?

d 💬 Which of the things are you best at? Which do you find very difficult? Talk about your ideas.

- talking to older people
- talking to younger people
- talking to people from different countries
- expressing my opinions
- expressing my feelings
- listening when people criticise me
- avoiding arguments

> I like talking to older people, but I'm not very good at talking to children.

5 SPEAKING

a Tick (✓) the things you have done recently. Make notes about the experience.

☐ met someone new
☐ had a communication problem with someone from another generation
☐ spoken to a large audience
☐ spoken a foreign language outside class
☐ met a famous person
☐ communicated with someone you don't know online
☐ sent or received a letter

b Look at the experiences your partner ticked and write three questions to ask them.

> *met someone new*
> *Who was it?*
> *Where were you?*
> *What did you talk about?*

c 💬 Ask your partner about their experiences.

> Who was the person you met?

> It was a new neighbour.

> What did you talk about?

> We talked about the neighbourhood. She asked me to recommend some shops in the area.

Learn to describe experiences in the present
- **G** Present simple and continuous
- **V** Gradable and extreme adjectives

Dy bannee diu   Guten Tag   **Gouden Dai   Salut**

Сәлем!   Bonjour   Halito   Salute

Hallo   Håfa ådai   **Ç'kemi**   Guuten takh

Héébee   Bon die!   **Servas**   Tungjatjeta

Ola   Ahoj   **Вітаю**   Góðan dag   Hoi

Salud   Hola / Bonos díes   **Bon dia**

1 SPEAKING

a 💬 Discuss the questions.
1 How many languages can you say 'Hello' in?
2 How many languages can you order a meal or have a simple conversation in?
3 What language are you best at (apart from your own)?

b Choose one idea below and continue using *because*. Write your idea.

Learning a new language is like …
- falling in love
- going on an endless journey *because*
- being a child *how you learn new!*
- growing plants in a garden
- learning a musical instrument

Learning a language is like falling in love, because it's exciting at the beginning, and then it becomes hard work.

c 💬 Read your sentences to each other. Do you agree with each other's ideas?

d 💬 Look at photos a–d and discuss the questions.
1 What are the advantages and disadvantages of each way of learning a language?
2 Which have you tried? Have you tried any other ways?

11

2 READING

a Read *Can you really learn a language in 22 hours?* quickly and answer the questions.

1 What is Memrise?
2 Why is Jon Foster using it?
3 How much has he learnt?

b Read the article again and choose the correct answers for questions 1–4.

1 The writer wants to learn Lingala because he …
  a loves new languages.
  b wants to talk with the people who speak it.
  c wants to try Memrise.
2 Ed Cooke wants learners to …
  a enjoy learning more.
  b improve quickly.
  c do more vocabulary practice.
3 'Mem' is …
  a the Lingalese word for 'engine'.
  b a translation of a new word.
  c a picture that helps people remember new words.

4 Where do the mems come from?
  a Ed Cooke creates them.
  b Users can create mems for themselves and other users.
  c Every user creates mems only for themselves.

c Match the words in **bold** in the article with meanings 1–8 below.

1 getting better
2 changes a word from one language into another
3 what someone wants to do
4 learnt something so that you remembered it exactly
5 something difficult which tests your ability
6 able to communicate freely and easily
7 to make someone remember something
8 do something again

d 💬 Would you like to use Memrise? Why / Why not?

CAN YOU REALLY LEARN A LANGUAGE IN 22 hours?

WE ALL KNOW THAT PEOPLE LEARN BETTER IF THEY ENJOY LEARNING.
Jon Foster reports on an app that makes learning a new language like playing a game.

I've never been much good at languages. But next month, I'm travelling to a remote area of Central Africa and my **aim** is to know enough Lingala – one of the local languages – to have a conversation. I wasn't sure how I was going to manage this – until I discovered a way to spend just a few minutes, a few times a day, learning all the vocabulary I'm going to need.

To be honest, normally when I get a spare moment at home, I go on Facebook or play games on my phone. But, at the moment, I'm using those short breaks for something more useful. I'm learning a foreign language. And thanks to Memrise, the app I'm using, it feels just like a game.

'People often stop learning things because they feel they're not **making progress** or because it all feels like too much hard work,' says Ed Cooke, one of the people who created Memrise. 'We're trying to create a form of learning experience that is fun and is something you'd want to do instead of watching TV.'

And Memrise is fun. It's a **challenge**. It gives you a few new words to learn and these are 'seeds' which you plant in your 'greenhouse'. (This represents your short-term memory.) When you practise the words, you 'water your plants' and they grow. When the app believes that you have really remembered a word, it moves the word to your 'garden'. You get points as your garden grows, so you can compare yourself to other Memrise users. I want to get a high score and go to the next level. And if I forget to log on, the app sends me emails that **remind** me to 'water my plants'.

The app uses two principles about learning. The first is that people remember things better when they link them to a picture in their mind. Memrise **translates** words into your own language, but it also encourages you to use 'mems' – images that help you remember new words. You can use mems which other users have created or you can create your own. I **memorised** *motele*, the Lingalan word for 'engine', using a mem I created – I imagined an old engine in a motel room.

The second principle is that we need to stop after studying words and then **repeat** them again later, leaving time between study sessions. Memrise helps you with this, because it's the kind of app you only use for five or ten minutes a day.

I've learnt hundreds of Lingalan words with Memrise. I know this won't make me a **fluent** speaker, but I hope I'll be able to do more than just smile and look stupid when I meet people in the Congo.

Now, why am I still sitting here writing this? I need to go and water my vocabulary!

motele

3 GRAMMAR
Present simple and continuous

a Match present simple sentences a–c with uses 1–3.

2 a When I get a spare moment at home, I normally **go** on Facebook or **play** games on my phone.

3 b I **know** this won't make me a fluent speaker.

1 c People **learn** better if they enjoy learning.

We can use the present simple:

1 to talk about things which are generally true (sentence ___)
2 to talk about habits and routines (sentence ___)
3 with state verbs – verbs about thoughts (e.g. *understand*), feelings (e.g. *want*) and possession (e.g. *own*). (sentence ___)

b Match present continuous sentences a–c with uses 1–3.

2 a I'**m learning** a foreign language.

1 b Now, why **am** I still **sitting** here writing this?

3 c Young people **are spending** more and more time playing on the computer.

We can use the present continuous to talk about:

1 actions in progress at the same time as speaking/writing (sentence ___)
2 actions in progress around (before and after) the time of speaking/writing (sentence ___)
3 changing situations (sentence ___)

c ▶ Now go to Grammar Focus 1B on p.132

d 💬 Make questions with the words below. Then discuss the questions.

1 you / think / you / communicate / well in your own language?
2 How often / you / hear / foreign languages where you live?
3 you / think / you / have / a good memory?
4 What / helps / you / learn / English grammar?
5 What / you / thinking / about / right now?
6 you / preparing / for an exam at the moment?
7 more people / learning / languages in your country than before?

> Do you think you communicate well in your own language?

> I think so, but I prefer writing to speaking.

e ▶ Communication 1B 💬 Student A: Look at the picture on p.127. Student B: Look at the picture on p.129. Describe your picture to your partner. Find eight differences between your pictures.

4 VOCABULARY
Gradable and extreme adjectives

a ⏵1.10 Listen and underline the correct words.

1 James is *a bit* / <u>*very*</u> tired.
2 Linda *likes* / <u>*doesn't like*</u> the book.
3 Tony thinks the girl can do something *quite* / <u>*very*</u> impressive.
4 The teacher thinks Olivier <u>*will*</u> / *won't* be able to pronounce 'squirrel'.

b ⏵1.10 Complete the sentences with the words in the box. Listen again and check.

exhausted   fantastic   impossible   useless

1 I'm absolutely _____ .
2 This book's _____ .
3 That's _____! I can only speak one language.
4 It's _____! I'll never get it right.

c Read about gradable and extreme adjectives. Complete sentences 1–6 with *absolutely* or *very*.

> • With some adjectives (*good, bad, difficult*), we can use words like *quite, very, really* and *extremely* to make their meaning stronger or weaker (e.g. *His pronunciation is quite good. The exam was extremely difficult.*).
> • Other adjectives already have a strong or extreme meaning (e.g. *perfect, useless*). We can use words like *completely* or *absolutely* before these adjectives to add emphasis (*Her English is absolutely perfect.*).

1 Online dictionaries are often very useful.
2 That cake's really/quite enormous.
3 I think Anna's very confident.
4 I went for a swim in the river and the water was absolutely/completely freezing.
5 There are only seven houses in my village – it's absolutely tiny.
6 It's very important to learn pronunciation as well as vocabulary.

d ⏵1.11 Pronunciation Listen and check. Then answer the questions below.

1 Which word is stressed in each sentence?
2 Do we usually stress gradable adjectives or extreme adjectives?

e ⏵1.11 Listen again and repeat the sentences.

f ▶ Now go to Vocabulary Focus 1B on p.153

5 SPEAKING

a 💬 Talk about learning a foreign language. Use the questions below.

- What do you want to be able to do with English?
- What level of English do you hope to reach?
- How often do you review what you have learned?
- How often do you watch or read things in English?
- How often do you communicate with native speakers?
- What are you doing at the moment to learn English?
- Are you having any problems with English at the moment?

b Report back to the class about what you found out.

1C Everyday English
Well, if you ask me …

Learn to give and respond to opinions
- **P** Word groups
- **S** Using *me too* / *me neither*

1 LISTENING

a 💬 Discuss the questions.

1 Do you enjoy meeting new people?
2 Do you usually decide what you think of someone from a first impression? Or do you get to know them first?

b 💬 Look at the photo above. What do you think the customer is buying?

c ▶1.14 Watch or listen to Part 1 to check.

d ▶1.14 Watch or listen again and <u>underline</u> the correct answers.

1 Becky is buying flowers because she's *going to someone's house* / *getting married*.
2 She doesn't want roses because *she doesn't like them* / *they're too romantic*.
3 She *likes* / *doesn't like* the tulips.
4 She will *buy flowers in another shop* / *come back later*.

e 💬 Look at the photo below right and answer the questions.

1 Where are the people?
2 What are they doing?

f ▶1.15 Watch or listen to Part 2 to check.

g ▶1.15 Watch or listen again and answer the questions.

1 What will happen to the bookshop?
2 What problem will this cause for Rachel?
3 What is Mark's advice?
4 What does Rachel say happened at work?

2 USEFUL LANGUAGE
Giving and responding to opinions

a ▶1.16 Listen and complete the sentences with one word.

1 Well, in my _____, roses are always a good option.
2 I _____ something like tulips might be better.
3 I _____ it's going to be impossible with another florist's in the same street.
4 Well, if you _____ me, it's not worth worrying about until we know for sure.

b Put the words in the correct order to make more formal phrases for giving an opinion.

1 it / me / seems / that / to   2 as / as / concerned / far / I'm

c Look at five ways of responding to an opinion. Does the speaker agree (A) or disagree (D)?

1 I know what you mean, but … ___
2 I know exactly what you mean. ___
3 I'm not so sure about that. ___
4 That's right. ___
5 I see where you're coming from, but … ___

d Tick (✓) the sentences you agree with. Change the other sentences so you agree with them.

1 ☐ English is an easy language to learn.
2 ☐ It's difficult to communicate with older people.
3 ☐ First impressions are important when you meet someone.

e 💬 Give your opinions from 2d and respond.

3 PRONUNCIATION Word groups

a ▶ 1.17 Listen to these sentences. Notice where the speaker pauses to make the message clearer.

I'm really worried. Jo phoned today with some bad news.

b ▶ 1.18 Listen to this similar sentence. Does the speaker pause?

I'm really worried I won't make enough money.

c Look at the conversation. Write // where you think the speakers pause.

Rachel	Oh, I'm sorry, love. I'm just a bit worried. Jo phoned today and said that the old bookshop is going to be turned into another florist's.
Mark	The bookshop on the corner? I didn't know they'd sold it.
Rachel	Me neither. But what am I going to do? It's hard enough already to make money, but I think it's going to be impossible with another florist's in the same street.

d ▶ 1.19 Listen and check.

4 CONVERSATION SKILLS
Using *me too / me neither*

a ▶ 1.20 Listen and <u>underline</u> the correct words.

1

Mark	The bookshop on the corner? I didn't know they'd sold it.
Rachel	Me *too / neither*.

2

Mark	Hey, don't worry about it. Let's just forget about work. Personally, I need a relaxing evening!
Rachel	Me *too / neither*.

> 1 We use *Me too* and *Me neither* to say we agree or are in the same situation.
> 2 We use *Me too* after a positive sentence.
> 3 We use *Me neither* after a negative sentence.

b Complete the exchanges with appropriate responses.

1 **A** I need a nice cup of tea.
   B _____

2 **A** I don't really like watching football.
   B _____ .

3 **A** I wasn't invited to the wedding.
   B _____ .

4 **A** I'm looking forward to the party.
   B _____ .

5 **A** I don't really eat chocolate.
   B _____ .

6 **A** I hate going out in the rain.
   B _____ .

5 LISTENING

a 💬 Look at the photo. What is happening? What do you think will happen next?

b ▶ 1.21 Watch or listen to Part 3 and check your ideas.

c 💬 Discuss the questions.

1 How would you feel in Becky's situation?
2 How would you feel in Rachel's situation?
3 Have you ever made a bad first impression?

6 SPEAKING

a Think of an example of:

- a good way to meet new people
- a good way to make a good first impression
- a good topic of conversation with someone you don't know well
- a good reason to dislike someone you've just met

b 💬 Discuss your ideas in 6a.

> If you ask me, the best way to make a good impression is to use people's names a lot.

> I'm not so sure about that.

⟳ Unit Progress Test

CHECK YOUR PROGRESS

You can now do the Unit Progress Test.

1D Skills for Writing
Different ways of learning

1 SPEAKING AND LISTENING

a 💬 What do you think are some good ways to learn new vocabulary in English? Talk about the ideas in photos a–e, or your own ideas.

b ▶1.22 Listen to Maria and Gilberto talking about learning vocabulary. Are you more like Maria or Gilberto?

c ▶1.22 Listen again and answer the questions.
1 What system does Maria use for learning vocabulary?
2 What system does Maria's sister use?
3 Does Gilberto think either system will work for him?

d Read the descriptions of each style. What kinds of learners are Maria and Gilberto?

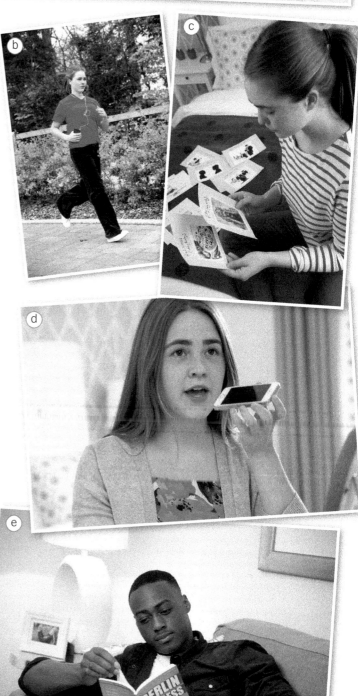

Visual learners

They prefer to learn by seeing or reading things and need to see new information written down.

Auditory learners

They prefer to learn by listening to new information. They also like to talk about the new things they've learnt.

Kinaesthetic learners

They prefer to learn by doing something. They don't like sitting still for very long.

e 💬 Talk about what kind of learner you are and why.

2 READING

a Read *What kind of learner are you?* on p.17. Answer the questions.
1 Which of Maria's ideas is mentioned?
2 Does the article talk more about understanding new information or remembering it?

b Read the article again. Make notes about the key study techniques for each learning style.
• visual • auditory • kinaesthetic

WHAT KIND OF LEARNER ARE YOU?

Different people learn in different ways. In order to find the most useful way to learn new information, it's a good idea to think about the kind of learner you are: visual, auditory or kinaesthetic. Knowing your learning style helps you study more effectively, so you remember what you have learnt more easily. Remember, you don't just learn when you study – this advice can also be useful for learning at work or in your free time.

VISUAL LEARNERS

It helps to study in a quiet place so that you can concentrate. To learn new information, try to think of an image in your head, or make a diagram to highlight different points. [1]**This technique helps your memory and it means you can find the information easily when you look at your notes again**.

AUDITORY LEARNERS

Going to a lecture is a good way for you to learn. Read your notes aloud, then cover them and try to say them again from memory. Also, try to use new words when you're talking to people. If you are studying words on a particular topic, you can listen to podcasts that include this vocabulary. [2]**These ideas should help you remember what you need to know.**

KINAESTHETIC LEARNERS

In order to learn new information, you need to be doing something. It helps to study in a place where you can walk around the room, touch things and move as freely as possible. Make sure you take regular breaks and go for a walk. [3]**This will help you to concentrate and remain interested in what you are studying.**

These descriptions are only a guide. Most people have a mixture of learning styles. To study successfully, you need to experiment and find the most suitable method.

3 WRITING SKILLS
Introducing a purpose; referring pronouns

a Look at these sentences from the article. Circle the words or phrases in the underlined parts which introduce the purpose in each sentence.

  1 <u>In order to find the most useful way to learn new information</u>, it's a good idea to think about the kind of learner you are …
  2 Knowing your learning style helps you study more effectively, <u>so you remember what you have learnt more easily</u>.
  3 <u>To learn new information</u>, try to think of an image in your head.

b <u>Underline</u> other examples of purpose words/ phrases in the article.

c Join the sentences using purpose words/ phrases. More than one answer is possible.

  1 I write the new words in a vocabulary notebook. I remember them.
  2 I practise pronunciation. I record myself saying words on my phone.
  3 I write grammar rules on a piece of paper. I understand them better.

d Look at sentences 1–3 in **bold** in the article and <u>underline</u> the correct words in the rules.

  a *This* and *these* refer to *ideas already mentioned / new ideas*.
  b In sentences 1 and 3, *this* refers back to *one word / a complete idea*.
  c We sometimes put *a noun / an adjective* after *this* and *these*.

4 WRITING A guide

a Think of a skill you know how to do well. It can be something to do with study, work, sport or a free-time activity. Make notes using these questions.

  1 How easy is it to learn this skill?
  2 What are the problems people have when learning it?
  3 What are good ways to learn this skill?
  4 Why are they good ways?

b Write a guide on how to learn this skill. Use words/phrases to introduce purpose and *this* or *these*, if possible, to refer back to ideas.

c 💬 Work in pairs. Read your partner's guide. How easy do you think it would be to learn their skill?

UNIT 1
Review and extension

1 GRAMMAR

a 🗩 Complete the questions. Then ask and answer the questions.

1 You live with someone.
   Who ___*do you live*___ with?
2 Something woke you up this morning.
   What _____ this morning?
3 You talk to someone every day.
   Who _____ every day?
4 You read something yesterday.
   What _____ yesterday?
5 Something has made you laugh recently.
   What _____ recently?
6 Someone speaks to you in English.
   Who _____ in English?
7 You know different ways of learning English.
   Which different ways of learning English _____?
8 Some ways of learning English work best for you.
   Which ways of learning English _____?

b Four of the sentences below have a mistake.
Tick (✓) the four correct sentences.

1 ☐ John's having a shower.
2 ☐ I think we need a new laptop. Are you agreeing?
3 ☐ I'm hardly ever writing letters.
4 ☐ You look sad, Maria. What do you think about?
5 ☐ Monkeys communicate with sounds.
6 ☐ I don't know at the moment.
7 ☐ Carrie doesn't work this week because she's ill.
8 ☐ I'm getting cold.

2 VOCABULARY

a Complete the sentences with the verbs in the box.

argue complain give express
keep persuade speak tell

1 Are you going to _____ about the terrible food?
2 Let's _____ in touch.
3 Can you _____ a joke?
4 I don't want to _____ a presentation.
5 He prefers to _____ his opinions in writing.
6 She's trying to _____ me to go on holiday with her.
7 When did you last _____ in public?
8 I try not to _____ with my boss – even when he's wrong!

b Match the extreme adjectives in the box with gradable adjectives 1–8.

awful brilliant enormous exhausted
filthy freezing furious tiny

1 big   _____   5 tired   _____
2 dirty _____   6 angry   _____
3 small _____   7 bad   _____
4 cold   _____   8 good   _____

3 WORDPOWER *yourself*

a Match sentence beginnings 1–6 with endings a–f.

1 ☐ Why do you keep **talking**
2 ☐ This room needs a lot of work, but you can **do**
3 ☐ Come in! **Make yourself**
4 ☐ Good luck at the interview! Just **be**
5 ☐ Bye! Have a wonderful time! **Look**
6 ☐ Are you OK? Have you

a **after yourself** and have fun – **enjoy yourself**!
b **yourself** and **tell yourself** 'I can do this!'.
c **to yourself**? Is it because you're **teaching yourself** German?
d **hurt yourself**?
e at home, and **help yourself** to food and drink.
f **it yourself** – you don't need to pay someone.

b Underline the correct words in the rule.

We use *yourself* in the phrases in **bold** in 3a because the object of the verb is *the same as* / *different from* the subject of the verb.

c Underline the correct words.

1 Is it possible to *help* / *teach* yourself how to swim?
2 You could pay someone to clean the car or you could *do* / *do it* yourself.
3 There's a lot of food in the fridge. Please *help* / *make* yourself.
4 Don't copy other people. *Be by* / *Be* yourself.
5 Sit down. Make yourself *to* / *at* home!
6 You should *tell* / *tell to* yourself 'I'm wonderful!' every day.

d Complete the questions with the correct form of the verbs in the box and *yourself*.

enjoy hurt look after talk to teach

1 Have you ever _____ how to do something? What was it? Was it easy or difficult to learn?
2 Do you _____? Do you eat well and get enough sleep?
3 Have you ever _____ at home? Did you have to go to hospital?
4 Do you ever _____? What do you say?
5 Are you _____ right now? If not, what would make you happy?

e 🗩 Discuss the questions in 3d.

↻ REVIEW YOUR PROGRESS

How well did you do in this unit? Write 3, 2 or 1 for each objective.
3 = very well   2 = well   1 = not so well

I CAN ...

talk about different forms of communication.	☐
describe experiences in the present.	☐
give and respond to opinions.	☐
write a guide.	☐

CAN DO OBJECTIVES

- Talk about experiences of work and training
- Talk about technology
- Make and respond to suggestions
- Write an email giving news

UNIT 2
Modern life

GETTING STARTED

a ▶1.23 Look at the photo. Where do you think the woman is? Listen and check your ideas.

b 💬 Discuss the questions.

1 What else do you think there might be in this office building? (Think of the furniture, rooms and entertainment.)
2 Would you like to work in an office building like this? Why / Why not?
3 What would your ideal workplace be like?

1 READING

a Discuss the questions.

1 Have you ever had a job interview?
2 Was it a good experience? Why / Why not?

b Read *Not the best interview I've ever had!* Who got the job? Who didn't get the job?

c Read the stories again. Match a–d with headings 1–4.

1 [a] Wrong word!
2 [c] Better to tell the truth
3 [d] The interviewer probably felt worse than me!
4 [b] An unlucky call

d Tell your partner which story you liked best. Have you had any embarrassing experiences like the ones in the stories?

> I've received a phone call at a bad moment.

> Really? What happened?

Not the best interview I've ever had!

Most people feel nervous when they go for a job interview, but some interviews are worse than others. Fortunately, they don't all end in disaster!

a 'They wanted to test how fast I could type. My fingers were over the keyboard, ready to type. The interviewer said 'Right click to open the file', but all I heard was 'Write click' so I typed 'click' on a window that was already open. I felt so embarrassed when I realised my mistake, but we both laughed and I got the job. I've worked there for eight months now.'
Laura

b 'I've never forgotten to switch my phone off in the cinema, but for some reason I forgot when I went for my first job interview. My friend phoned me to wish me good luck – right in the middle of the interview. Oops! I didn't get the job.'
Andy

c 'I've had lots of good interviews, but this one was a disaster. I had put on my CV that I could speak 'some French'. I learnt some French at school, but I've never really used it and my listening skills are really bad. The three interviewers began the interview by speaking to me in French, and I didn't understand a word. No, I didn't get the job, and yes, I've changed my CV!'
Dan

d 'I had a job interview with two people last week. One of them was leaning back on his chair when suddenly it fell right back and it was soon clear that he couldn't get up again. I didn't know if I should try to help or not and I was worried I was going to start laughing. Fortunately, the other interviewer asked me to wait outside the room for a minute, and then the interview carried on as if nothing had happened. Guess what? They've just offered me the job!'
Ellie

2 VOCABULARY Work

a Look at photos a–f below and match them with sentences 1–6.

1 🔲 Hundreds of people **applied for** the job but only six **candidates** were invited for an interview.
2 🔲 It's hard to balance family life and a **career**.
3 🔲 I'm proud of my practical skills and medical **knowledge**.
4 🔲 There are 200 **employees** in this organisation, but I'm only **in charge of** a small team.
5 🔲 I've got good **grades** but I haven't got much experience to put on my **CV**.
6 🔲 I've got a lot of **business contacts** who work for **employers** in different countries.

b Match the words in **bold** in 2a with these meanings.

1 the jobs you do during your working life
2 people you know who might be able to help your career
3 contacted a company asking for a job
4 people who work for a company
5 the results of your exams at school or university
6 the things you know from experience or study
7 people who are trying to get a job
8 responsible for something or someone
9 the people that you work for
10 a document which describes your education and the jobs you have done

c 💬 What do managers look for when they employ someone new? Choose the four qualities that you think are most important.

- creative thinking
- good grades
- work experience
- self-confidence
- good problem-solving skills
- a friendly personality
- the ability to work in a team
- a positive attitude to work
- practical skills

3 GRAMMAR

Present perfect simple and past simple

a Look at these sentences from the stories on p.20. Which verbs are in the present perfect and which is in the past simple?

1 I**'ve** never **forgotten** to switch my phone off in the cinema.
2 I**'ve had** lots of good interviews, but this one was a disaster.
3 I **had** a job interview with two people last week. *PS*
4 They**'ve** just **offered** me the job! *PPS*

b Underline the correct words to complete the rules.

1 We use the *past simple / present perfect* to talk about recent past events that have an effect on the present.
2 We use the *past simple / present perfect* to talk about our experiences.
3 We use the *past simple / present perfect* when we give details (e.g. when, where, etc.) or talk about specific past events.

c ▶1.24 Pronunciation Listen and choose the sentence you hear, a or b.

1 a I worked there for eight months.
  b I've worked there for eight months.
2 a I had lots of good interviews.
  b I've had lots of good interviews.

d ▶1.25 Listen and practise saying the sentences.

e ▶ Now go to Grammar Focus 2A on p.134

f Complete the sentences with the present perfect or past simple form of the verbs in brackets.

1 I *'ve never had* (never/have) a really terrible job interview.
2 Once, I *'ve forgot* (forget) to switch off my phone when I was at the cinema.
3 I don't have very much work experience, but I *'ve been* (be) in charge of a small team.
  I *'ve been* (be) the leader on a project at school.
4 I *'ve got* (get) some useful work experience last year.
5 I *'ve studied* (study) hard this year, so I hope I can pass my exams.
6 I *'ve been always* (always/be) able to express myself clearly since I was a child.
7 I *'ve already worked* (already/work) for more than three organisations.
8 I *knew* (know) what career I wanted when I was a child.

g 💬 Tell your partner which sentences are true for you and give more information.

> Number 1 is true for me. I've only had two or three job interviews, but they've all been OK.

4 LISTENING

a 💬 Think of five reasons why an employer might <u>not</u> offer a candidate a job. Compare your ideas with a partner.

b ▶️1.29 Listen to the beginning of a radio interview. Answer the questions.   *N S*

1 Are any of your ideas in 4a mentioned in the report?
2 What one quality does Nancy believe all employers are looking for at a job interview? *likeability*

c ▶️1.29 Listen again and complete each sentence with one or two words.

1 People with likeability can ~~*work well*~~ *work* with other people.
2 Nancy believes likeability is more important than other abilities in the first ~~*in*~~ *18 mon* *months* of a new job.
3 She advises job hunters to spend time with *other people*
4 Nancy encourages people to apply for jobs even if they don't have the right ~~*qualification*~~ ~~*impress*~~ *qualifications*
5 During an interview, it's important to ~~*impress*~~ the interviewers by showing that you're friendly, positive and can communicate well.

d ▶️1.30 Listen to five speakers. Do they agree that being likeable is more important than other skills? Write A (agree) or D (disagree).

Speaker 1 _A_   Speaker 3 _D_   Speaker 5 _D_
Speaker 2 _A_   Speaker 4 _A_

e ▶️1.30 Listen again and answer the questions.

1 According to Speaker 1, why don't people know that likeability is important? *employers not like to talk about it*
2 According to Speaker 2, what's the advantage of developing your 'soft skills'? ~~*Be good*~~ *ability to get work*
3 How does Speaker 3 behave towards his patients? *listening*
4 What problem does Speaker 4 have with 'soft skills'? ~~*he has no win*~~
5 According to Speaker 5, what are the most important things you can offer an organisation? *Education - working hard - practice*

f 💬 Discuss the questions.

1 Which do you think is more important when getting a new job – likeability or good qualifications? Why? Think of different kinds of jobs.
2 Do you think schools and colleges should help students develop 'soft skills'? How could they do this?

5 SPEAKING

a You are going to talk about your experiences. Tick (✓) three things you have done. Then make notes about your experiences.

- ☐ got qualifications (which?)
- ☐ learned practical skills (what?)
- ☐ studied/worked in a foreign country (where?)
- ☐ chosen a career
- ☐ worked for no money
- ☐ visited an interesting office or factory
- ☑ written a CV
- ☑ given a talk or presentation
- ☐ done some online learning
- ☑ studied or worked as part of a team
- ☐ been in charge of a project

b 💬 Take turns to talk about your work and training experiences. Ask questions to find out more information.

> I've been in charge of a project. It was a small team and we all worked well together.

> Was this at work or at school?

2B I've been playing on my phone all morning

1 VOCABULARY Technology

a 💬 Think of things you can do on a smartphone. Compare ideas with other students. Who has the most ideas?

b Match words 1–5 with definitions a–e.

1 [e] app   3 [d] icon   5 [a] username
2 [c] browser   4 [b] text message

a a name you need to type (with a password) to start using something
b a written message that you send from one phone to another
c a computer program that you use to read information on the internet
d a small picture on a computer/phone screen that you click on to open a program or an app
e a small computer program that you can download onto a mobile phone or other device

c Cross out the wrong verb in each group.

1 ~~turn off~~ / send / delete an email
2 download / ~~press~~ / ~~share~~ a video
3 ~~install~~ / share / ~~upload~~ some photos
4 install / download / ~~press~~ a new app
5 turn off / turn on / ~~delete~~ a phone
6 ~~upload~~ / press / click on a button or icon
7 connect to / ~~send~~ / browse the internet
8 type / change / ~~turn on~~ a password

d 💬 Think of five things that you've done recently using phrases from 1c. Tell a partner.

> I've just changed my email password.

> Why? Did you forget it?

e 💬 Discuss the questions.

1 What apps have you got on your phone or tablet?
2 Which apps do you like or use most?
3 Look at the apps on this page. What do you think they do?

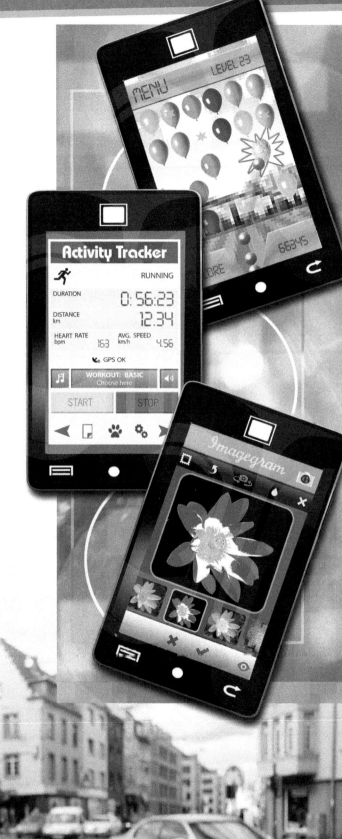

2 READING

a Read *What's your favourite app?* below and answer the questions.

Which app … ?
1 is good for music lovers
2 helps you learn about the stars
3 keeps you interested because you can keep improving
4 helps busy people organise themselves
5 helps you create and keep photos online
6 helps you make funny photos
7 is useful if you've got too many apps on your phone
8 records your fitness information

b Read the article again and answer the questions.
1 What do you get from ThingsToDo at the end of each week?
2 How do you find a planet with SkyWatch?
3 What changes can you make to photos with Imagegram?
4 Why does Enzo play Balloon Pop every day?
5 What information does ActivityTracker give you when you run?
6 What information can Tunespotter tell you about a song?
7 How can StopApp make your phone work better?
8 What kinds of photos does Luke think are funniest on Crazy Faces?

c 💬 Discuss the questions.
1 Do you use any apps like the ones in the article? Which ones? How useful are they?
2 Would you like to use any of the apps in the article? Which ones? Why?

3 GRAMMAR Present perfect simple and continuous

a Read sentences a–d. Then answer questions 1–5.
a **I've seen** photos where people have baby faces on adult bodies.
b **I've been playing** it on the bus every day.
c **I've been recommending** it to all my friends.
d **I've just installed** the ThingsToDo app.

1 Which sentences use the present perfect continuous?
2 Which sentence talks about one completed past activity (without mentioning a time)?
3 Which sentence talks about something the speaker has experienced?
4 Which sentences talk about activities which started in the past and are not finished yet?
5 Which sentences talk about something which happened regularly or more than once?

What's your favourite

I've just installed the ThingsToDo app. It's so easy to use – which is really important when you've got lots of things to do and not much time! You just create a list and then add items to it. Once a week it sends you a list of everything you've done. **Juan**

My favourite game at the moment is Balloon Pop. You select groups of coloured balloons and pop them. I've been playing it on the bus every day, because I always want to get to the next level – it's very addictive! **Enzo**

Have you heard about SkyWatch? It's great. You just point your phone at the night sky and it tells you what the stars are. You can also type in the name of a planet and the program tells you where to look for it. **Katya**

ActivityTracker is a great app for running. You just press the start button when you begin your workout and the app records your speed, distance and heart rate. After the workout, you can then upload your information to social networking websites and compare with your friends. I've never found an app as good as this before. **Fay**

I love Imagegram and I've been using it more and more recently. You can use different effects to make photos look different, like old-fashioned photos, or with brighter colours. Then you can store them online and share them with your friends. **Paul**

I've just downloaded Tunespotter. If you hear a song you like but you don't know what it is, you can use this app. It identifies the name of the song and the singer. And if you like it, you can buy the song really easily. I've had it for a week and I've been using it a lot. **Martin**

b Complete the sentences with the present perfect simple or present perfect continuous form of the verbs in brackets.
1 I ____ a new phone. (just/buy)
2 I ____ for my own name online. (never/search)
3 I ____ a lot of films in the last two weeks. (watch)
4 I ____ for a new tablet, but I haven't got enough money yet. (save up)
5 I ____ about not using my smartphone for a few weeks, just to see if I can survive! (think)

c ▶1.31 **Pronunciation** Listen to sentences 1–4 and <u>underline</u> the correct words in the rule.
1 I've used an app.
2 I haven't used an app.
3 I've been using an app.
4 I've just been using an app.

In present perfect sentences, we usually stress the *main verb* / *auxiliary verb*. If it is a negative sentence, or we add a word like *just*, then we *also* / *don't* stress the main verb.

d ▶1.31 Listen again and repeat the sentences.

e ▶ Now go to Grammar Focus 2B on p.134

f ◯ Are the sentences in 3b true for you? Change the false sentences so that they are true for you. Tell your partner about your sentences.

4 SPEAKING

a You are going to find out which of your classmates is most addicted to technology. Think of six questions to ask about what people have used recently. Use the topics below or your own ideas.

---

apps/mobile phones   computer games
the internet   social-networking sites

How often have you been on Facebook in the last two days?
What apps have you been using recently?

b ◯ Use your questionnaire to interview different people in the class. Who has used the most and least technology recently? Who in the class do you think is a technology addict?

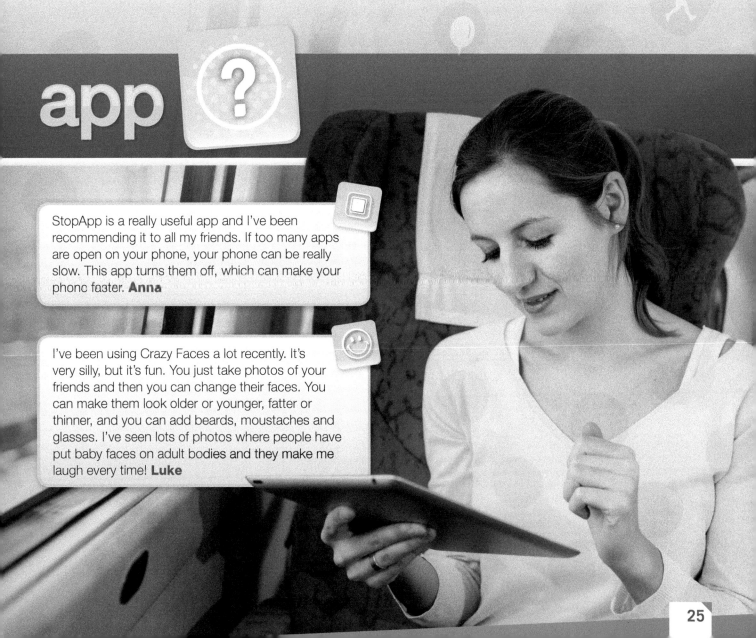

app ?

StopApp is a really useful app and I've been recommending it to all my friends. If too many apps are open on your phone, your phone can be really slow. This app turns them off, which can make your phone faster. **Anna**

I've been using Crazy Faces a lot recently. It's very silly, but it's fun. You just take photos of your friends and then you can change their faces. You can make them look older or younger, fatter or thinner, and you can add beards, moustaches and glasses. I've seen lots of photos where people have put baby faces on adult bodies and they make me laugh every time! **Luke**

Learn to make and respond to suggestions
- **P** Sentence stress
- **S** Sounding sympathetic or pleased

1 LISTENING

a 💬 Talk about a problem you have had recently. What was the problem? Did you solve it? How?

b 💬 Look at the photos. What has just happened?

c ▶1.33 Watch or listen to Part 1 to check.

d 💬 What do you think Rachel and Becky will do next?

e ▶1.34 Watch or listen to Part 2. Do they mention any of your ideas?

f ▶1.34 Watch or listen again. Are the sentences true (T) or false (F)?

1 Becky's screen is still working.
2 Rachel thinks removing the SIM card might help.
3 Becky is worried about losing all her phone numbers.
4 Becky bought the phone very recently.
5 Becky has got insurance.
6 Rachel heard on the radio about using rice to dry phones.

2 USEFUL LANGUAGE Making suggestions

a Choose the correct words.

1 Have you tried *turning* / *turn* it off and on again?
2 What about *taking* / *take* the SIM card out and drying it?
3 Could you *taking* / *take* it back to the shop?
4 Can you *claiming* / *claim* on your insurance?
5 You could *trying* / *try* that.

b ▶1.34 Watch or listen to Part 2 again and check your answers to 2a.

c Complete the responses with the words from the box.

why	idea	worth	give

1 **A** How about just leaving it until it dries out?
   B I'll _____ it a try. What have I got to lose?
2 **A** Why don't you try drying it with a hair dryer?
   B That's _____ a try, but wouldn't the heat damage the phone?
3 **A** Shall we phone Mark and see if he has any ideas?
   B Yes, _____ not? He might know what to do.
4 **A** Let's go to the phone shop and ask for advice.
   B That's a great _____. They should be able to help.

d What solutions can you think of for these problems? Make notes.

1 You missed your bus home and the next one is in an hour. It's raining.
2 You don't have any ideas about what to buy your friend for his/her birthday.
3 You've spilt coffee on your shirt and you have an important meeting in 20 minutes.
4 The battery in your phone is low and you need to make an important call in an hour.

e 💬 Take turns to ask for advice and make suggestions.

3 LISTENING

a 💬 Look at the photo. Who do you think Becky is talking to?

b ▶1.35 Watch or listen to Part 3. Does the phone work now? Why / Why not?

4 CONVERSATION SKILLS
Sounding sympathetic or pleased

a ▶1.36 Listen and complete the conversations.

1 **Rachel**   How's the phone?
   Becky   Not good. The screen's frozen.
   Rachel   _____! Have you tried turning it off and on again?

2 **Becky**   I hope I haven't lost all my contacts. I haven't saved them anywhere else.
   Rachel   Oh no, _____.

3 **Becky**   My phone's working. That rice trick worked.
   Rachel   That's _____! I'm really _____ to hear that.

b Look at the completed conversations in 4a. Which phrases sound sympathetic? Which phrases sound pleased?

c 💬 Take turns to say sentences 1–6 below. Respond, sounding sympathetic or pleased. Then ask for more details.

1 I've lost my phone.

2 I've found a new place to live.

3 My car has broken down.

4 I was woken up very early this morning.

5 My sister is coming to visit.

6 I've been offered a great new job.

5 PRONUNCIATION Sentence stress

a ▶1.37 Listen to these sentences. Underline the stressed syllables.

1 Have you tried turning it off and on again?
2 What about taking the SIM card out and drying it?
3 Could you take it back to the shop?
4 Can you claim on your insurance?

b We usually put stress on the words which are important for our message. Which syllables do you think are stressed in these sentences?

1 I can't find my phone!
2 My computer's broken. I've lost all my work!
3 I have a very annoying colleague at work – he complains about everything.
4 I'm really worried. I have a big exam tomorrow.
5 My car has been making a strange noise recently. I hope there isn't a problem.

c ▶1.38 Listen and check. Then practise saying the sentences.

6 SPEAKING

a Think of a problem you have or might have (e.g. with a colleague, your studies, a car, your computer). Make notes about the problem.

b 💬 Take turns to explain your problem and make suggestions.

Unit Progress Test

CHECK YOUR PROGRESS

You can now do the Unit Progress Test.

application

Dear Sir/Madam,

I'm writing to enquire about the possibility of work in your company. I'm an application software developer. I've been [1]_____ for my current company for just over [2]_____ _____ now, but I'd like a change. I'm good at [3]_____ thinking and I have excellent [4]_____ - _____ skills. In addition, I also have a positive [5]_____ towards my work and colleagues.

I don't speak Cantonese, but I'm very interested in [6]_____ _____ and would love the opportunity to live and work there. I'd be interested in any information you can send me.

Please find my CV attached.

Yours faithfully,

Tania Sampson

1 SPEAKING AND LISTENING

a What changes would you like to make to your life? Make notes about one of the topics below.

your job   the apartment/house you live in
the town/city you live in   your free-time activities
your studies   your friends

b 💬 Talk about the changes you would like to make to your life. Give reasons.

c ▶1.39 Listen to two friends, Tania and Lin, talking in a café. What two changes is Tania thinking about?

d ▶1.39 Tania writes an email to an IT company in Hong Kong called PayHK. Listen to the conversation again and complete gaps 1–6 in the application email above right.

e 💬 Ask and answer the questions.

1 How common is it for people in your country to work abroad?
2 What are the main reasons they go?
  • better work opportunities
  • more money
  • a cultural experience
  • language learning
  • other reasons

2 READING

a Read Tania's email to Lin about Hong Kong and answer the questions.

1 Has Tania got good or bad news?
2 When does she hope to see Lin?

b Read the email again and answer the questions.

1 What did Tania do the day after the interview?
2 What kind of apps will she create in her new job?
3 Will she only work on the company's current products?
4 Is the new job well paid?
5 What else would she like to do in Hong Kong?

Hong Kong!!!

Hi Lin,

I'm sorry I haven't been in touch for the past few days, but it's been a very busy time.

On Monday I had a job interview with PayHK, the IT company in Hong Kong that I emailed. Then the next day, I had to do a practical test. [1]**You won't believe this, but** they've just rung to offer me the job!

The work sounds really interesting – they want me to work on developing apps that can be used for making mobile payments. [2]**And what's really exciting is that** they also want me to think of ideas for new products. The job offer is very generous. Apart from giving me a good salary, they're also going to pay me a bonus if I do well. And they'll pay for my flights and help me with accommodation when I arrive.

[3]**But the best thing is that** I'm going to live in Hong Kong! Besides the food, I'm also looking forward to learning Cantonese. Everyone at PayHK speaks English, but I'd like to be able to talk to local staff in their first language. I've always wanted to learn a second language well, and I'm sure I'll be able to do it when I'm living there.

We must get together before I leave, so you can tell me all about Hong Kong. Would you like to meet up for dinner some time in the next week? Let me know a day that suits you.

Tania

3 WRITING SKILLS Adding new information

a Look at **bold** phrases 1–3 in the second email. Why does Tania use them? Choose the correct reason.

1 to summarise her news
2 to introduce new information
3 to show she is very busy

b Rewrite phrases 1–3 in the second email using the words in brackets.

1 _____
(will never)
2 _____
(fascinating)
3 _____
(most fantastic)

c Put the words in the correct order to make sentences.

1 but I've / believe this / bought a house / you'll never
_____

2 is / more amazing / what's even / the location
_____

3 it wasn't / thing is that / too expensive / but the best
_____

d Read sentences a–c and underline the correct words in the rules below.

a I have good problem-solving skills. **In addition**, I also have a positive attitude towards my work.
b **Apart from** giving me a really good salary, they're also going to pay me a bonus.
c **Besides** the food, I'm also looking forward to learning Cantonese.

- We can use phrases like *in addition (to)*, *apart from* and *besides* when we want to add information.
- We use them at the [1]*beginning / end* of a sentence.
- We use *in addition (to)* in more [2]*formal / informal* writing.
- After *apart from* and *besides*, we use an [3]*infinitive form / -ing form or a noun*.
- In the other part of the sentence, we can use [4]*and / also* to emphasise that we are adding information.

e Read the sentences. Do the words/phrases in **bold** mean *as well as* or *except for*?

1 They're going to pay all my expenses **apart from** meals.
2 **Apart from** my travel expenses, they're also going to pay for my meals.
3 **Besides** the food, I'm also looking forward to learning Cantonese.
4 I've done everything I can to prepare, **besides** learning Cantonese.

f Rewrite these sentences using the words in brackets. Write two sentences if necessary. There may be more than one possible answer.

1 I have a degree in software development and I have a diploma in interactive media design. (in addition)
2 They'll pay for a hotel when I arrive and they'll pay the first month's rent on an apartment. (apart from)
3 They're going to give me a return airfare now and they're going to pay for another return airfare in the middle of my contract. (besides)

4 WRITING An informal email

a Imagine you have some exciting news. Choose one of the topics below or your own idea. Make notes about extra things you can say about this news.

1 You've won a trip to a tropical island. (How did you win it? When are you going?)
2 You've got a new job. (What's the job? Why did you apply?)

b 💬 Compare your ideas with a partner.

c Write an email to a friend explaining your good news. Use phrases to introduce new information, if possible.

d Work in pairs. Read your partner's email. Is their news similar to yours? Do they use phrases to add information correctly?

UNIT 2
Review and extension

1 GRAMMAR

a 💬 Underline the best answers. Then ask and answer the questions.

1 What job *did you want / have you wanted* to do when you were a child?
2 How long *have you used / have you been using* this book?
3 How many emails *have you written / have you been writing* today?
4 Have you ever *lost / been losing* your phone?
5 How long *have you known / have you been knowing* your colleagues or classmates?
6 *Have you taken / Have you been taking* a driving test yet?

b Complete the text using the present perfect simple, present perfect continuous or past simple.

^{1}_____ (you/ever/imagine) what it's like to be a successful games designer? That's my goal.
I ^{2}_____ (always/love) playing games. In fact, I ^{3}_____ (play) computer games since I was just three!
I ^{4}_____ (leave) school at 18 and studied computer animation at college. Then I ^{5}_____ (work) for a software company. I ^{6}_____ (develop) some useful skills there, but it wasn't the right job for me.
Then, six months ago, I got an apprenticeship with a games company. It doesn't pay very much, but I ^{7}_____ (already/gain) a lot of experience.
I ^{8}_____ (work) on an idea for a game in my free time for the last six months. When it's ready, I'll present it to my company. I know I'll be a success.

2 VOCABULARY

a Complete the words.

1 We have 72 e __ p __ __ __ __ __ s at this company. Some of them have worked here for a long time.
2 We have two c __ __ d __ __ __ __ __ s for the job. We need to choose one.
3 Schools should teach p __ __ c __ __ __ __ l skills, like cooking and driving.
4 He's got great p __ __ b __ __ m s __ __ v __ __ g skills.
5 My uncle had a long c __ __ e __ r in the army.

b Match the words in the box with definitions 1–6.

app   browser   device   display   keyboard   password

1 a software program that allows users to find and read information on the web _____
2 a secret phrase that you use to log in to a website _____
3 you type by using this _____
4 a computer program designed for one purpose _____
5 a tablet, laptop or mobile phone _____
6 the screen on a phone, tablet or computer _____

3 WORDPOWER look

a Match questions 1–8 with answers a–h.

1 ☐ What do employers usually **look for**?
2 ☐ Did you see John's office?
3 ☐ What does 'disconnect' mean?
4 ☐ What are you **looking at**?
5 ☐ Are you coming to the meeting tomorrow?
6 ☐ How do you feel about your trip to Moscow?
7 ☐ What do you think of my new SmartWatch?
8 ☐ **Look out**! Didn't you see that bicycle?

a It **looks** good. Can I try it?
b I don't know. **Look** it **up** online.
c No, I have to **look after** some customers.
d Someone who is reliable and hard-working.
e No! It came out of nowhere!
f No, we didn't **look around** the building.
g It's an advert for a sales job.
h I'm really **looking forward to** it.

b Match the phrases in the box with definitions 1–8.

look + adjective   look after someone/something
look at someone/something   look around (somewhere)
look for something/someone   look forward to something
look out   look (something) up

1 try to find _____
2 feel excited about a future event _____
3 check a meaning or other fact in a book or online _____
4 explore _____
5 be responsible for _____
6 seem _____
7 be careful _____
8 watch _____

c Complete the sentences with the correct form of *look* and a particle (*after*, *up*, etc.) if necessary. Sometimes, more than one answer is possible.

1 Do you like _____ trees, flowers and other plants?
2 Do you enjoy _____ small children?
3 Have you ever _____ a factory?
4 Do you know anyone who's _____ a job at the moment?
5 Where do you usually _____ new English words?
6 What are you _____ to doing this year?
7 Does the weather _____ good today?
8 In what situation would you shout '_____!' to someone?

d 💬 Discuss the questions in 3c.

REVIEW YOUR PROGRESS

How well did you do in this unit? Write 3, 2 or 1 for each objective.
3 = very well   2 = well   1 = not so well

I CAN ...

talk about experiences of work and training.	☐
talk about technology.	☐
make and respond to suggestions.	☐
write an email giving news.	☐

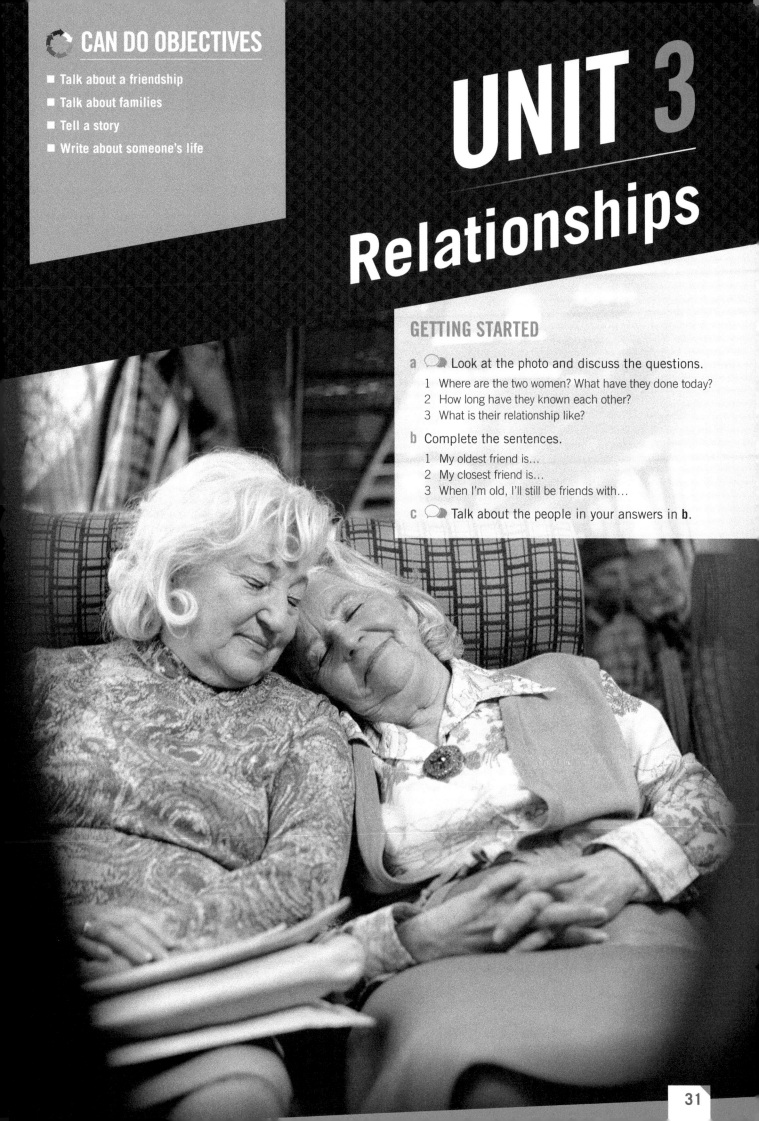

CAN DO OBJECTIVES

- Talk about a friendship
- Talk about families
- Tell a story
- Write about someone's life

UNIT 3
Relationships

GETTING STARTED

a Look at the photo and discuss the questions.

1 Where are the two women? What have they done today?
2 How long have they known each other?
3 What is their relationship like?

b Complete the sentences.

1 My oldest friend is…
2 My closest friend is…
3 When I'm old, I'll still be friends with…

c Talk about the people in your answers in **b**.

1 VOCABULARY Relationships

a 💬 Write down the names of three people you know well and show them to your partner. Ask and answer the questions about each person.

1 How long have you known him/her?
2 When did you meet?
3 How often do you see each other?
4 What do you do together?

b Underline the correct answers.

1 My friends and I like the same music but that's the only thing we *have in common* / *get on*.
2 I don't like it when *strangers* / *relationships* start talking to me.
3 I generally *get on with* / *get to know* people of all different ages.
4 I have a good *friendship* / *relationship* with my cousins.
5 I think you can only *keep in touch* / *get to know* people well when you live with them.
6 I don't need emotional *friendship* / *support* from my friends. I just want to have fun with them.
7 Most of my friends come from the same *background* / *personality* as me.
8 A lot of my *relatives* / *strangers* live in the same town as I do.
9 I can be friends with anyone who has the same *sense of humour* / *relationship* as me.
10 I'm not very good at *getting on* / *keeping in touch* with friends who live far away.
11 My longest *friendship* / *relative* started when I was at primary school.
12 I have shared *interests* / *support* with most of my close friends.

c 💬 Which sentences in 1b are true for you?

2 PRONUNCIATION Linking sounds

> In a sentence, when one word ends in a consonant sound and the next word starts with a vowel sound, we often link these words. We say them without any pause between the words.

a ▶ 1.40 Listen to the sentences. Can you hear the linking between the words in **bold**?

1 That's the only thing we **have in** common.
2 I don't **need emotional** support.
3 I generally **get on** with people **of all ages**.

b Underline the words which you think will be linked in this way (consonant sound + vowel sound).

1 I fell in love with my husband the moment I saw him.
2 Kate lives in the USA, but we keep in touch online.
3 My friends and I have a very silly sense of humour.
4 I don't think a shared background is important.
5 My relatives are all very close.

c ▶ 1.41 Listen and check. Then practise saying the sentences.

3 READING

a 💬 Look at the film poster on the right and the 'Film Facts' below and answer the questions.

1 What do you think the connection between the two men is?
2 Why is one man in a wheelchair?

b Read the first part of *Untouchable: the true story of an unlikely friendship* below and check your ideas.

c 💬 Before you read the rest of the article, guess the answers to these questions.

1 In what ways did Abdel help Philippe?
2 How long did Abdel work for Philippe?
3 In what ways did Philippe help Abdel?
4 What is their relationship like now?

Film Facts

 Untouchable (2011)

 Directed by Olivier Nakache and Éric Toledano

 France's number one film for ten weeks

 France's second biggest box office hit

 Nominated for nine Césars

 Made over $160 million in France and $400 million worldwide

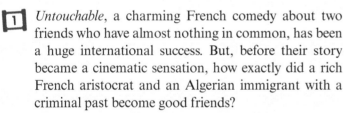

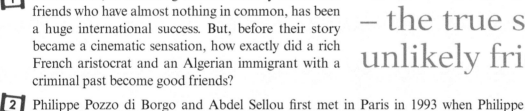

Untouchable
– the true story of an unlikely friendship

1 *Untouchable*, a charming French comedy about two friends who have almost nothing in common, has been a huge international success. But, before their story became a cinematic sensation, how exactly did a rich French aristocrat and an Algerian immigrant with a criminal past become good friends?

2 Philippe Pozzo di Borgo and Abdel Sellou first met in Paris in 1993 when Philippe was looking for a nurse. Philippe was from a very wealthy family. At one time he had been a successful businessman, living a life of great luxury. Then he had a terrible paragliding accident and lost the use of his arms and legs. Life in a wheelchair was lonely and boring. Philippe was struggling to imagine the future, and he needed practical help with his day-to-day life.

3 Philippe interviewed more than 80 people for the job of nurse, but none of them seemed right. Then he met Abdel, who had quit a life of crime in Algeria and moved to France to look for work. He was lively, intelligent and quick-thinking, with a crazy sense of humour. Philippe got on with Abdel immediately, and he offered him the job.

4 The two men didn't have much in common. Abdel loved pop music, but Philippe preferred classical music. Philippe loved modern art, but Abdel hated it. Philippe's family were sure that he had made a bad choice. They believed that Philippe needed someone much more sensible. Meanwhile, Abdel wasn't planning on staying in the job for long.

d Read the second part of the article and check.

5 However, their working relationship quickly developed into a close friendship. Abdel gave Philippe the support he needed. More importantly, his energy and sense of humour brought fun and excitement back into Philippe's life. Abdel helped Philippe make trips to other countries. Back home in Paris their adventures included travelling around the streets of Paris with Abdel on the back of Philippe's wheelchair or driving Philippe's Rolls-Royce – often much too fast!

6 In the end, Abdel worked for Philippe for ten years. Philippe believes it was Abdel's energy and sense of fun that kept him alive. 'I suddenly found I was enjoying life again,' he says. 'I felt like I didn't know what was coming next.' As for Abdel, getting to know Philippe had kept him out of prison and introduced him to a new way of life.

7 Philippe and Abdel now live in different countries, each with a wife and family. They keep in touch regularly. Over the years they have learnt, among other things, to enjoy each other's favourite music. All that really matters to their friendship, though, is their shared love of laughter and adventure.

e Find words or phrases with these meanings in the article.
1 someone from a high level in society (paragraph 1)
2 rich (paragraph 2)
3 sad because you are not with other people (paragraph 2)
4 full of energy (paragraph 3)
5 help or encouragement (paragraph 5)
6 ability to enjoy life and not be too serious (paragraph 6)

f 💬 Discuss the questions.
1 Why do you think people liked the film so much?
2 Do you have a lot in common with your friends? Or do they introduce you to new things and ideas? Which is more important?
3 How long can a friendship last when you keep in touch but don't spend time together?

4 GRAMMAR Narrative tenses

a Underline the correct words.

The two men [1]*first met / were first meeting* in Paris in 1993, when Philippe [2]*looked for / was looking for* a nurse. At one time, he [3]*was / had been* a successful businessman, living a life of great luxury. Then, after a terrible paragliding accident, he [4]*had lost / lost* the use of his arms and legs. Philippe [5]*struggled / had struggled* to imagine the future. Philippe [6]*liked / had liked* Abdel immediately and he [7]*offered / had offered* him the job of being his nurse.

b Answer the questions.
1 Did Philippe look for a nurse once or for a long time?
2 When was Philippe a businessman: when he met Abdel or before he met Abdel?

c Find and underline two more examples of the past continuous and two more examples of the past perfect in the first part of the article on p.33.

d Complete the story with the correct form of the verbs in brackets. Use narrative tenses (past simple, past continuous, past perfect).

I [1]_____ (meet) my friend Amy in 2009. She [2]_____ (work) in a café at the time and I [3]_____ (go) there quite often. She [4]_____ (not be) very happy because she [5]_____ (just/finish) a degree in Art History and she couldn't find an interesting job. One day she [6]_____ (notice) that I [7]_____ (read) a book about Leonardo da Vinci and we [8]_____ (start) talking about art. We realised we had a lot in common, including a love of Italian art. A few months later, Amy [9]_____ (hear) about an Art History course in Italy and we [10]_____ (decide) to do it together. We both still live in Rome and we love it here.

e ▶ Now go to Grammar Focus 3A on p.136

5 SPEAKING

a Think about yourself and a close friend, or two people you know who are close friends. Prepare to tell the story of how the friendship started. Make notes about these topics:
• life before you/they first met
• what happened when you/they met
• what happened next
• things in common.

b 💬 Take turns to tell your stories.

> I met my best friend at high school. We had been at the same primary school, but we were in different classes.

3B We used to get together every year

Learn to talk about families
G *used to, usually*
V Family; Multi-word verbs

1 VOCABULARY Family

a 💬 Look at the photos and guess the family relationships between the people. Make at least two guesses for each picture.

> They could be sisters.
>
> Perhaps they're cousins.

b Match sentences 1–8 with photos a–h.

1. ☐ I haven't got any brothers or sisters, so I'm an **only child**.
2. ☐ My brother has got a son and a daughter, so I've got a **nephew** and a **niece**. They're twins.
3. ☐ Judy was born a year before me, so I've got an **older sister**.
4. ☐ My brother is two years older and my sister is three years younger. I'm the **middle child** in our family.
5. ☐ I've got five brothers and sisters who are all younger than I am. I'm the **oldest child** in the family.
6. ☐ My family lived in Malta until I was 12 years old, so I spent all my **childhood** there.
7. ☐ Helena has given up work to stay at home and **raise** her young children.
8. ☐ I've just become a grandmother, so there are now three **generations** in our family!

c 💬 Use the **bold** words and phrases in 1b to talk about your family.

> I'm not an only child – I've got an older sister.

> I spent my childhood in the country.

2 LISTENING

a ⤸ Discuss the questions.

1 Do you know any twins? If so, how well do you know them? How similar/different are they?
2 What do you think are the advantages and disadvantages of having a twin?

b ▶1.45 Listen to two twins talking about their lives. Answer the questions.

Charlotte

1 What were the twins like when they were children?
2 What changed in their relationship when they were teenagers?
3 What's their relationship like now?

Megan

1 What kind of sister was Charlotte?
2 What changed in their relationship when they were teenagers?
3 In what ways are they similar now?

c ⤸ Do you think Megan and Charlotte like being twins? Why / Why not?

d ▶1.45 Listen again and answer the questions. Write C (Charlotte), M (Megan) or B (both).

Who says … ?

1 she can tell what the other twin is thinking _____
2 they used to swap clothes _____
3 they looked very similar when they were children _____
4 they didn't use to argue very much _____
5 they wanted to be different from each other when they were teenagers _____
6 they get in touch frequently now _____

e ⤸ Discuss the questions.

1 Do you have brothers and sisters? Is your relationship similar to the relationship between Megan and Charlotte?
2 Would you like to have a twin? Why / Why not?

3 VOCABULARY Multi-word verbs

a Match the multi-word verbs in **bold** in sentences 1–9 with meanings a–i.

1 ☐ As we **grew up**, we created our own identities.
2 ☐ We usually speak on the phone two or three times a day, and we **get together** as often as we can.
3 ☐ We looked so similar – our parents used to **mix** us **up**.
4 ☐ We didn't use to argue much, but in our teenage years we started to **grow apart**.
5 ☐ We saw that we'd both **cut** all our hair **off**!
6 ☐ We wanted to **hang out with** each other more.
7 ☐ My parents **ring** me **up** every Sunday night for a chat.
8 ☐ My grandmother **brought** me **up**, so I'm very close to her.
9 ☐ I think I mainly **take after** my dad – we look similar and we're both good at science.

a to be similar to an older member of the family
b to meet (when you have organised it before)
c to make a phone call to someone
d to gradually have a less close relationship
e to think one person/thing is another person/thing
f to remove or make shorter, using scissors or a knife
g to spend time with someone
h to gradually become an adult
i to look after a child until he/she is an adult

b Complete rules 1–3 with the verbs in **bold**.

• I mainly **take after** my dad.
• We started to **grow apart**.
• We'd both **cut** all our hair **off**.
• We'd both **cut off** all our hair.
• We'd both **cut** it **off**.

1 Some multi-word verbs have no object (e.g. _____).
2 Some multi-word verbs are separable (e.g. _____). This means that the object can go either between the verb and the particle or after the particle. (When the object is a pronoun (e.g. *you, him, it*), it must go between the verb and the particle.)
3 Some verbs are not separable (e.g. _____). When we use a pronoun with these, it goes after the particle.

c ▶1.46 Pronunciation Listen to these sentences. Which word in **bold** is stressed?

1 As we **grew up**, we wanted to create our own unique identities.
2 We wanted to **hang out with** each other.
3 We saw that we'd **cut all our hair off**!

We usually stress the particle in multi-word verbs, not the main verb. If the multi-word verb has two particles, we stress the first one. If the multi-word verb is separated by an object (e.g. *all our hair*), then we often stress the object.

d ▶1.46 Listen again and repeat the sentences.

e 💬 Discuss the questions.

1 Where did you grow up?
2 Who brought you up?
3 When did your whole family last get together?
4 How much do you take after your parents?

4 GRAMMAR *used to, usually*

a ▶1.47 <u>Underline</u> the words used in the recording. Then listen and check.

1 Megan *dressed / used to dress* as differently from me as she could.
2 Megan *started / used to start* wearing flowery dresses!
3 We *were / used to be* very close.
4 We *usually speak / used to speak* on the phone two or three times a day.

b Complete the rules with the words in the box.

always   the past simple   *usually*   *used to*

1 We can use _____ to talk about events that happened only once in the past.
2 We can use _____ + infinitive to talk about past habits.
3 We can use _____ and _____ with the present and past simple to talk about present and past habits.

c ▶ Now go to Grammar Focus 3B on p.136

d Complete the sentences so they are true for you.

• The whole family usually … once a year.
• My mum/dad/parents used to … when I was a child.
• My mum/dad/parents didn't use to … when I was a child.
• My grandmother/grandfather/uncle/aunt used to …
• My brother/sister usually …
• Families in my country usually …
• Families in my country used to …

e 💬 Talk about your sentences from 4d.

> The whole family usually gets together once a year.

> Really? How big is your family?

> There are about 20 of us.

5 SPEAKING

a You are going to talk about a tradition in your family. Make notes using these questions and use the ideas in the photos to help you.

• What's the tradition?
• How often does it happen?
• When/Where does it happen?
• Which family members are involved?
• How did the tradition start?
• Was there anything you used to do which you don't do now?
• Do you like the tradition?
• Do you think the tradition will carry on in the future?

b 💬 Tell each other about your family traditions. Are your traditions similar?

> We always go out for dinner on my birthday. We used to go for a pizza, but now I usually choose a Japanese restaurant – I love sushi!

3C Everyday English
You won't believe what I did!

Learn to tell a story
- Ⓟ Stress in word groups
- Ⓢ Reacting to what people say

1 LISTENING

a 💬 Discuss the questions.

1 When was the last time you bought a present for a friend or relative? What was it? Did they like it?
2 Do you do a lot of shopping online? Do you buy different things online and in 'real' shops? Which do you prefer?

b 💬 Look at the photo below and the words in the box. What story do you think Mark is telling Tom?

a desk   Mark's dad   online shopping
very small   for children

c ▶1.49 Watch or listen to Part 1 and check your ideas. What mistake did Mark make?

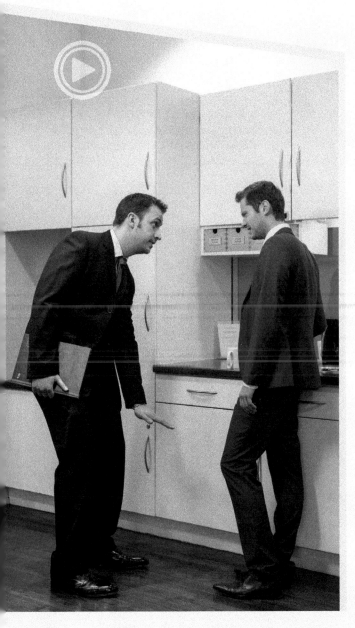

2 CONVERSATION SKILLS
Reacting to what people say

a ▶1.49 Watch or listen to Part 1 again. Match Mark's comments 1–4 with Tom's replies a–d.

1 [b] You won't believe what I did.   a Great!
2 [c] It was a fantastic price too.   b What?
3 [a] So I ordered it.   c Sounds good.
4 [d] It turned out I'd ordered a desk for a child.   d No way!

b Match responses a–d in 2a with the descriptions below.

1 responding positively ___, ___
2 showing surprise ___
3 asking for more information ___

c Underline two other ways to show surprise in the exchange below.

A I've just bought my sister's birthday present. She loves running, so I got her a sports watch.
B Wow! That's a coincidence. I ordered one for myself yesterday.
A Really? What make did you get?

d Complete the sentences so they are true for you.

1 I like / don't like …   3 I really want to …
2 Last week, I …   4 I haven't been to …

e 💬 Take turns to say your sentences and then react to what your partner says. Use the phrases in 2a and 2c.

> I don't like chocolate cake.

> Really? I thought everyone liked chocolate cake.

3 LISTENING

a What do you think Mark did when he discovered his mistake?

b ▶1.50 Watch or listen to Part 2. What did Mark do next? Did he get a desk for his dad in the end?

c ▶1.50 Watch or listen again. Are the sentences true (T) or false (F)? Correct the false sentences.

1 The company Mark bought the desk from didn't offer a refund.
2 Looking on a freecycling website for a new desk was Rachel's idea.
3 Freecycling is where people can give away unwanted things.
4 Tom already knew about the website Freecycle.
5 Mark is waiting for the desk to be delivered.

d 💬 Have you ever had any problems with online shopping? What happened?

4 USEFUL LANGUAGE
Telling a story

a ▶1.51 Complete each sentence with one or two words. Then listen and check.

1 **You won't** _believe_ **what** I did.
2 **The** _____ **thing** is, it was really, really small.
3 **It** _____ I'd ordered a desk for a child.
4 But _____, I still had to find a desk.
5 **In the** _____, Rachel suggested I try one of those 'freecycling' websites.
6 I found the perfect desk straight away, and **the** _____ **thing is** it's free.

b Add the phrases in 4a to the list below.

* starting a story:
  You'll never guess what (happened to me last week).
  _____

* adding new information:
  _____
  _____
  _____

* finishing a story (or part of a story):
  _____
  _____

c 💬 Tell each other stories using the notes below and the phrases in 4b.

1 • went to the shops
  • saw an old friend I hadn't seen for years
  • had lunch
  • she knew my wife/husband from work
2 • went shopping
  • wanted new clothes for wedding
  • found perfect dress/suit
  • got 25% discount

5 PRONUNCIATION
Stress in word groups

a ▶1.52 Listen to these sentences from the conversation. Notice how the speaker pauses between word groups. Use // to mark where the speaker pauses.

1 The funny thing is, it was really, really small.
2 In the end, Rachel suggested I try one of those 'freecycling' websites.
3 Well, I phoned the company to explain and luckily they agreed to give me a refund.

Notice how, in each word group, one syllable is stressed more than all the others in the group. This is the main stress.

b ▶1.52 Listen again. Underline the syllable in each group which is stressed more strongly than the others.

c ▶1.52 Listen again and repeat the sentences.

6 SPEAKING

a Think of an interesting thing that happened to you (or someone you know) recently. Choose from the topics below or your own ideas:

* making a stupid mistake
* meeting a new person
* going on an interesting trip

Make notes about what happened. Think about which phrases from 4a you can include when you tell your story.

b 💬 Tell each other your stories. Make sure you react to what your partner is saying.

🔄 **Unit Progress Test**

CHECK YOUR PROGRESS

You can now do the Unit Progress Test.

1 SPEAKING AND LISTENING

a 💬 Discuss the questions.

1 How much do you know about past generations of your family?
2 Do you know more about your mother's or your father's side of the family? Why?

b ▶1.53 Bryan is talking to his cousin, Susie, about their family. What relatives are they talking about?

c Look at the photos. How do you think Bryan and Susie's relatives met?

d Make notes about someone in your family who interests you. Why do they interest you?

e 💬 Tell a partner about the person in your family.

2 READING

a Read Bryan's email to Susie. Why did their grandparents decide to live in Canada?

> **Mail**
>
> Hi Susie,
>
> I've done a bit of investigating about Gran and Grandad, and how they ended up living in Canada. I told you that Grandad worked as a chef on cruise ships from 1937 until 1939, when World War II started. And you know that while he was working on one of the ships, he met Gran. She was the ship's nurse.
>
> Well, apparently, that ship's destination was Vancouver. When the ship arrived, they spent a couple of days there. That's when Grandad proposed to Gran, and she said yes. During their stay in Vancouver, they decided that they really liked the city and that they would start a new life in Canada.
>
> However, World War II started and Grandad had to go back to England and join the British army. Meanwhile, Gran stayed in Canada, because it was much safer. They were separated for five years and missed each other very much. Gran was quite lonely at first, but after a couple of months she got a job in a hospital and she made friends there – she was always very friendly and good at talking to people.
>
> In 1946, Grandad returned to Canada and they got married. Five years later, my father was born. And then two years after that, your mother was born.
>
> Gran and Grandad lived in the same house for 30 years. I used to go and visit them in Vancouver over the summer when I was at school. Would you like me to take you to see the house one day?
>
> Bryan

b Read the email again and put pictures a–e in the correct order.

1 ☐ 2 ☐ 3 ☐ 4 ☐ 5 ☐

3 WRITING SKILLS Describing time

a Look at the words in **bold** in the examples. Do they all describe a *point* in time or a *period* of time?

1 **From** 1937 **until** 1939, he worked as a chef on cruise ships …
2 **While** he was working on one of the ships, he met Gran …
3 **During** their stay in Vancouver, they decided that they really liked the city …
4 They were separated **for** five years …
5 **Meanwhile,** Gran stayed in Canada and Grandad went back to England …
6 I used to visit them **over** the summer.

b Underline the correct words to complete the rules.

1 We can use *while / during* before a noun or noun phrase.
2 We can use *while / during* before a verb phrase.
3 We *can / can't* use 'during' before lengths of time (e.g. six months).
4 *Meanwhile / Over* means 'at the same time' and is always at the start of a sentence.
5 *Meanwhile / Over* can mean the same as 'during'.

c Underline the correct words.

1 I lived alone *from / until* 1993 *from / until* I got married.
2 I worked as a chef *while / during* the 1990s.
3 I usually go abroad *over / from* the winter months.
4 I lived in London *while / meanwhile* I was working for the government.
5 I had a job in Los Angeles *from / for* about two years. *Meanwhile / While*, I was planning to move to New York.

d Complete the sentences.

1 He was a soldier in the army _____ five years.
2 He went to India twice _____ he was working on the boat.
3 He was in Italy _____ 1943 until 1945.
4 She was in Rome for about six months. _____, her husband stayed in Milan.
5 From 1950 _____ two years later, he worked as a chef in an Italian restaurant.

e Make notes about some important events in your life (e.g. your job, your studies, the people you know, etc.).

Over the summer holidays, I worked at a swimming pool.
I started work four years ago. Meanwhile, I was studying for a diploma.

f 💬 Take turns to read your events to your partner. Ask questions to find out more.

4 WRITING

a You are going to write a biography of someone you know or know about. Choose who to write about and make notes about these topics:

1 why this person is important to you
2 what you remember most about this person
3 what the key events in this person's life are.

b Write the biography. Use words and phrases to describe time (*from, while*, etc.).

c 💬 Work in pairs. Read your partner's biography. Do they use time words correctly? Ask a question about the person they described.

UNIT 3
Review and extension

1 GRAMMAR

a Complete the sentences with the past simple, the past continuous or past perfect of the verbs.

1 When I _____ (get) home, everyone _____ (wait) for me. My family and friends _____ (plan) a surprise party for my birthday!
2 When I _____ (wake up) this morning, I _____ (have) a shock. The wind _____ (blow) a tree down and it _____ (block) the front door.
3 As soon as the doctor _____ (show) me the X-ray, I _____ (know) I _____ (break) my leg.
4 As I _____ (sit) on the grass, I _____ (realise) I _____ (put on) odd socks. I _____ (feel) very silly.

b Underline the correct words.

1 We *occasionally / used to* had a big family party.
2 My parents *used to give / gave* me a bike on my eighth birthday.
3 Did you *used / use* to be shy when you were a child?
4 Terry and his twin brother *always wear / used to wear* the same clothes. They wear the same clothes to work and at the weekend, too.
5 My sister and I *always used to walk / walked always* home from school together when we were young.
6 My aunt doesn't *used to / usually* celebrate her birthday, but I always phone her.
7 I didn't *use to / hardly ever* like George, but now we're best friends.
8 My grandfather says, 'Young people *used to be / always were* more polite than they are now'.

2 VOCABULARY

a Complete the words.

1 Someone with no brothers or sisters is an o_____ c_____ .
2 Your brothers, sisters, parents, cousins, uncles, aunts and grandparents are your r_____s.
3 Someone who you don't know is a s_____ .
4 Your brother or sister's daughter is your n_____ .
5 Your brother or sister's son is your n_____

b Complete the sentences with a multi-word verb which has a similar meaning to the words in brackets.

~~bring~~ grow cut hang grew
apart off out ~~up~~ up
---

1 It's a book about how to <u>bring</u> <u>up</u> children. (raise)
2 When did he _____ all his hair _____? (remove)
3 Where did you _____ _____? (live when you were a child)
4 We used to be good friends, but we _____ _____ when she changed schools. (become less close)
5 I often _____ _____ with Martin and his cousin. (spend time relaxing)

3 WORDPOWER *have*

a Complete the conversations with sentences a–g.

a Yes, we did, but we **had an accident** in the car we rented.
b Yes, I did. Well, I **had a go**. I wasn't very good!
c Shall we **have lunch** out today?
d Neil **has three brothers**, doesn't he?
e I **have no idea**. What Spanish restaurant?
f Does he **have brown eyes and a beard**?
g You should **have some lessons**.

A ¹_____
B Yes, but I only know the oldest one, Carl. I sometimes **have a drink** with him after work.
A ²_____
B Yes, he does.

A How was your holiday? Did you **have fun**?
B ³_____
A ⁴_____
B Yes, I'd like that. Where's that new Spanish restaurant?
A ⁵_____
B It's a new place. Let's go into town and **have a look**.

A How was the wedding? Did you dance?
B ⁶_____
A ⁷_____
B Yes, maybe I will.

b Add the phrases with *have* in **bold** in 3a to the table.

eating/drinking	possession	experience	other phrases
		have fun	

c Complete the sentences with the correct form of *have* or *have a/an*.

1 How many cousins do you _____?
2 When was the last time you _____ special meal?
3 Are any of your friends or family _____ language lessons at the moment?
4 Your sister's private diary is open on her bed. Do you _____ look?
5 Do you usually _____ breakfast with your family or on your own?
6 Have you ever _____ accident in a car, or on a bike?
7 Did you _____ good time last weekend? Why / Why not?
8 For fun, some people are trying to lift a 50kg weight. Do you _____ go too?

d 💬 Ask and answer the questions.

REVIEW YOUR PROGRESS

How well did you do in this unit? Write 3, 2 or 1 for each objective.
3 = very well   2 = well   1 = not so well

I CAN ...

talk about a friendship.	☐
talk about families.	☐
tell a story.	☐
write about someone's life.	☐

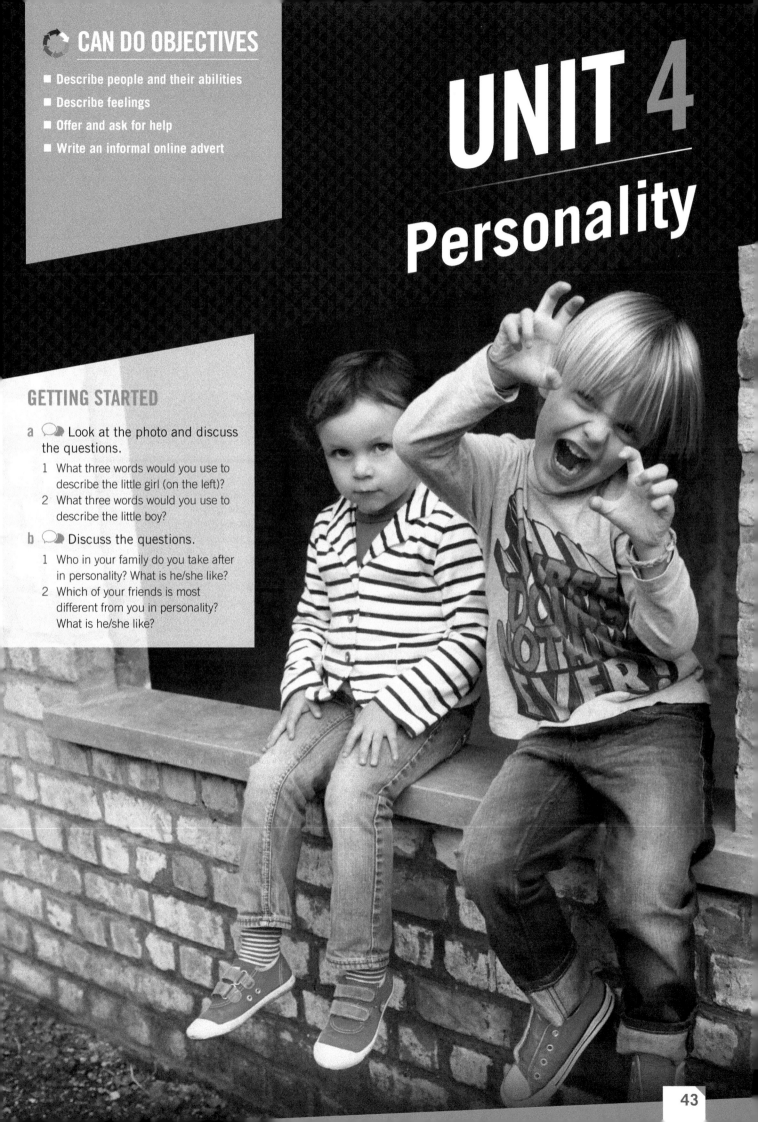

CAN DO OBJECTIVES

- Describe people and their abilities
- Describe feelings
- Offer and ask for help
- Write an informal online advert

GETTING STARTED

a 💬 Look at the photo and discuss the questions.

1. What three words would you use to describe the little girl (on the left)?
2. What three words would you use to describe the little boy?

b 💬 Discuss the questions.

1. Who in your family do you take after in personality? What is he/she like?
2. Which of your friends is most different from you in personality? What is he/she like?

1 VOCABULARY Ability

a Write down three things you are good at. How long have you been able to do these things?

b 💬 Talk about what you are good at.

> I'm good at drawing people's faces. I've always enjoyed drawing and painting.

c Read *What happens to talented children when they grow up?* Did the children become successful as adults?

d Read the article again and <u>underline</u> the correct words.

e Look at the words and phrases in the box. Which are about … ?

1 how clever you are
2 your feelings/emotions
3 what you have done
4 stopping something

talented   confident   brilliant
ability   intelligent   a positive attitude
successful   achievement   give up   bright

f Complete the sentences with the correct prepositions.

1 She is **good** _____ making friends.
2 He's **brilliant** _____ playing the piano.
3 I'm not very **talented** _____ art.
4 It's important to have **a positive attitude** _____ your work.
5 She has the **ability** _____ pass exams without even trying.

g Complete the sentences so they are true for you.

1 It's important to have a positive attitude and not give up because …
2 I'm talented at …
3 I'm not very good at …
4 If you want to be successful in life, you need to …
5 One of my biggest achievements is …

h 💬 Talk about your sentences in 1g.

WHAT HAPPENS TO TALENTED CHILDREN WHEN THEY GROW UP?

Do successful children become successful adults? We look at two talented children and see what happened to them when they became adults.

ANDREW HALLIBURTON

Andrew Halliburton has an IQ of 145 and was very [1]*succeeded / talented* at maths at a young age. But, rather than making a fortune in banking or computers, he ended up clearing tables in a fast-food restaurant. As a child, his parents pushed him very hard, but he didn't spend enough time making friends. He thinks that the other children at school didn't like him because he was always so clever. He went to university to study computing, but he thought the course was too easy, so he [2]*gave up / succeeded* after six months. He got a job in a burger bar instead, and worked there for several years.

OPRAH WINFREY

Oprah Winfrey is a [3]*success / successful* TV presenter in the USA. She had a very difficult family life and she never had any money. But she was very [4]*intelligent / talent* and did well at school. She always had a [5]*positive attitude / positive thinking* towards life and she was [6]*determined / brilliant* to work on TV. At the age of 19, she got a job with a local radio station. In the mid 1970s, she became the first black female newsreader on American TV. This was the beginning of her [7]*successful / success* story. Her TV show, where she interviewed famous people like Tom Cruise, Michael Jackson and Barack Obama, became famous around the world. Now she is one of the richest women in America.

2 LISTENING

a 💬 Look at the photos below of four talented people and discuss the questions.

1 What is each person good at?
2 Do you think they always had this talent?
3 What age do you think they were when they became successful?

b ▶1.54 Listen to a radio programme about age, talent and success. Check your ideas from 2a.

c ▶1.54 Listen again. Are the sentences true (T) or false (F)?

1 Tsung Tsung first became famous when he appeared on a TV show.
2 As a boy, Messi could play football better than the older boys.
3 A recent study showed that most talented children do much better than other adults when they grow up.
4 Vivienne Westwood used to be a teacher.
5 Bocelli's solo classical album became an international success when he was in his 40s.
6 Ed believes that talented people don't usually make mistakes.

d 💬 Do you agree with these statements?

1 Talented children don't succeed as adults because they don't develop good social skills.
2 It's better to be successful when you are young – you can enjoy it more.
3 If you want success in a creative job, hard work is more important than talent.

Vivienne Westwood

Tsung Tsung

Lionel Messi

Andrea Bocelli

3 GRAMMAR
Modals and phrases of ability

a Underline the words and phrases used to talk about ability in these sentences.

1 Tsung Tsung could play the piano when he was three.
2 He wants to be able to play like Mozart.
3 He was so good that he was able to join the Barcelona junior team when he was 11.
4 Less than 5% managed to become very successful adults.
5 Andrea Bocelli has been able to sing well since he was a child.
6 Say to yourself: 'I can do it!'
7 She'll be able to play the piano when she's a bit older.

b Look at the sentences in 3a. Complete rules 1–5 with the words in the box.

> be able to   can   will be able to
> could   manage to   was/were able to

1 We use _____ and *be able to* to talk about ability in the present.
2 In the past, we usually use _____ to talk about general ability and _____ to talk about a single time.
3 There is no present perfect or infinitive form of *can*, so we use forms of _____ instead.
4 We can't say 'will can', so we say _____ instead.
5 The verb _____ means to succeed in doing something difficult.

c ▶1.55 **Pronunciation** Listen to this sentence from 3a. Which is stressed more: *could* or *play*?

Tsung Tsung could play the piano when he was three.

d ▶1.56 Now listen to this sentence. Which word is stressed the most?

Say to yourself: 'I can do it!'

e Underline the correct words in the rules below.

1 We *usually / don't usually* stress words and phrases to talk about ability, unless we are emphasising something.
2 We *usually / don't usually* stress the main verb we are focusing on (e.g. *play the piano*).

f Complete the sentences. More than one answer may be possible.

1 I took my exam today and I _____ finish all the questions before the end.
2 After trying for 20 minutes, we _____ open the door.
3 I've _____ ski since I was five years old.
4 Ellie _____ already read simple books when she was three years old.
5 I live near the sea, but I _____ swim.
6 My Spanish is getting better. I'll _____ speak to my Spanish friends on the phone soon.

g ▶ Now go to Grammar Focus 4A on p.138

h Make notes about these topics.

1 three things you could do when you were a child which you can't do now
2 two things you managed to do after a lot of hard work
3 one thing you want to be able to do better in the future
4 two things you didn't manage to do last week because you had no time

i 💬 Talk about the topics in 3h. Ask each other questions to find out more information.

4 SPEAKING

a Think about ways in which you have succeeded (e.g. learnt a new skill, passed an exam, solved a problem). Tick (✓) the things that helped you to be successful.

☐ a positive attitude
☐ patience
☐ working long hours
☐ knowing the right people
☐ good luck
☐ good health
☐ talent
☐ support from friends and family
☐ self-confidence
☐ intelligence

b 💬 Which of the things from 4a helped you to be successful? Which do you think are most important?

> My parents helped me a lot when I was at university. You definitely can't succeed without the support of your family.

1 VOCABULARY -ed/-ing adjectives

a 💬 Discuss the questions.

1 Do you prefer spending time alone or with other people?
2 Do you think you are an extrovert or an introvert? Why?

b Read the description and the reviews of *Quiet* by Susan Cain. What good things do you think the book says about introverts?

c Match the words in **bold** in the reviews with the meanings 1–7.

1 very unhappy
2 unhappy because something is not interesting
3 making you feel pleased because you have what you need or want
4 unhappy because something didn't happen
5 very afraid
6 not interesting or exciting
7 extremely interesting

d ▶1.58 **Pronunciation** Listen to these adjectives. How is the final -ed sound pronounced? Complete the table.

amused   bored   depressed   disappointed
fascinated   interested   relaxed   satisfied   terrified

/d/	/t/	/ɪd/

e ▶1.59 Listen and check. Repeat the adjectives.

f Match the sentence halves.

1 We use -ing adjectives
2 We use -ed adjectives

a to describe feelings.
b to describe the things or people that cause the feelings.

g Complete the sentences with the correct form (-ing or -ed) of the words in brackets.

1 Jo and I are going to a concert next week. Are you _____? (interest)
2 Some people find winter _____ but I like it. (depress)
3 Everyone says the new restaurant is very good but I thought it was very _____. (disappoint)
4 I thought Clare would like the picture, but she wasn't _____. (amuse)
5 When I saw the spider on my leg I was _____! (terrify)
6 Japan is a wonderful country. I'm _____ by the culture. (fascinate)

h Write short answers for these topics.

• a time you felt disappointed
• a book or film that you found really interesting
• music that you find relaxing
• something or someone that you find amusing
• something you think is boring
• what you do if you feel depressed

i 💬 Take turns to read out your answers.

NEW YORK TIMES BESTSELLER

Quiet

The Power of Introverts in a World That Can't Stop Talking

SUSAN CAIN

by Susan Cain (2013)

Are you an extrovert (confident and sociable) or an introvert (quiet and happy to be alone)?

Your personality type influences your friendships, your relationships and your career. It even affects your need for sleep and the way you learn.

In societies that value conversation and self-expression, introverts are often seen as 'second place' to extroverts. In this beautifully written book, Susan Cain explores the many good things that introverts bring to the world.

BOOK REVIEWS 📖

Home   Shop   **Reviews**   Login

by BookMan ★★★★
This is the most **fascinating** book I've read on the introvert/extrovert topic for a long time. Cain describes her personal experience of being an introvert as well as writing about famous introverts who have changed the world.

by JD ★★★★
As a child I was often **terrified** at school because of the emphasis on public speaking and discussion. Perhaps some of the ideas from Susan Cain's book will change the education system in the future.

by Alan Gibson ★★★
A well-written book. I found the ideas very interesting, but I was **disappointed** that Susan Cain only writes about society in the USA without exploring how other cultures view introverts and extroverts.

by BLil ★★★★★
A great book! Everyone who thinks that introverts are **depressed** or **boring** should read it!

by Thinker ★★★
I was a bit **bored** by all the stuff about business, but I'm an introvert myself so it was very **satisfying** to see such praise of my personality type!

2 READING

a Complete the quiz. Then go to p.128 to see your results. Do you agree with how the results describe you?

b Look at the four photos of famous people below and on p.49. Then answer the questions.

1 What do you know about them?
2 Do you think they were/are introverts or extroverts?

c Read *Why the world needs introverts* quickly to check your ideas.

d Read the article again and answer the questions.

1 What is the attitude that Susan Cain calls the 'Extrovert Ideal'?
2 How do people organise classrooms and offices to make them better for extroverts?
3 How are extroverts useful to introverts?

e 💬 Discuss the questions.

1 Do people in your culture think that being quiet is a good thing?
2 Are schools and offices in your country designed for extroverts? How?

Are you an introvert? 🔳 **Quiz**

Read each statement and tick *Yes* or *No*.

1 I can be alone for a long time without feeling lonely.
Yes ◯   No ◯

2 In class, I prefer listening to talking in groups.
Yes ◯   No ◯

3 I express myself better in writing than speaking.
Yes ◯   No ◯

4 I don't always answer the phone when it rings.
Yes ◯   No ◯

5 I prefer working on my own or in a small group of people.
Yes ◯   No ◯

6 I don't like other people seeing my work before I've finished it.
Yes ◯   No ◯

7 People often describe me as quiet.
Yes ◯   No ◯

Number of *Yes* answers = ▢

Why the world needs introverts

'It's good to be **sociable**! It's good to be confident! It's good to be loud!' In her book *Quiet*, Susan Cain points out how deeply this belief is held by society. Very often the qualities of extroverts – being **active** and **lively**, making quick decisions and working well in a team or group, for example – are valued more than the **shy**, serious and **sensitive** qualities of introverts. Susan Cain calls this attitude the 'Extrovert Ideal'. In her book she looks at the way society places such value on the Extrovert Ideal that many modern schools and workplaces are built around it. Desks in classrooms are pushed together so that students can work in groups more easily. In Europe and the USA, employees are frequently put in shared offices so that they can work in teams. Students and employees are also expected to be confident and **talkative**.

Why are the needs of introverts ignored in this way when introverts have so much to offer? Introverts need less excitement around them than extroverts, it's true, but that doesn't make them less exciting people. Many of the world's greatest ideas, art and inventions have been produced by introverts. The Indian leader Mahatma Gandhi was an introvert, as were the artist Vincent Van Gogh and the physicist Albert Einstein.

Mahatma Gandhi was an introvert, as were Van Gogh and Albert Einstein

Then there was Rosa Parks, who started the US civil rights movement in 1955 by bravely and quietly saying 'no' when a white passenger wanted to sit in her seat on a bus.

Famous introverts in modern times include Angelina Jolie and Mark Zuckerberg. Jolie, a hugely successful actor, supports charities that help people in war zones. She describes herself as an introvert, saying she loves to spend time alone or with small groups of people because it helps her develop as a person.

And despite the huge success of his social networking site, co-founder of Facebook Zuckerberg remains a private person who doesn't like speaking in public.

But let's not forget that we need extroverts too. Because of course, introverts can come up with great ideas, but they also need help in communicating those ideas to the world. Songwriters need singers. Designers need sales people. In other words, extroverts and introverts need each other.

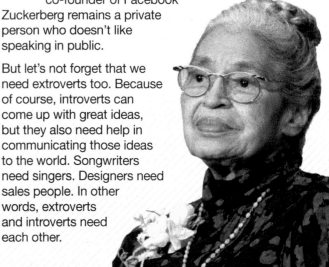

3 VOCABULARY Personality adjectives

a Complete the definitions with the personality adjectives in **bold** in the article on p.48.

1 _____ people talk a lot.
2 _____ people are easily upset and feel emotions deeply.
3 _____ people like spending time with other people.
4 _____ people do a lot of things or move around a lot.
5 _____ people are full of energy and enthusiasm.
6 _____ people are not confident, especially with new people.

b Read about these people. What adjectives describe them?

1 Bella loves romantic poetry. It often makes her cry.
2 Louis doesn't say much when he's with people he doesn't know.
3 Stefan always has something to say.
4 Jon loves parties and meeting new people.
5 Anna organises various clubs, and is always out doing new things.
6 Monica is always so energetic and busy.

4 GRAMMAR Articles

a Read the text and underline the correct answers. Ø means 'no article'.

I have always been [1]*an / the* introvert, but I pretend to be lively. At [2]*the / Ø* school, I was always really shy, but I acted loud and confident. I have always preferred to spend hours alone with [3]*the / a* good book or go for a long walk with my dog. I hate [4]*Ø / the* clubs and groups. For example, I went to [5]*a / the* birthday party last week, and I felt really shy and nervous. But I tried to look happy and active at [6]*a / the* party because I didn't want people to think I was strange. My husband is [7]*the / a* friendliest person in [8]*a / the* world. He loves going out and being with people. And he appreciates the effort I make to fit in when we socialise. But every so often he says, 'You really don't like [9]*Ø / the* people, do you?'.

b Complete the rules with *a/an*, *the* or *Ø* (no article).

1 We use _____ when it is clear what or who we are talking about.
2 We use _____ when we are not talking about one specific thing or person.
3 We use _____ when there is only one of something.
4 We use _____ when we talk about things in general, or the general idea of something.

c ▶ Now go to Grammar Focus 4B on p.138

d Write a short paragraph about one of the topics below. Try to use articles correctly.

- someone you know who is an extrovert/introvert
- an interesting book you would recommend
- a famous person you admire

e Read and check your partner's paragraph. Are there any mistakes with articles?

5 SPEAKING

a You are going to talk about a time when you experienced strong feelings. Choose one of the ideas in the box, or your own idea. Make notes about how you felt at different stages of the experience. Write down key words and phrases.

a time you helped someone	a terrible shock
an interesting journey	a nice surprise
an expensive mistake	a scary situation

b 💬 Tell your group about your experience. Has anyone else had a similar experience? If so, did they feel the same?

> I had to give a speech to 200 people. I'm quite shy, so I was terrified!

1 LISTENING

a 💬 Discuss the questions.

1 Do you think that you're a helpful person? Why / Why not?
2 Do you know anyone who's very helpful? Have they helped you?

b 💬 Look at the photo. What do you think Tom is offering to do to help?

c ▶1.61 Watch or listen to Part 1 and check your answers to 1b.

d ▶1.61 Watch or listen to Part 1 again. Underline the correct answers.

1 Becky is showing Rachel photos of her *holiday* / *house*.
2 Rachel asks Becky to take photos for *her website* / *fun*.
3 Mark is going to *buy* / *pick up* the desk on Saturday.
4 Becky suggests that *Mark goes alone* / *Tom helps Mark*.

e What favour do you think Tom might ask Rachel?

2 CONVERSATION SKILLS
Question tags

a ▶1.62 Listen to the questions below and look at the question tags in **bold**. Match the question tags with uses a or b.

1 ☐ That's the hotel you stayed in, **isn't it**?
2 ☐ You know I'm making a new website, **don't you**?

a a statement checking something you already think is true
b a real question

b Match 1–4 with a–d to complete the rules.

1 ☐ We usually use a positive question tag
2 ☐ We usually use a negative question tag
3 ☐ If there is an auxiliary verb (*do/have/be*), or the main verb isn't *be*,
4 ☐ If there is no auxiliary verb, or the main verb isn't *be*,

a after a positive sentence.
b after a negative sentence.
c use *do/don't* in the question tag.
d use the auxiliary verb in the question tag.

c Complete the question tags.

1 You don't drink coffee, _____?
2 It's cold in here, _____?
3 You've eaten, _____?
4 It was you I saw, _____?
5 Steve's gone to France, _____?
6 You didn't come to class yesterday, _____?

3 PRONUNCIATION
Intonation in question tags

a ▶1.63 Listen to this sentence. Here, the speaker thinks she knows the answer. Does the intonation go up or down on the question tag?

> That's the hotel you stayed in, isn't it?

b ▶1.64 Now listen to the same sentence with a different intonation on the question tag. This time, the speaker isn't sure about the answer. It is a real question. Does the intonation go up or down on the question tag?

> That's the hotel you stayed in, isn't it?

4 LISTENING

a ▶1.65 Watch or listen to Part 2 and <u>underline</u> the correct words.

1 Tom wants Rachel to help him to *ask Becky to marry him / buy a ring*.
2 Rachel *agrees / refuses* to help Tom.

b 💬 Look at the photo. What do you think is happening?

c ▶1.66 Watch or listen to Part 3 and check your ideas.

d 💬 Which of these things have you done to help a friend? Were you happy to do it? What happened?

- move furniture/help them move house
- use your creative skills (e.g. taking photos)
- talk through a problem they have
- buy a present
- give them a lift in your car

5 USEFUL LANGUAGE
Offering and asking for help

a ▶1.67 Complete each sentence with one word. Listen and check.

1 **Do you think you** _____ take them?
2 **Do you** _____ **a hand?**
3 **Could I** _____ **you a favour** in return?
4 So **what do you** _____?
5 **I** _____ **if you could** come with me to buy the ring.

b Add the phrases in **bold** in 5a to the table.

Offers to help	Asking for help

c Add these questions to the table in 5b.

1 Can you do something for me?
2 Can you give me a hand (with something)?
3 Is there something I can do?
4 How can I help you?

d Complete the conversations with the phrases in 5b. There may be more than one answer.

1 **A** I'm having a fridge delivered this evening.
  B _____?
  A No, it's fine, thanks.

2 **A** _____ with this report?
  B Of course, what do you need?
  A _____ check it and see if it makes sense?

3 **A** _____?
  B Depends what it is.
  A _____ look after my plants while I'm away.

6 SPEAKING

a ▶ Communication 4C 💬 Student A: Go to 6b below. Student B: Go to p.128.

b You are going to have two conversations offering and asking for help. Read the information and think about what you are going to say.

Student A
1 You need some help to buy a new computer. You think Student B knows about computers. You would like Student B to come shopping with you.
2 You have a bad back so you can't lift things. However, Student B is available at the weekend, but he's not available on Friday.

c 💬 Have conversations using the language in 5b.

○ Unit Progress Test

CHECK YOUR PROGRESS

You can now do the Unit Progress Test.

1 SPEAKING AND LISTENING

a 💬 Discuss the questions.

1 Have you ever used the internet to … ?
   - buy or sell something
   - rent a room
   - meet other people or join a group
   - find work or offer other people work
2 What do you think are the advantages and disadvantages of using the internet for these things?

b ▶1.68 Listen to three people talking about websites they have used. What is the purpose of each website?

c ▶1.68 Listen again. What do the speakers in brackets say about each topic?

1 how she travelled in India (Sheena)
2 her personality (Sheena)
3 earning money (Alya)
4 teaching children (Alya)
5 his skills (Brad)
6 being serious (Brad)

d 💬 Would you use websites like these? Why / Why not?

2 READING

a Read adverts a–c below and on p.53 quickly. Which of these topics does each advert mention?

dates or times	money	travelling	types of people	work

b Read the adverts again and answer the questions.

Advert a
1 Where is the trip?
2 How many people are they looking for?
3 What kind of person are they looking for?

Advert b
1 What are the main responsibilities of the job?
2 When does the work start?
3 What kind of person are they looking for?

Advert c
1 What does the job involve?
2 What experience is needed?
3 How long is it for?

ⓐ

🏠 HOME

TRAVEL GROUPS

1 **North India and the Himalayas – come and join us in October!**
Hi there,

2 We're planning a trip to North India and the Himalayas this October and we're looking for people to join us. We'll be doing some climbing (not too much!) and also travelling around in North India. We're meeting up in Delhi in mid-October and spending about four weeks on the road.

3 We're looking for one or two people, male or female, under 30, reasonably fit and able to live cheaply. Climbing experience preferred (and experience of India would be good too). Ideally you should be sociable and not too serious (like us).

4 If this sounds like the trip for you, send a reply plus a photo and we'll get back to you!
Cristina, Matt and Rob

●●●● ▶

ⓑ

ⓒ

VC Volunteer Community Project

home   about us   community projects   accommodation   applications

Volunteer needed

Duties include teaching English, art, maths, etc., as well as leading educational play groups. Support will be given by local teachers or project staff. Occasionally, volunteers will be asked to help with domestic duties such as preparing meals and keeping the classrooms and gardens clean to help create a happy and healthy atmosphere for the children.

Volunteers should be available to start work next month. No qualifications required, but candidates should have a positive and outgoing personality and be good with young children.

Please send a CV and a short personal profile.

3 WRITING SKILLS The language of adverts

a Read about the language used in the adverts. Which adverts do sentences 1–6 describe? Write a, b or c.

1 Sentences start with *we* or *you*. _a, c_
2 Sentences start with impersonal nouns like *jobs* or *duties*. _____
3 Sentences use formal words like *candidates* or *volunteers*. _____
4 Passive verb forms are often used. _____
5 The advert uses conversational expressions (*Hi there*, *get back to*, *fixing things*). _____
6 Some sentences and phrases end in exclamation marks. _____

b Which features in 3a make the adverts seem …?

a more personal and friendly
b more impersonal and official

c Look at advert a. What is the purpose of each section? Match sections 1–4 with these descriptions.

a ☐ tells the reader what to do next
b ☐ gives details of the situation (work, travel, plans, etc.)
c ☐ shows briefly what the advert is about
d ☐ says what kind of person they're looking for

ⓒ

SHORT WORK

Home   Profile   Account

Wanted – help with garden and house

We're a big family (three small children) and we need help with work on our garden and house for two weeks.

Jobs that need doing include general work in the garden, painting in the house, fixing electrical problems.

No experience needed but you should be good at fixing things and happy to work hard. Payment to be arranged.

Reply to: Mel and Nick

d In adverts and messages, we often use fixed 'reduced' expressions. Find expressions in the adverts which mean the following:

1 You don't need any experience.
2 We'd prefer a person with climbing experience.
3 We need a volunteer.
4 We don't require you to have any qualifications.

e Look at some more examples of reduced expressions in writing. How can you express the same ideas in full sentences?

1 Assistance urgently needed.
2 Driving licence required.
3 Male or female under 40 preferred.
4 Accommodation included.

4 WRITING An informal online advert

a Write an advert. Choose one of these situations.

• You're travelling somewhere and you want more people to join you to make a group.
• You're organising charity work and you want to take on some volunteers to help you.
• You want to employ someone to work for you for a couple of weeks.

Follow this plan.

1 Give a heading to draw attention to the advert.
2 Describe the situation (the job, your plans, etc.).
3 Say what kind of person you're looking for.
4 Ask for a reply.

b Read and check your advert.

1 Do you think it's too formal, not formal enough, or about right?
2 Have you used any reduced expressions?

c Read another student's advert and write a reply.

1 Say you're interested.
2 Give details about yourself.
3 Ask any further questions.

UNIT 4
Review and extension

1 GRAMMAR

a Tick (✓) the correct sentences. Sometimes both are correct.
1 ☐ a I can kick a ball, but I can't play football!
  ☐ b I manage to kick a ball, but not manage to play football!
2 ☐ a Were you able to answer all the questions?
  ☐ b Did you manage to answer all the questions?
3 ☐ a Unfortunately, I couldn't relax.
  ☐ b Unfortunately, I wasn't able to relax.
4 ☐ a You need to can swim.
  ☐ b You need to be able to swim.

b Underline the correct words (Ø means 'zero article').

The colourful world of
Aelita Andre

Aelita Andre is [1]a / Ø six-year-old artist from Melbourne, Australia. She loves [2]the / Ø colours, and her paintings are bright and wild. She sometimes adds [3]the / Ø small toys to her pictures, such as plastic dinosaurs and butterflies.
[4]A / The young painter has already earned more than £100,000, and [5]Ø / the people have described her as 'the youngest professional artist in [6]Ø / the world'. When Aelita was five, her work was on show in [7]the / an art gallery in New York.
Aelita's mother says, 'You know how [8]Ø / the young children paint for a few minutes and then lose interest? When Aelita was two, she often painted for an hour without stopping.'

c 💬 Complete the questions with a, an, the or Ø. Then ask and answer the questions.
1 Do you like spending time in ___ countryside?
2 How many times ___ year do you go to ___ cinema?
3 Can you remember ___ first time you went to school?
4 Have you ever called ___ police?
5 Did you go anywhere interesting ___ last week? If so, where?
6 Can you play ___ piano or any other musical instrument?
7 Would you like to be ___ artist? Why / Why not?

2 VOCABULARY

a 💬 Underline the correct words. Which sentences are true for you?
1 People think I'm confidence / confident, but I'm not.
2 I'd like to be a successful / success businessperson.
3 I've already succeeded / achieved a lot of my goals.
4 I'm very patient / patience with young children.
5 I'm very talkative / sensitive, so people often tell me to be quiet.

b Complete the sentences with the correct -ing or -ed forms of the words in brackets.
1 I hate this kind of music. It's really _____! (depress)
2 I thought the plane was going to crash. It was _____! (terrify)
3 Ivan was very _____ that he didn't get the job. (disappoint)
4 I like travelling by train. It's more _____ than driving. (relax)
5 I hope Jane was _____ with her exam results. (satisfy)

3 WORDPOWER so and such

a Match statements and questions 1–6 with responses a–f.
1 ☐ How many people were in the group?
2 ☐ Julie works so hard!
3 ☐ How many pages have you written?
4 ☐ Simon's a bit of an introvert.
5 ☐ You're getting married. That's such good news!
6 ☐ We're going to need a lot of stuff!

a Yes, paper, glue, paint, scissors and so on.
b About 20 or so, I think. I didn't speak to all of them.
c So he doesn't like working in big groups, then?
d Yes, I'm so happy!
e Ten so far, but I haven't finished yet.
f I know. And she's such a nice person, too.

b Find examples of rules 1–3 in 3a.
1 We use so + clause to describe a result. ___
2 We use so before an adjective or adverb to add emphasis. ___ , ___
3 We use such before an adjective + noun to add emphasis. ___ , ___

c Match the words in the box with the meanings.

and so on   so far   or so

1 up to now _____
2 there are more things on the list _____
3 more or less _____

d Complete the sentences with one, two or three words. One of the words must be so or such.
1 Emma speaks _____ quickly!
2 We need to leave in 10 minutes _____.
3 It was too difficult _____ I asked for help.
4 She's _____ interesting person.
5 I've been trying to find a present for my brother, but I haven't had much success _____.
6 I don't like _____ hot weather.
7 We need simple food for the picnic, like bread, cheese, eggs, tomatoes _____.
8 It was _____ big achievement for me.

e 💬 Think of famous people who match the descriptions below.
1 ... is such an amazing singer.
2 ... is so funny.
3 ... is so rich.
4 ... does such good things for other people.

↻ REVIEW YOUR PROGRESS

How well did you do in this unit? Write 3, 2 or 1 for each objective.
3 = very well   2 = well   1 = not so well

I CAN ...

describe people and their abilities.	☐
describe feelings.	☐
offer and ask for help.	☐
write an informal online advert.	☐

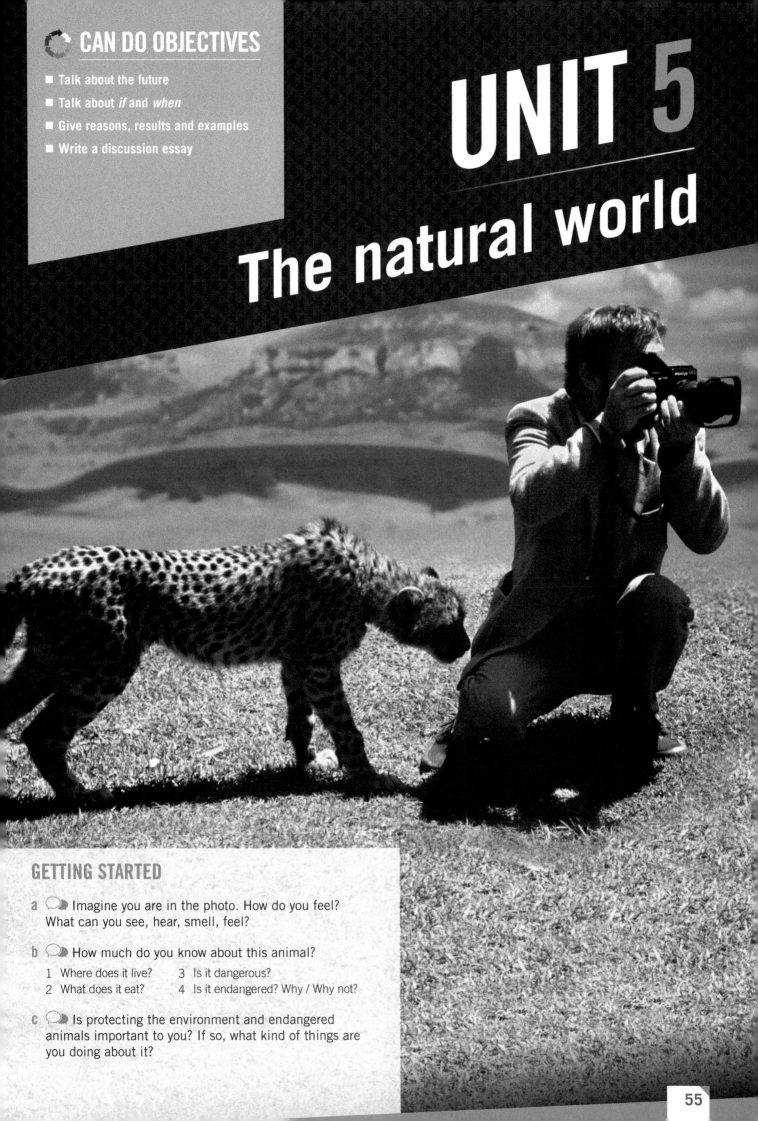

CAN DO OBJECTIVES

- Talk about the future
- Talk about *if* and *when*
- Give reasons, results and examples
- Write a discussion essay

UNIT 5
The natural world

GETTING STARTED

a 💬 Imagine you are in the photo. How do you feel? What can you see, hear, smell, feel?

b 💬 How much do you know about this animal?

1 Where does it live?   3 Is it dangerous?
2 What does it eat?   4 Is it endangered? Why / Why not?

c 💬 Is protecting the environment and endangered animals important to you? If so, what kind of things are you doing about it?

1 VOCABULARY Environmental issues

a Match the words in **bold** in sentences 1–8 with the descriptions in a–h.

1 Is air **pollution** a problem where you live? If yes, how can we **prevent** it?
2 What **wildlife** or natural environments are **endangered** in your country?
3 Are there any **conservation projects** to help **protect** these animals and plants or **save** these places?
4 Do most people support these projects?
5 Have new roads and buildings **damaged** the environment near you?
6 Do most people in your country care enough about **climate change**?
7 What can ordinary people do to help **the environment**?
8 Are you **environmentally friendly**? For example, do you **recycle** glass and paper?

a a noun that means the air, land and water where people, animals and plants live
b four verbs that are used to talk about solutions
c a verb which means 'destroyed' or 'hurt'
d two nouns that are environmental problems
e a noun that can be a solution to environmental problems
f a noun that means 'animals and plants'
g an adjective that describes animals and plants that may disappear
h a phrase that means 'not harmful to the environment'

b ▶2.2 **Pronunciation** How is the <u>underlined</u> letter *a* pronounced in each word below? Complete the table. Listen and check.

~~animals~~   ch<u>a</u>nge   clim<u>a</u>te   conserv<u>a</u>tion   d<u>a</u>maged
end<u>a</u>ngered   gl<u>a</u>ss   n<u>a</u>tural   p<u>a</u>per   pl<u>a</u>nts

/eɪ/	/aɪ/	/æ/	/ə/
			animals

c ▶2.2 Listen again and repeat the words.

d 💬 Choose two questions from 1a that interest you. Discuss your answers to the questions.

e ▶ Now go to Vocabulary Focus 5A on p.154

2 READING

a Read about the Whitley Fund for Nature below and answer the questions.

1 Who do they give money to?
2 How much money do they give?
3 What can winners do with the money?

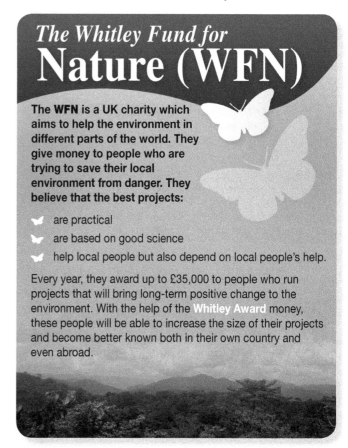

The Whitley Fund for Nature (WFN)

The **WFN** is a UK charity which aims to help the environment in different parts of the world. They give money to people who are trying to save their local environment from danger. They believe that the best projects:

- are practical
- are based on good science
- help local people but also depend on local people's help.

Every year, they award up to £35,000 to people who run projects that will bring long-term positive change to the environment. With the help of the **Whitley Award** money, these people will be able to increase the size of their projects and become better known both in their own country and even abroad.

b You are going to read about three people who won £35,000 to help their local environments. Look at the photos on p.57. What do you think their projects are?

c Work in groups of three, a, b and c. Read your part of the article on p.57 and answer the questions below.

1 Where does the person work?
2 How did they first get interested in conservation?
3 What wildlife are they trying to protect?
4 Does the person work with local people? What does he/she do?
5 What does the person hope will happen in the future?

d 💬 Work in your group. Use the information in 2c to discuss these questions.

1 What do the people and their projects have in common?
2 Do you think one project is more important than the others?
3 Which project would you like to visit or help? Why?

WFN
WHITLEY FUND FOR NATURE

a Ekwoge Enang Abwe

The Ebo forest in Cameroon covers almost 2,000 km^2 and is home to a unique mix of 11 primates, including gorillas and the Nigeria-Cameroon chimpanzee, the most endangered of the chimpanzees. These amazing chimps use tools to fish and open fruit. In addition, the spectacular Goliath frog, the largest frog in the world, lives here.

The Cameroon government is considering turning the Ebo forest into a national park with a focus on conservation research and tourism, but there are still threats from local people and large companies who want to use the land for farming.

Ekwoge Enang Abwe grew up in a village in Cameroon, so his love for chimpanzees began at an early age. He has played an important role in the area for almost a decade and, since 2010, he has been managing the Ebo Forest Research Project.

As well as encouraging local communities to be proud of the forest's unique biodiversity, this project has been doing biological research in the forest. The project has regular contact with communities through environmental and conservation education. They hope they will be able to create a safe future for the Ebo forest.

b Dr Aparajita Datta

In 1995, Dr Aparajita Datta arrived at the Pakke Tiger Reserve in north-east India to study the local wildlife. Her attention was captured by a species of beautiful birds called hornbills. These birds are endangered because of hunting and the destruction of their forest home. Aparajita now leads a programme to conserve them.

India's north-eastern region is known for its biological and cultural diversity. The area contains the world's most northerly tropical rainforests with an estimated 7,000–8,000 species of flowering plants, and over 600 bird and 150 mammal species, including tigers and elephants. The region also has small tribal communities and these communities often depend on using the resources from the forest to survive. Aparajita and her team are working with local people and the government. They hope to find a balance between the conservation of wildlife and the needs of the local communities. Aparajita is spreading knowledge of the importance of hornbills to the forest – plants need them to spread their seeds. There is also a nest adoption programme, with money going to villagers who help to protect the birds.

c Çağan Şekercioğlu

Turkey has a huge variety of natural environments, from Mediterranean forests to coastal mountains. But many of these areas are threatened by the construction of new dams and roads. ÇağanŞekercioğlu has been working hard to protect some of these areas. He is the first conservationist to win two Whitley Gold Awards.

In 2008, he won his first award for his work to protect the natural environment around Lake Kuyucuk, home to over 40,000 birds of 227 species. This work included research into the local wildlife, environmental education programmes for schools, and promoting nature tourism to support the local economy.

He won the award again in 2013 after he persuaded the government to create Turkey's first Wildlife Corridor. Approximately 4.5 million trees will be planted to connect the Sarıkamış-Allahuekber National Park to the forests along the Black Sea coast and the Caucasus mountains in neighbouring Georgia. This will allow large animals, such as the wolf, brown bear and Caucasian lynx, to move freely and safely.

Çağan's interest in conservation began when, as a teenager in Istanbul, a local wetland area where he had played as a small child was destroyed. This early experience inspired his life's work of protecting Turkey's wildlife habitats. For his next mission, he hopes to stop the construction of a dam that could destroy one of the world's most important wetlands.

3 GRAMMAR Future forms

a ▶ 2.4 Masha is going to Costa Rica to work on an environmental project. Listen to her talking about it. How much does she know about the project?

b ▶ 2.4 Listen again. Are these sentences true (T) or false (F)?

1 The government in Costa Rica wants to save the rainforests.
2 Masha will find out more about her project soon.
3 She knows exactly who she's going to work with.
4 She promises to send Phil regular emails.

c Match the future verb forms in 1–4 with uses a–d.

1 ☐ It takes quite a long time for forests to recover.
   They'll probably get better, but not immediately.
2 ☐ Tomorrow **I'm meeting** someone who worked on the project.
3 ☐ **I'm going to make** the most of my time in Costa Rica and learn some Spanish too.
4 ☐ **I'll write** regular updates on the blog, and you can follow that.

a to talk about an intention (a future plan)
b to make a prediction about the future
c to make an offer, promise or quick decision to do something in the future
d to talk about something you have arranged to do in the future

d Look at the future forms in **bold** below. Do they sound very sure, or a bit sure? What changes their meaning?

1 **They'll probably get** better, but not immediately.
2 But **I'll definitely be able** to save some turtles!
3 **Perhaps I'll work** with local people, too.
4 **I'm sure you'll have** a good time.

e Underline the best phrases in the blog below.

MY BLOG   Home About me Follow

Welcome to the first entry in my blog! ¹*I'm going / I'll go* to Costa Rica tomorrow for six weeks! It's all arranged. ²*I'll work / I'm working* on a turtle conservation project on the west coast. ³*It will definitely be / It's definitely being* hard work – but so interesting! ⁴*I'm going to work / I'm working* with turtles every day – counting them and collecting their eggs.

⁵*I'm going to have probably / I'm probably going to have* some Spanish lessons while I'm there. Perhaps ⁶*I'll be / I'm being* fluent in a few weeks!

⁷*I'll leave / I'm leaving* tomorrow and I'm back at the beginning of March.

⁸*I'll write / I'm writing* again soon with more details. Probably not tomorrow, because ⁹*I'll be / I'm being* tired after the flight. But definitely as soon as I can.

f ▶ Now go to Grammar Focus 5A on p.140

g Work in pairs. Write six predictions about your partner using the ideas in the box.

travel around the world	get your hair cut
learn another language	get a new job
live in a different country	be famous

1 I think you'll …
2 Perhaps you'll …
3 I'm sure you'll …
4 You'll probably …
5 You probably won't …
6 You definitely won't …

h 💬 Discuss your predictions.

> I'm sure you'll get a good job and become very rich in the next few years.
> I hope so!

4 SPEAKING

a Read predictions 1–6. Do you agree with them? If not, change them so you do.

In the future …
1 people will stop killing endangered animals and cutting down trees.
2 we will lose some animal or plant species for ever.
3 people will discover new wildlife species.
4 pollution will continue to get worse in big cities.
5 more areas of my country will become national parks.
6 people will behave in a more environmentally friendly way (recycle more, use public transport more, etc.).

b 💬 Discuss your ideas. Do you generally agree with each other? Are you optimistic or pessimistic about the future?

> In general, our group is quite hopeful because we think that pollution will get better, not worse. We think that people will recycle more in the future.

5B If you go to the beach, you can see dolphins

(a)

1 LISTENING

a 💬 Look at photos a and b and discuss the questions.

1 What do you think each photo shows?
2 What is the material in photo b used for?
3 What is the connection between the things in the two photos?

b Read the TV guide and check your ideas.

ON 📺 TONIGHT...

Nature knows best, Channel 4, 21:30

In this series, Professor Leslie Cook takes a closer look at common objects which were invented by humans, but inspired by nature.

Professor Cook begins the programme by talking about Velcro: a material we use every day on our shoes, clothes, purses and bags. It was inspired by the 'hook and loop' system that some plants use to move their seeds. In 1948, Swiss engineer George de Mestral was walking with his dog in the countryside when he noticed that little seeds from a plant were sticking to his dog's fur. He studied the plants more closely and saw how the hooks on the plant attach themselves to the loops and curls of an animal's fur. This gave him the idea of making Velcro.

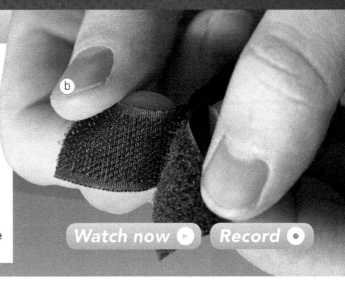
(b)

Watch now ▶   **Record** ⏺

c 💬 Match the things from the natural world (1–3) with the related objects (a–c).

(1) a thorny dragon lizard
(2) a spider
(3) a typical seashell

(a) a robot spider
(b) a safety helmet
(c) a glass of water

d ▶2.8 Listen to part of the TV programme and check your ideas.

e ▶2.8 Listen again and complete the summary with one word in each gap.

- One reptile, the thorny dragon lizard, can pull up water through 'pipes' in its [1]_____. It has inspired a device which can [2]_____ water. This will help people who live in very [3]_____ environments.
- Most spiders can move [4]_____ and make themselves very small. This has inspired the invention of a [5]_____ robot which will help people who are trapped in [6]_____ spaces.
- Seashells are very [7]_____ and light. This has inspired the production of material for safety [8]_____ such as gloves and helmets.

f Which of the inventions do you think is most useful? Why?

g 💬 Compare your ideas in 1f. Do you agree about the most useful invention?

2 GRAMMAR Zero and first conditional

a Read the conditional sentences from the TV programme and <u>underline</u> the correct words in rules 1 and 2.

- Zero conditional: *If the lizard puts a foot somewhere wet, its skin pulls the water up and over its whole body.*
- First conditional: *If we are successful, the device will provide water for people who live in very dry environments.*

1 The *zero / first* conditional talks about what will probably happen in the future as a result of something.
2 The *zero / first* conditional talks about what always happens as a result of something.

b <u>Underline</u> the correct words in rules 1 and 2 below.

1 We can use *if / when* to talk about things which will possibly or can happen.
2 We can use *if / when* for things which will definitely happen.

c Complete the text below with the correct form of the verbs in the box.

try   succeed   save   attach   make   fall off

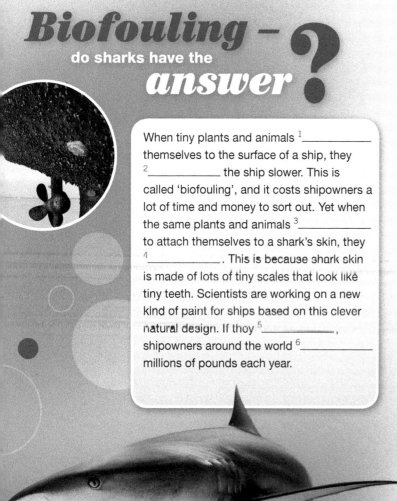

Biofouling –
do sharks have the
answer?

When tiny plants and animals ¹_____ themselves to the surface of a ship, they ²_____ the ship slower. This is called 'biofouling', and it costs shipowners a lot of time and money to sort out. Yet when the same plants and animals ³_____ to attach themselves to a shark's skin, they ⁴_____. This is because shark skin is made of lots of tiny scales that look like tiny teeth. Scientists are working on a new kind of paint for ships based on this clever natural design. If they ⁵_____, shipowners around the world ⁶_____ millions of pounds each year.

d ▶ Now go to Grammar Focus 5B on p.140

e 💬 Complete the sentences so they are true for you. Work in pairs and compare your sentences.

1 When I get a cold, I …
2 When I need to study for an exam, I …
3 If I go to a party where I don't know anyone, I …
4 If it rains today, I …
5 If I'm not too busy this weekend, I …
6 If I get up early tomorrow, I …

3 READING AND VOCABULARY
The natural world

a Look at the photos on p.61. Which animals or plants can you see? Read *Animals have adapted to survive everywhere* quickly and check your answers.

b Look at the words in the box. Which can you see in the photos?

branch   feathers   fur   leaf   paws
petals   scales   skin   tail   web

c Read the article again on p.61 and complete the gaps with the words in 3b.

d ▶2.11 **Pronunciation** Words with several consonants together can sometimes be difficult to pronounce correctly. Listen and practise saying these words, paying attention to the <u>underlined</u> parts.

a<u>dap</u>t   ba<u>ckgr</u>ound   bra<u>nch</u>   de<u>str</u>uction
mu<u>shr</u>oom   <u>scr</u>eam   <u>spl</u>ash   <u>spr</u>eading   <u>thr</u>eatened

e 💬 Which animal or plant on p.61 do you think is the most amazing? Do you know any other animals which can do amazing things?

f 💬 Describe the animals and plants in the box using the words in 3b. Do not say what you are describing. Try to guess your partner's word.

chicken   goldfish   monkey   orang-utan   palm tree
parrot   pine tree   rose   shark   snake   spider

> It's tall, and has short branches. It has little leaves. It doesn't lose its leaves in the winter.
>
> A pine tree?

g ▶ Now go to Vocabulary Focus 5B on p.155

ANIMALS HAVE
ADAPTED to survive
EVERYWHERE

Polar bears are a good example. They have layers of fat under their [1]_____, which means that they can swim in freezing water. Not only this, but it's very difficult for other animals to see them in the snow. Because they have completely white [2]_____, they can easily run up to other animals and attack with their huge [3]_____.

Another amazing animal is the ptarmigan. This Arctic bird is also white, which helps it hide in the snow. However, when the snow melts, the bird's [4]_____ change colour. From its head to its [5]_____, it turns grey to match the rocky environment.

Plants have adapted, too. This bee orchid looks exactly like it has a real bee resting on its [6]_____. This 'bee' is actually part of the flower, and it's nature's way of attracting real bees to the orchid.

Many fish can change the colour of their [7]_____ instantly to match their background.

At first, you might think that this is a [8]_____. But it's really an Indian leaf butterfly, sitting on the [9]_____ of a tree. Because it doesn't look like a butterfly, it can hide from other animals that would like to eat it.

This Amazon jungle spider also has an inventive way of protecting itself. It creates a [10]_____ which looks like a much larger spider, possibly to frighten other animals.

4 SPEAKING

a You are going to recommend the best place to experience the natural beauty of your country. Make notes on these topics:

- beautiful places
- what you can see there (rivers, forests, beaches, etc.)
- animals or plants you can see
- what you can do
- the best time of year to go

b 💬 Practise talking about the places on your list. Try to use conditional sentences.

> If you go to the beach near here, you will be able to see dolphins.

> If you like forests, you can go to …

c 💬 Work with another pair. Take turns to describe your places.

1 LISTENING

a 💬 Discuss the questions.

1 What hobbies and interests do you have?
2 Could any of your hobbies become a job? Would you like to do those jobs?

b 💬 You are going to watch Rachel and Becky talking about Rachel's job. Discuss the questions.

1 Why do you think Rachel became a florist?
2 What might the advantages of the job be?

c ▶2.14 Watch or listen to Part 1. Do Rachel and Becky mention your ideas?

d ▶2.14 Watch or listen to Part 1 again. Complete each sentence with one or two words.

1 Tina spent the morning _____ .
2 Tina _____ to be in the photos.
3 Becky thinks that being a florist is good because you can be your own _____ .
4 Becky doesn't like dealing with other people's _____ .
5 Rachel suggests that Becky could be a _____ .

2 USEFUL LANGUAGE
Reasons, results and examples

a Complete the sentences with the words/phrases in the box.

for instance   such as   like   because of

1 That's _____ Tina. She spent the morning cleaning up!
2 Oh, lots of things. _____ , all I seem to do is deal with other people's problems, _____ issues with their pay or holidays.
3 **Becky** I wish I had a job where I could travel the world, spread my wings, be free!
   Rachel _____ ?

b ▶2.15 Listen and check your answers.

c Add the words/phrases in the box to the table.

because   for instance   like   as a result   due to
for example   since   because of   so   such as

Giving reasons	Giving results	Giving examples

d Read this conversation and underline the correct words/phrases.

A So, do you still want to be a vet?
B Sure. That's my dream. I've always wanted to work with animals, [1]*for example / due to*, in a zoo or something like that.
A A zoo! Wow, that would be good.
B Well, I need to do lots of things first, [2]*since / like* finding the best college to go to.
A I see. And is it easy to become a vet?
B Not really. It takes years at university [3]*because of / so* all the things you have to study. But that's OK. I really want to do it, [4]*so / for example* I'm sure I won't find it too difficult.
A Well, if there's anything I can do to help, [5]*so / such as* looking at college websites, let me now!

3 LISTENING

a Look at photos a–c above. Which one would be best for Rachel's website?

b ▶2.16 Watch or listen to Part 2. Which photo does Rachel suggest using first? Does Becky agree?

c Answer the questions.
1 What is Rachel looking at on the computer?
2 Do they choose a photo for Rachel's website in the end?

d 💬 Do you think that Becky should give up her job and become a photographer?

4 CONVERSATION SKILLS
Giving yourself time to think

a ▶2.17 Listen and complete the extract.
Becky Rachel, we can't see you in that one.
Rachel OK, _____, I think this one.

b Complete the exchanges with the words in the box.

Just   Let   sure   Well   That's

1 **A** When did you meet Frankie?
  B _____ me see, I think it was in 2004.
2 **A** This thermometer says it's 21° in here.
  B I'm not _____. I think that's wrong.
3 **A** How old were you when you decided to work with animals?
  B _____ a good question … I was about 15, I think.
4 **A** What time does the restaurant open?
  B _____ a second, I'm not sure. I'll check on their website.
5 **A** Why did you decide to resign?
  B _____, I was bored in my job.

c 💬 Ask and answer the questions. Give yourself time to think using phrases from 4b.
1 What's your dream job?
2 What's your favourite natural place? (e.g. the beach, mountains, forest)

> Let me see … I think my dream job involves working with animals …

5 PRONUNCIATION
Voiced and unvoiced consonants

a ▶2.18 Listen to these words from the conversation which begin with the sounds /p/ and /b/.

pay   people   Becky   being

b Repeat the words in 5a. Touch your throat when you try to say them. Then complete the rules with /b/ and /p/.

1 When you say _____, there is a sound in the throat.
2 When you say _____, there is no sound in the throat.

c ▶2.19 Listen and underline the words you hear.
1 pay / bay   4 rope / robe
2 pie / buy   5 pride / bride
3 pair / bear

d ▶2.20 Listen and repeat the words in 5c. Which sounds are voiced in the throat? Which sounds are not voiced?

6 SPEAKING

▶ Communication 5C   💬 Student A: Read the information below. Student B: Go to p.128.

Student A
1 You don't like your job and you want to quit. Think about the answers to these questions.
 • Why don't you like it?
 • What are you going to do next? Why?

2 Student B will tell you he/she is going to move to another part of the country. Ask him/her about their decision, including why he/she has decided to do this.

⟳ Unit Progress Test

CHECK YOUR PROGRESS

You can now do the Unit Progress Test.

1 SPEAKING AND LISTENING

a 💬 How much do you know about whales?

b 💬 Look at the Whale File on the right. Which sentence is NOT true? Check your answer on p.127.

c ▶2.21 Liz Kerr is an environmental journalist who is helping whales that have come ashore. Listen to her audio diary and answer the questions.

1 How many whales is Liz looking after?
2 Is she working alone or in a group?
3 What happened in the end?

d ▶2.21 Listen again and complete the suggestions for saving whales that have come ashore. Write one word in each gap.

1 Don't try and do things on your own – talk to the Marine _____ Service.
2 Put on a wetsuit – it can get quite _____ .
3 Cover the whale with _____ towels.
4 Pour buckets of water over the whale to keep her _____ .
5 Make sure you don't _____ the whale's blowhole.
6 Make a _____ in the sand around the whale to fill with water.
7 When the tide comes in, _____ the whale out to sea again.

THE WHALE FILE TRUE OR FALSE?

1 Whales aren't fish, so they need to come to the surface to breathe.
2 All whales have teeth.
3 Female whales are bigger than male ones.
4 Whales never sleep because they need to breathe.
5 Whales breathe every 15 minutes.
6 Whales can communicate by singing to each other.
7 Whales sometimes swim onto the shore and can't get back to sea.

2 READING

a Read Tomas' essay about water pollution below. In his opinion, who should do something about this kind of pollution?

b Read the essay again. Are the sentences true (T) or false (F)?

1 Tomas suggests that we probably don't complain when people throw rubbish in water.
2 He suggests there's more rubbish in lakes than on beaches.
3 Eating plastic can make animals and birds ill.
4 Forgotten bits of fishing net can kill fish.
5 Tomas thinks water pollution is worse than air pollution.

c 💬 What do you think should be done about water pollution?

Keeping our water clean

1 If you walk down the street and see someone throw a plastic bottle on the ground, you'll probably get annoyed. You might even say something to that person. But do we react in the same way when we see people throwing rubbish into the sea? We all know how rubbish damages the environment on land, but we often forget the effect that it can have on environments like the sea, lakes and rivers, too.

2 First of all, water pollution looks terrible. Beautiful beaches can become covered in rubbish when whatever we have thrown into the water comes ashore. It's just not pleasant to swim in rivers and lakes that have plastic bags floating in them.

3 Secondly, rubbish can hurt animals and birds that live in or by the water. If they see a plastic bottle, they may think it is food. However, when they try and eat the bottle, it can get caught in their mouth or stomach and stop them from eating anything else. Plastic bottles can also stop dolphins from breathing. Sometimes, fishing boats leave bits of fishing net behind in the water. Fish can get caught in this and die.

4 Finally, people forget that plastic contains chemicals which stay in the water. This is very bad for both fish and plants. If you eat fish containing these chemicals, then you can also get sick.

5 In conclusion, I would say that we need to worry about water pollution as much as we care about land or air pollution. We should all look after the seas, lakes and rivers, and remember to take our rubbish away with us.

3 WRITING SKILLS
Organising an essay; signposting language

a How is the essay organised? Tick (✓) 1 or 2.

1 ☐ introduction → a discussion of different points connected to the topic → conclusion
2 ☐ introduction → points in favour of the topic → points against the topic → conclusion

b Look at the sentence below and answer the questions.

First of all, water pollution looks terrible.

1 Which paragraph of the essay does the sentence come from?
2 Does the signposting phrase in **bold** refer to something that has already been mentioned or introduce a new topic?
3 What other signposting phrases in the essay are similar to this one?

c Read the essay again and answer the questions.

1 In the first paragraph, does *you* refer to 'people in general' or 'the reader'?
2 In the first paragraph, what does *we* refer to?
3 Why does Tomas use these two pronouns?
4 In paragraph 5, what phrase does Tomas use to introduce his opinion?

4 WRITING

a Plan an essay on an environmental issue. Choose one of the topics below or your own idea. Make notes about your topic. Try to think of at least three main points with examples.

air pollution   cutting down forests   electric cars
taking too many fish from the sea   wasting food

b 💬 Compare your ideas with a partner.

c Write the essay. Use the structure in 3a. Use signposting expressions to organise your ideas. Make sure you communicate directly with the reader in the introduction and conclusion.

d 💬 Read each other's essays. Do you agree with the other students' opinions?

UNIT 5
Review and extension

1 GRAMMAR

a <u>Underline</u> the correct words.

1 The flowers close when you *will touch* / *touch* them.
2 They've decided they aren't *building* / *going to build* a road through the forest.
3 *Shall* / *Will* I pick the apples or do you want to do it?
4 Unless the government does more to stop hunting, tigers *are dying out* / *will die out*.
5 If you find a plant that you haven't seen before, *don't* / *you won't* touch it, please.
6 Don't eat wild mushrooms *unless* / *if* you know they're safe.

b Complete the sentences with the correct future form of the verbs in brackets. (Sometimes there is more than one possible answer.)

1 This weekend, I _____ (not/do) anything special – just staying at home.
2 _____ (you/carry on) learning English when you _____ (finish) this course?
3 It's very cold. I think it _____ (snow) this evening.
4 If the sky _____ (be) red in the morning, it _____ (rain) later in the day.

2 VOCABULARY

a <u>Underline</u> the correct words.

1 The children jumped across the *stream* / *river* / *lake*.
2 A *valley* / *rainforest* / *national park* is a tropical, wet place with lots of trees.
3 The sun was shining, but it was completely dark inside the *bay* / *coast* / *cave*.
4 We could see the monkey hanging from the *leaf* / *skin* / *branch* of a tree.
5 The fish's *scales* / *feathers* / *wings* were blue, white and black.
6 Dogs and bears have *webs* / *shells* / *paws*.

b Complete the words.

1 The w _ _ d _ _ _ e in the national park is amazing – from butterflies to flowers to elephants.
2 The Blue Whale and the Mountain Gorilla are both e _ _ _ _ g _ _ _ d s _ _ _ _ _ s.
3 Most countries r _ c _ _ _ e paper, glass and cardboard.
4 The cl _ _ a _ e is changing; some places are getting hotter and some are getting colder.
5 Building new roads d _ m _ _ es the environment.
6 They want to c _ t d _ _ n the trees so they can use the land for farming.

3 WORDPOWER *problem*

a Match pictures a–f with sentences 1–6.

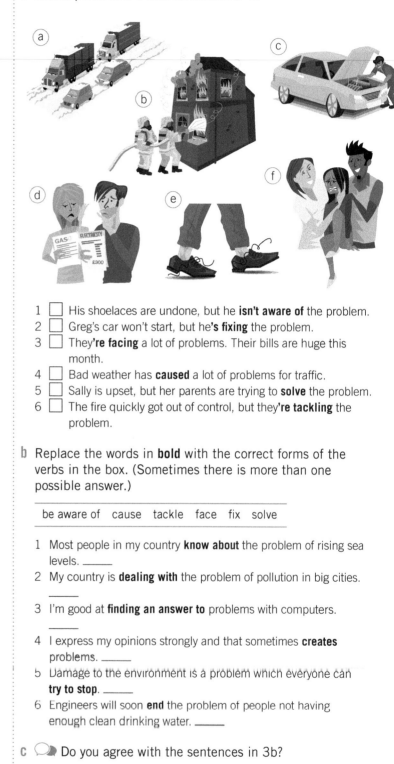

1 ☐ His shoelaces are undone, but he **isn't aware of** the problem.
2 ☐ Greg's car won't start, but he**'s fixing** the problem.
3 ☐ They**'re facing** a lot of problems. Their bills are huge this month.
4 ☐ Bad weather has **caused** a lot of problems for traffic.
5 ☐ Sally is upset, but her parents are trying to **solve** the problem.
6 ☐ The fire quickly got out of control, but they**'re tackling** the problem.

b Replace the words in **bold** with the correct forms of the verbs in the box. (Sometimes there is more than one possible answer.)

be aware of   cause   tackle   face   fix   solve

1 Most people in my country **know about** the problem of rising sea levels. _____
2 My country is **dealing with** the problem of pollution in big cities. _____
3 I'm good at **finding an answer to** problems with computers. _____
4 I express my opinions strongly and that sometimes **creates** problems. _____
5 Damage to the environment is a problem which everyone can **try to stop**. _____
6 Engineers will soon **end** the problem of people not having enough clean drinking water. _____

c 💬 Do you agree with the sentences in 3b?

⟳ REVIEW YOUR PROGRESS

How well did you do in this unit? Write 3, 2 or 1 for each objective.
3 = very well   2 = well   1 = not so well

I CAN ...

talk about the future.	☐
talk about *if* and *when*.	☐
give reasons, results and examples.	☐
write a discussion essay.	☐

Communication Plus

1B GRAMMAR Student A

▶ Now go back to p.13

5D SPEAKING AND LISTENING

The wrong statement is: 4 Whales never sleep because they need to breathe.

In fact, whales do sleep. They appear to take turns letting one side of their brain sleep. The other side of the brain stays awake so they remember to breathe.

▶ Now go back to p.64

Results

Research shows that about 70% of the population are extroverts and about 30% of the population are introverts, but not many people are either extreme introverts or extreme extroverts.
Are you a confident introvert? A shy extrovert? Or something else?

How many 'yes' answers did you have?

7	6	5	4	3	2	1	0

Introvert   **Extrovert**

Introverts don't need much external excitement in order to feel happy. They feel alive when they have time to focus on the thoughts and feelings inside them. If you had four or five 'yes' answers, then you're a sociable introvert. You really enjoy spending time with people, but you always need to balance it with time on your own to recharge your batteries.

Extroverts feel happiest when they have lots of external excitement. They get ideas from any kind of conversation and discussion, and they enjoy having people and activity around them. If you had more 'no' answers, then you're probably a quiet extrovert. You don't always say much when you're around other people, but you love the energy you get from their company.

Now go back to p.48

4C SPEAKING Student B

1 Student A wants help. You know quite a bit about computers and you like helping people. But you have your French class on Tuesdays and Thursdays, so you can't go shopping on those days.
2 You need help moving some furniture and you think that Student A has a big car. You would like to move it on Friday. Ask for Student A's help.

Now go back to p.51

5C SPEAKING Student B

1 You are going to move to another part of the country. Think about the answers to these questions.
   • Why are you moving?
   • How do you feel about this?
2 Student A will tell you about his/her job. Ask him/her about what he/she is going to do.

Now go back to p.63

1B GRAMMAR Student B

This week's aims: The Present Continuous;
sports vocabulary

Class trip to Science
Museum: Monday 9th June

▶ Now go back to p.13

Grammar Focus

1A Subject and object questions

Most questions in English need an auxiliary verb (e.g. *do, be, have* or a modal verb) before the subject. The auxiliary verb can be positive or negative.

▶ 1.5

Question word	Auxiliary verb or *be*	Subject	Main verb	
	Can	I	borrow	your pen?
	Do	you	have	much homework?
Why	were	you		late?
Who	are	you	waiting	for?
How many people	have	you	invited	to the party?

▶ 1.6

When we ask about the subject of the verb, we use the same word order in the question as in the statement (subject – verb – object). Don't add an auxiliary verb to subject questions:

*Who **told you the news**? (*Stuart **told me the news**.)
*What **happened yesterday**? (*Nothing **happened yesterday**.)

Question word	Verb	
Who	told	you the news?
What	happened	yesterday?
How many people	are coming	to the party?
Which team	won	the match?

In questions with prepositions, the preposition goes at the end of the question:

A **Who** did you go to the cinema **with**?   **B** *My sister.*
A **What**'s he talking **about**?   **B** *His job.*

> **Tip**

> ***What ... like?*** and ***How ... ?***
> Use *What ... like?* to ask for a description of a person:
> **A** **What's** your teacher **like**?
> **B** *She's very friendly.*

> Use *How ... ?* to ask about a person's health:
> **A** **How**'s your sister?
> **B** *She's very well, thanks.*

> You can use *What ... like?* or *How ... ?* to ask for a description of a thing or event:
> **A** **What** was your holiday **like**? / **How** was your holiday?
> **B** *It was excellent.*

1B Present simple and present continuous

▶ 1.8 **Present simple**
We use the present simple for:
* facts which are true all the time.
  *The sun **rises** in the east. The bus **doesn't go** past my house.*
* habits and routines.
  *I **study** for about an hour a week. We never **get** much homework.*
* opinions and beliefs.
  *Do you **agree**?   I **don't know** the answer.*

▶ 1.9 **Present continuous**
We use the present continuous for:
* actions which are in progress at the moment of speaking.
  *Why **are** you **carrying** an umbrella? It**'s not raining**.*
* actions or situations around the moment of speaking.
  *He**'s studying** Russian at university.*
* future arrangements (see 5A p.140).
  *I**'m meeting** Andrew **tonight**.*

States and actions
The present continuous is not normally used to describe:
* mental states: *know, agree, understand, believe,* etc.
* likes and preferences: *like, want, love, hate, need, prefer,* etc.
* other states: *be, own, belong, forget, hear, seem, depend,* etc.

Special cases
Some verbs (e.g. *think, see, have*) can be used as states or actions, with different meanings:
State: *I **think** you're wrong.* (= my opinion)
Action: *I**'m thinking** about my birthday.* (= a mental process)
State: *I **see** what you mean.* (= I understand)
Action: *I**'m seeing** the doctor tomorrow.* (= I'm meeting him/her)
State: *I **have** a car / a sister.* (= possession, relationship, etc.)
Action: *I**'m having** a party / a shower / dinner.*

1A Subject and object questions

a Make questions with the words below.

1 listening / why / me / isn't / to / anybody

_____

2 you / question / I / ask / can / a

_____

3 borrow / did / book / whose / you

_____

4 about / are / worrying / what / you

_____

5 has / cake / who / my / eaten

_____

b Correct the mistake in each question.

1 What time you will be here? _____
2 Happened what to your leg? _____
3 To what are you listening? _____
4 Which speaker did gave the best presentation?

_____

5 How's your new friend like? _____

c Write a subject and an object question for each statement. Ask about the information in bold.

1 **400** people have commented on **your photo**.
   How many people have commented on your photo?
   What have 400 people commented on?

2 **A fire** damaged **the roof**.

_____

_____

3 **Joanna** is afraid of **spiders**.

_____

_____

4 **His brother** told them a joke about **elephants**.

_____

_____

d ▶ Now go back to p.9

1B Present simple and present continuous

a Match the pairs.

1 b He drives to work
2 a He's driving to work

3 ☐ He wears a red shirt
4 ☐ He's wearing a red shirt

5 ☐ I think
6 ☐ I'm thinking

7 ☐ I have dinner
8 ☐ I'm having dinner

a at the moment, so he can't answer the phone.
b every day.

c every time he goes to a football match.
d so you'll find him easily.

e it's going to be a nice day.
f about what to do at the weekend.

g right now. Can I call you back?
h at a restaurant every week.

b Complete the conversation with the present simple or present continuous form of the verbs in brackets.

A What [1]___are you reading___ (you / read)?
B It's an article about learning languages. It's really interesting!
A Really? [2]_____ (it / have) any good advice?
D Yes, it does. The writer [3]_____ (learn) Japanese.
He [4]_____ (want) to learn ten new words a day.
He [5]_____ (always revise) them again at the end
of each week to check he [6]_____ (still remember)
them. It [7]_____ (not sound) like much, but after a
year, he now [8]_____ (know) over 3,500 new words.
That's a lot!
A Wow, yes, I [9]_____ (see) what you mean. So
[10]_____ (you/think) of trying this technique?
B Yes, maybe. I [11]_____ (try) to learn Russian at the
moment, but I [12]_____ (not make) much progress.
A Really? Why [13]_____ (you/learn) Russian?
B I [14]_____ (go) to Moscow next year for six months.

Yes, I'm studying Russian at the moment. I study about an hour a day but I'm not making much progress... I don't know why.

c ▶ Now go back to p.13

2A Present perfect simple and past simple

▶ 1.26 Present perfect simple

We use the present perfect simple to talk about:

- experiences in our lifetime, or another unfinished time period.
  ***Have** you ever **had** a job interview?*
  *I**'ve** never **worked** in an office.*
  We can use adverbs like *ever, never, three times*, etc.
- news and recent events, often with a present result.
  *They**'ve** just **offered** me the job.* (result = I've got a job.)
  *The interviews **have** already **finished** – you're too late.*
  (result = You can't have an interview.)
  *She **hasn't called** me back yet.* (result = I'm still waiting to speak to her.)
  We can use adverbs like *just, already* and *yet*.
- unfinished states (when we want to talk about the duration).
  *I**'ve** only **had** this phone for a week.*
  *We**'ve lived** in London since 2010.*
  We use *for* to give the duration or *since* to give the starting point.

▶ 1.27 Past simple

We use the past simple for completed past actions in a completed past time period:
*She **didn't get** the job.*
*The interviews **finished** five minutes ago.*
*Why **did** you **miss** the bus?*
We often use past time phrases like *last week, a few days ago, when I was a child*.

▶ 1.28 Present perfect or past simple?

We often introduce a topic with the present perfect and then change to the past simple in the next sentence to talk about the details:
*I**'ve had** lots of job interviews. The last one **was** about three months ago – it **was** terrible.*
*I**'ve lost** my keys. Maybe I **left** them on the bus this morning.*
*He **hasn't worked** here long. He **started** a few weeks ago.*
Don't use the present perfect when you describe an action that happened at a particular time. Use a past tense instead:
*They **left** yesterday / at four o'clock / ten minutes ago.*

2B Present perfect simple and present perfect continuous

Unfinished actions and states (duration)

- We use the present perfect simple with state verbs:
  *We**'ve owned** this car **for** several years and it has never broken down.*
  *She**'s known** him **since** they were children. They're very good friends.*
- We use the present perfect continuous with action verbs:
  *How long **have** you **been waiting**?*
  *I**'ve been working** on my essay **since** 6 o'clock.*
  *He**'s been playing** very well **so far** in this match.*

> **Tip**
>
> Some verbs (e.g. *work, live*) can be used as action verbs or state verbs with no important change of meaning:
> *How long **have** you **worked** here? / How long **have** you **been working** here?*

Recent past actions with present results

- We use the present perfect simple when <u>completing</u> an action has a result now:
  *I**'ve** just **finished** my essay.* (result of finishing writing = I can relax, I can hand in the work, etc.)
  A *The house looks lovely.*
  B *Thanks! We**'ve** just **painted** it.* (result of finishing painting = the house looks nice)

- We use the present perfect continuous when <u>doing</u> an activity has a result now:
  *I'm tired because I**'ve been writing** an essay.* (result of writing = I'm tired.)
  A *What's that smell?*
  B *We**'ve been painting** the living room.* (result of painting = the house smells of paint)

New habits and repeated actions

- We use the present perfect continuous to describe repeated activities which started recently:
  *I**'ve been doing** a lot of exercise lately.* (In the past, I didn't do much exercise.)
  *She**'s been coming** to the gym with me three times a week.* (She has recently started coming.)

▶ 1.32 Present perfect continuous

	I / you / we / they	he / she / it
+	*I**'ve been using** a new app.*	*He**'s been using** a new app.*
–	*I **haven't been sleeping** well.*	*She **hasn't been sleeping** well.*
Y/N?	*Have they **been living** abroad? Yes, they **have**. / No, they **haven't**.*	*Has she **been living** abroad? Yes, she **has**. / No, she **hasn't**.*

trics

2A Present perfect simple and past simple

a Find and correct the mistakes.

1 **A** How long do you live here? **B** About two years.   *have you lived*
2 I haven't been to work yesterday – I was ill.   *I didn't go to work*
3 **A** We need to email the bank this afternoon.
   B Don't worry – I've done it yet.   *Already or just yet*
4 On her CV she says she's got lots of experience, but in fact
   she hasn't never had a job in her life!   *she has never had*
5 I've wanted to work for your company since I've been a student.   *was*
6 **A** Have you heard the news? Louise has left her job!
   B Yes, I know. She's told me last week.
7 I've worked there for about six months. I've started in January.

b Complete the conversation with the present perfect or past simple form of the verbs in brackets.

A There's a really good job advert here in the newspaper. [1] _Have you seen_ (you / see) it?
B No, I [2] _haven't_ (not / read) the paper yet. You [3] _have had_ (have) it for hours. Can you show me?
A It's this one. Senior Marketing Specialist for a bank. I think you should apply for it.
B Er … no, I don't think so. They want someone with lots of experience in banking, but I [4] _I've never worked_ (never / work) in a bank.
A No, but you [5] _have worked_ (work) for lots of marketing companies, and you've [6] _did done_ (do) lots of projects for banks. Remember? You [7] _worked_ (work) on a really big banking project about eight years ago. It [8] _had been was_ (be) really good.
B Yes, but eight years is a long time ago. Everything's [9] _changed_ (change) in banking recently. It's a different world now. But what about you? Maybe you should apply. You [10] _told_ (tell) me last month that you wanted to try something new.
A Yes, but that [11] _was_ (be) last month. I [12] _applied_ (apply) for a job at a newspaper last week, and they've [13] _just emailed_ (just / email) me to offer me the job.
B Wow! Congratulations! [14] _have you accepted_ (you / accept) the offer yet?
A Not yet, no. But I think I will.

c ▶ Now go back to p.21

2B Present perfect simple and present perfect continuous

a Match the pairs.

1 I've had — b
2 I've been having — a
3 I've just read this book. — c
4 I've been reading this book. — b
5 Have you eaten — f
6 Have you been eating — e

a tennis lessons for a month.
b this car for a year.
c I thought it was amazing.
d I can't wait to finish it.
e properly recently? You look very thin!
f lunch yet?

b Complete the sentences using the words in brackets and the present perfect continuous.

1 The baby's face is dirty because _she's been eating._ (she / eat)
2 He's tired because _he's been cutting_ (he / cut / the grass)
3 They're stressed because _they've been trying_ (they / try / to fix the computer)
4 I'm hot because _I've been cooking_ (I / cook)
5 We're all wet because _it's been raining_ (it / rain)
6 They've got muddy shoes because _they've been playing_ (they / play / outside)

c Underline the best verb form in each sentence.

1 Angela's on the phone right now – she's talked / *she's been talking* to one of her friends for the last two hours!
2 *I've just found* / I've just been finding my glasses. I'm so happy! I lost them two days ago.
3 *I've known* / I've been knowing Jon for about 15 years.
4 I'm so tired. I've worked / *I've been working* since 7 o'clock this morning.
5 I can't drive, but *I've wanted* / I've been wanting to learn for a long time.
6 They've studied / *They've been studying* every night recently because they have an exam next week.

d ▶ Now go back to p.25

3A Narrative tenses

 Past simple

We use the past simple to describe the main events of a story in the order they happened:
*We **met** a few years ago. He **offered** to help me fix my car.*
*Later, we **became** good friends.*

▶ **1.43** **Past continuous**

We use the past continuous:
- to describe the situation at the beginning of a story.
  *That day, I **was driving** home from university for the summer.*
- for longer actions in comparison with shorter actions in the past simple.
  *Where **were** you **going** when I **saw** you by the road?*
  *I **was trying** to get home with some heavy bags when he **stopped** to help me.*
- when actions are interrupted by main events in the past simple.
  *I **was skiing** in the French Alps when I **had** my accident.*

We can connect past simple and past continuous actions with *as*, *while* and *when*:
*Somebody **stole** my bag **while** I **wasn't looking**.*
*Your sister **phoned while** you **were working**.*
*He **looked** out the window **while** the train **was going** through the countryside.*
*The car **broke down as** I **was driving** down the road.*

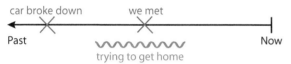

car broke down — *we met*

Past — trying to get home — Now

*As we **were walking** along the road together, we **chatted**.*

Don't use the past continuous for state verbs. Use the past simple instead:
*We met when I **was** a student.*
NOT *… when I was being a student.*

▶ **1.44** **Past perfect**

We use the past perfect to describe an event that happened before the story started, or earlier in the story than a main event:
*That summer, I **had** just **finished** my second year at university.*
*When we met, my car **had broken** down by the side of the road.*
*I **hadn't taken** my phone with me, so I couldn't phone for help.*

> **Tip**
>
> We can use *by* + a time with the past perfect to show what happened up to a point in the past:
> *I started reading it on Monday and **by Friday I'd read** the whole book.*
> *They were really late for the party. **By the time they arrived**, everyone else **had gone** home.*

3B used to, usually

We use *used to* to describe past habits and states:
*When I was at school, I **used to play** football every Saturday.* (past habit)
*The whole family **used to love** animals. We always had two or three pets in the house.* (past state)

The negative forms are *didn't use to* and *never used to*:
*My parents **didn't use to go** out much, so we spent a lot of time together.*
*We **never used to** understand my dad's jokes.*

There is no present tense of *used to*. Use adverbs of frequency instead:
*They **usually go** out to a restaurant once or twice a week.*
*How many times a month **do** you **usually visit** them?*

You can also use adverbs of frequency with the past simple and a past time phrase (e.g. *when I was a child, back then*):
*We **went** abroad for a holiday **quite often back then**.*

We can use the adverbials *not any more* and *not any longer* to say that a past habit or state has now stopped:
*I **don't** play football **any more**. I usually go to the gym instead.*
*They **don't** live in the same house **any longer**.*

We can use the adverb *still* to talk about a past habit or state that has not changed:
*I **still** love board games. I frequently play Chinese Chequers.*
*Do you **still** see him very often?*

Past simple or *used to*?

We use *used to* for situations that were true for a long time (e.g. a few months or years). For shorter periods of time, we usually use the past simple:
*When we were on holiday last week, we **went** swimming every day.*
NOT *… we used to go …*

We often use *used to* for situations that aren't true now.
*When I was a child I **used to love** ice cream, but now I don't really like it.*

Use the past simple, not *used to*, to describe something that happened once or a specified number of times.
*I **went** to the USA twice when I was a child.*
NOT *I used to go abroad twice …*

> **Tip**
>
> We often use a mixture of the past simple and *used to* to describe past situations. It sounds unnatural if you use *used to* for every verb.

3A Narrative tenses

a Underline the correct options.

I ¹*meeting* / *met* my friend Alex while I ²*was fixing* / *fixed* my bike last year. The wheel ³*fell* / *had fallen* off and I ⁴*was trying* / *had tried* to put it back on. Alex ⁵*had walked* / *was walking* down the street when he ⁶*saw* / *was seeing* me and he ⁷*was offering* / *offered* to help. After that, we ⁸*became* / *had become* friends.

I ⁹*met* / *had met* my friend Anna in a hospital. I ¹⁰*was being* / *was* there because I ¹¹*was falling* / *had fallen* over and ¹²*had broken* / *was breaking* my arm. Anna ¹³*was* / *had been* there because she ¹⁴*injured* / *had injured* her foot. We ¹⁵*started* / *were starting* talking while we ¹⁶*had waited* / *were waiting* to see the doctor. By the time the doctor ¹⁷*was arriving* / *arrived*, we ¹⁸*had become* / *became* good friends.

b Complete the interview with the most suitable form of the verbs in brackets. Sometimes there is more than one possible answer.

A When ¹_____*did*_____ the accident _____*happen*_____ (happen)?

B It ²_____ (happen) as I ³_____ (drive) along the High Street last night. I ⁴_____ (see) an old lady. Just as I ⁵_____ (turn) left, she ⁶_____ (fall) over onto the pavement right in front of me. I was pretty sure I could see why. A young man ⁷_____ (push) her over. Straight away I ⁸_____ (stop) my car and I ⁹_____ (jump) out. I ¹⁰_____ (run) over to the old lady. She ¹¹_____ (lie) on the ground and she ¹²_____ (cry).

A ¹³_____ (you / notice) anything else?

B Yes … a large flowerpot on the pavement. It ¹⁴_____ (be) broken.

A Where ¹⁵_____ (it / come) from?

B It ¹⁶_____ (fall) from a window above the street. The young man ¹⁷_____ (push) the old lady out of the way. He ¹⁸_____ (save) her life!

c ▶ Now go back to p.34

3B *used to, usually*

a Complete the text with the correct words/phrases.

<del>used to go</del>   use to have   used to be   went
used to have   usually visit   didn't use to go
don't go   live   lived   don't live   used to enjoy

When I was a child, I ¹____*used to go*____ to my grandparents' house in the mountains. We ²___*lived*___ in a city back then, and we visited them every year. We didn't ³*use to have* a car at that time, so we travelled by bus. It always took ages! We ⁴*didn't use to go* in the winter because there was too much snow.
I loved helping my grandfather in his garden (although I usually avoid gardening now!). He never ⁵*used to have* a lawnmower, so we had to cut the grass by hand. It was hard, but I ⁶*used to enjoy* it.
I still ⁷___*live*___ in the same city, but I ⁸___*don't go*___ to the mountains any more. My grandparents ⁹___*don't live*___ there any longer. They ¹⁰___*went*___ to live in a large town five years ago. Now, I ¹¹*usually visit* them in the summer, but it's not as nice as the mountains ¹²*used to be*

b If possible, change the verbs in **bold** to the correct form of *used to*. If it is not possible, put **✗**.

1 I **drank** a lot of cola, but now I don't. ☐ _*used to drink* …_
2 I **celebrated** New Year with my family last year. **✗**
3 She **had** long hair when she was younger. ☐
_____
4 Where **did** you **live** when you were a child? ☐
_____
5 I **went** for a run every day last week. ☐
_____
6 We **didn't wear** the same clothes all the time. ☐
_____
7 In the past, people **spent** more time at work. ☐
_____
8 **Did** you **play** with your sister when you were kids? ☐
_____
9 I **bought** this bag in London – it's my favourite bag. ☐
_____
10 They **weren't** friends in those days. ☐
_____

c ▶ Now go back to p.37

4A Modals and phrases of ability

General ability

We use *can* / *could* to talk about general abilities:
*I **can** ski, but I **can't** snowboard. I **couldn't do** maths at school.*

We only use *can* in the present tense and *could* in the past tense, so when we need another form we use *be able to*.
We use *be able to*:

* in the present perfect, past perfect and after modal verbs.
  *How long **have** you **been able to drive**?*
  *We hope we'**ll be able to come** on Saturday.*
  *Everyone **should be able to swim**.*
* after other verbs (e.g. *want*, *need*, *like*) or prepositions (e.g. *of*, *about*).
  *The person who gets the job **needs to be able to speak** English.*
  *I **like being able to visit** my parents regularly.*
  *Don't worry **about not being able to understand**. You'll be fine!*

Specific past achievements

Don't use *could* for specific past achievements:
*When I went to France last year, I **was able to** visit the Louvre.*
NOT *I could visit…*

I couldn't play the piano when I was a child but I can play very well now.

In negative sentences about specific past events, we use *couldn't* or *wasn't able to*:
*I went to France last year, but I **couldn't** remember / I **wasn't able to** remember any words in French.*
We can also use *managed to* for specific past achievements, especially to show that something was difficult:
*It was hard work, but I **managed to** finish the project.*

4B Articles

We use *a* / *an*, and *the* with singular countable nouns. We use *the* or no article with plural or uncountable nouns. The choice of article shows:

* if the topic is new.
  *I read **a great book** last week.* (= we haven't discussed this book before)
  *What was **the book** about?* (= the one we discussed earlier)
* if something is the only one.
  *Where are **the car keys**?* (= the only car keys we have.)
* if we are talking about things in general or in particular.
  Cats are clever animals. (= the animal)
  ***The** cats are in the garden.* (= our pets)

Other uses of *a* / *an*

* when you describe something or say what job someone has:
  *That's **a** beautiful photo. / He's **a** doctor.*
* in some frequency expressions:
  *I drink coffee once **a** week / three times **a** day.*

Other uses of *the*

* when the noun is defined by a defining relative clause:
  *I've just met **the** man who lives next door.* (= one specific man)
* before superlatives:
  *Kyoto is **the most beautiful city** in Japan.*
* with certain countries, oceans, rivers, or groups of islands:
  *I went to **the** USA / **the** Pacific / **the** Amazon / **the** Bahamas.*
* with some fixed expressions about:
  time: *all **the** time, most of **the** time, at **the** same time*
  places or seasons: *in **the** countryside / city; in **the** summer*
  free-time activities: *go to **the** cinema / **the** gym; listen to **the** radio (**but** watch TV)*

I've been reading a book.

I've been reading the book you lent me.

Other uses of no article

* in phrases about meals:
  *I **had breakfast** / **lunch** / **dinner** at 7am.*
  NOT *I had a/the breakfast …*
* in some fixed phrases about routines:
  *I usually **go home** / **go to bed** / **go to work** / **go to school** at … o'clock.*
* to talk about most countries, continents, cities, streets, etc.:
  I went to China / Africa / Paris / Bond Street.

> 💬 **Tip**
>
> Be careful with expressions with *next* / *last + week* / *month* / *year*:
> *I went there last week.* (= the calendar week before now)
> *I've been there twice in the last week.* (= the seven days before now)
> *We went there in the last week of the holidays.* (= a period of time with no connection to now)

4A Modals and phrases of ability

a <u>Underline</u> the correct option. If both options are possible, <u>underline</u> both of them.

1 I went to India last year but I *cannot / <u>could not</u>* take any pictures because my camera was broken.

2 *He's been able to swim / He can swim* since he was a child. ,

3 When they were children, they *could / were able to* run really fast.

4 She tried to read *War and Peace*, but she *wasn't able to / didn't manage to* finish it.

5 He *managed to / could* climb trees when he was a boy, but he *can't / couldn't* climb them now.

6 Katya needs to *can / be able to* speak Japanese in her new job.

7 You will *can / be able to* find a new person for the job soon, I'm sure.

8 I'm scared of *not being able to / can't* pass my exam tomorrow.

9 They *couldn't / didn't manage to* find a parking place.

10 I think everyone should *manage to / be able to* drive. It's an important skill.

b Complete each gap with a phrase from the box.

can swim   could all swim   ~~couldn't swim~~   couldn't walk   didn't manage to   was able to jump   was able to stand   needed to be able   to be able to   managed to climb

When I was a young child, I [1] <u>couldn't swim</u> – I only learnt to swim when I was about 14. I guess I thought that I didn't need [2]_____ swim, because I never went to swimming pools. But one day I went for a walk on a hill near the sea with my friends – we were about 13 at the time. Part of the path was missing in one place – we [3]_____ along it, so we decided to try to jump across. My friend Andy was quite big, so he [4]_____ across it very easily. But then it was my turn – I was a lot smaller, so I [5]_____ jump across. I fell down the hill and into the sea. My friends [6]_____, so they thought it was really funny to see me in the water, but I was really scared. Luckily, I [7]_____ on a rock under the water and then I [8]_____ out of the water. After that, I knew I [9]_____ to swim, so I started going to swimming lessons every week. And now I [10]_____ really well.

c ▶ Now go back to p.46

4B Articles

a Find the mistakes in these sentences.

1 Do you want to go to a cinema with me?   <u>Do you want to go to the cinema with me?</u>

2 Can you give me an advice?   _____

3 I want to buy new shirt.   _____

4 We had a good fun at the beach.   _____

5 I want to go to a countryside.   _____

6 I hope we have good weather at weekend.   _____

7 If you have problem, call me.   _____

8 I was in a shock for a few days.   _____

9 My brother is engineer.   _____

10 Please visit us if you have a time.   _____

b Complete the text with *a / an*, *the* or *Ø* (no article).

I don't like working in [1] <u>Ø</u> groups because I never know what to say when [2]_____ people talk to me. [3]_____ last year I joined [4]_____ language course and [5]_____ teacher made [6]_____ students work in [7]_____ groups for [8]_____ most activities. [9]_____ lessons that we had were good, but I wasn't happy about [10]_____ speaking activities. I know speaking is probably [11]_____ best way to learn to speak [12]_____ language, but I don't really need to speak in my job. [13]_____ only thing I want is to be able to write [14]_____ good emails without making [15]_____ mistakes. One day, after [16]_____ extremely difficult lesson, I decided to speak to [17]_____ teacher about [18]_____ problem. I explained [19]_____ situation and she listened carefully. She explained [20]_____ purpose of working in [21]_____ groups, and that she needs to find [22]_____ right balance for all of [23]_____ students in [24]_____ class. In [25]_____ end, I agreed to try to speak more, and she agreed to give me [26]_____ more time to work quietly.

c ▶ Now go back to p.49

5A Future forms

▶2.5 Decisions, plans and arrangements
We use *will* to make a spontaneous decision (= a decision while we are speaking):
OK, I'll come for a run with you.
We use *going to* to talk about future plans (= decisions we made earlier):
We're not going to stay at that hotel again.
We use the present continuous to talk about arrangements (= fixed plans, usually involving other people and specific times and places):
She's travelling to Central America on Sunday.

There is not a big difference in meaning between *going to* and the present continuous to talk about future plans / arrangements. Often both are possible:
I'm visiting / going to visit my sister this weekend.

▶2.6 Offers, promises and suggestions
We use *will* to make offers and promises:
I'll help you, if you like.
I'll always be here when you need me.

We use *shall + I / we* in questions to make offers and suggestions:
A *Shall I carry that for you?*   **B** *Oh, yes, please.*
A *Shall we go swimming on Saturday?*   **B** *That's a good idea.*

▶2.7 Predictions
We use *will* to make predictions based on our opinions:
I'm sure you'll learn a lot when you go travelling.
Don't put that there! It'll fall off.
We use *going to* to make predictions based on concrete facts (= things that we can see or information that we have read, etc.):
We should leave soon. The roads are going to be busy.
It's not going to rain. There isn't a cloud in the sky.

> **Tip** In negative sentences, say *I don't think + will.*
> **I don't think** *the forest* **will** *recover.* NOT *I think the forest* **won't recover.**

5B Zero and first conditional

Conditional sentences have two parts: the *if*-clause describes a possible event and the main clause describes the result of that event. The *if*-clause can come before or after the main clause. When the *if*-clause is first, put a comma between the two parts:
If *the lizard gets scared, it hides.*
The lizard hides **if** *it gets scared.*

▶2.9 Zero conditional
The zero conditional describes events and results that happen regularly or are always true. *If* and *when* both mean 'every time': every time the event happens, the same result happens. We use a present tense in both the *if*-clause and the main clause:
If *the lizard* **gets** *scared, it* **hides.**
If *I* **go** *to the city centre, I always* **eat** *in that restaurant.*
Anyone **can succeed** *if they* **work** *hard.*
Butter **doesn't burn** *in the pan if you* **add** *a little oil to it.*

▶2.10 First conditional
The first conditional describes possible future events and the expected results of those events. We use a present tense in the *if*-clause and a future form in the main clause:
If *the scientists* **succeed,** *many people* **will live** *longer.*
If *I* **don't work** *hard, I* **won't be** *successful.*
Will *you* **have to commute** *if you* **get** *the job?*
He'll **cook** *you an amazing meal* **if** *you* **ask** *him to. He loves showing off!*

Imperative conditionals
We can use imperatives in the main clause. The meaning can be present or future:
If you're tired (now), **go** *to bed (now).*
If you're tired when you arrive (this evening), **go** *to bed (then).*

Unless
Unless means 'if not'. We can use it in zero or first conditionals and with imperatives:
We play every Saturday **unless** *it rains.*
It won't hurt you **unless** *you run away.*

> **Tip**
> In general, don't use a future form (e.g. *will, going to*) in the *if*-clause (or after *when* or *unless*):
> **If** *the government* **changes** *the law, this area will become a national park.* NOT *If the government will change …*
> *We're going to miss the bus* **unless** *we leave right now.* NOT *… unless we're going to leave …*

5A Future forms

a Underline the best option in each sentence.

1 **A** It's a bit hot in here.
   B Yes … *I'll / I'm going to* open a window.
2 I'm going to the shop. *Will / Shall* I get you anything?
3 **A** Why are you carrying those flowers?
   B Because *I'll / I'm going to* ask Sara to marry me!
4 **A** I'm so tired.
   B *I'll / I shall* make you a coffee, if you want.
5 I've got a bad stomach. I think *I'll / I'm going to* be ill …

b Complete the sentences with *will*, *shall* or *going to* and the verbs in brackets.

1 ___Shall I carry___ (I / carry) your bag down the stairs?
2 What time _____ (we / meet)?
3 _____ (you / cook) me a nice meal tonight?
4 I _____ (go) to bed when this programme is finished – I'm tired.
5 I _____ (come) back one day – I promise.
6 I _____ (have) a steak – no, I _____ (have) fish, please.
7 According to the website, she _____ (talk) about some of her trips.
8 I think you _____ (like) my chocolate cake a lot.

c Complete the telephone conversation using the verbs in brackets with *will / shall*, *going to* or the present continuous. Sometimes there is more than one possible answer.

A Hi Dan, it's Tony. Listen, I [1] _'m coming_ (come) to Bristol for a couple of days next week for a big meeting with a client. I [2] _____ (try) to see some of my old friends while I'm there. Do you want to meet up one evening?
B Sounds good. It [3] _____ (be) good to see you again after all these years.
A Yeah, I know. [4] _____ (we / say) Tuesday evening?
B Er … no, that's no good for me. I [5] _____ (take) the kids to the cinema on Tuesday. We've already got tickets.
A OK, no problem. What about Wednesday?
B Yes, that's fine. What time [6] _____ (you / be) free, do you think?
A The meeting [7] _____ (probably / finish) at about 5 o'clock – that's what the client said, anyway.
B OK, so around 7 then? [8] _____ (I / pick) you up at your hotel? Where [9] _____ (you / stay)?
A [10] _____ (I / be) at the King's Hotel. I reserved a room last week.
B Perfect. Listen, I [11] _____ (phone) you before I leave, at about 6.30, to check you're ready.
A Don't worry – I [12] _____ (be) ready.

d ▶ Now go back to p.58

5B Zero and first conditional

a If a pair of sentences has the same meaning, write (S). If they have different meanings, write (D).

1 a I'll send you a text if Petra arrives.
   b I'll send you a text when Petra arrives. ☑ D
2 a If a snail is in danger, it hides in its shell.
   b When a snail is in danger, it hides in its shell. ☐
3 a The animals won't come out if we don't stay quiet.
   b The animals won't come out unless we stay quiet. ☐
4 a If you need some money, I'll lend you some.
   b When you need some money, I'll lend you some. ☐
5 a If you see a bear in the forest, don't run!
   b When you see a bear in the forest, don't run! ☐
6 a Lizards don't bite unless they feel scared.
   b Lizards don't bite if they feel scared. ☐

b Underline the correct options.

1 If I *eat / will eat* too much, I feel sleepy.
2 Simon isn't very talkative when he *wakes up / will wake up*.
3 *I send / I'll send* you some photos if you give me your email address.
4 If we don't leave now, we *don't / won't* get to the airport on time.
5 If you *go / will go* to London, visit the British Museum.
6 I go to the cinema every Friday unless *I'm not / I'm* busy.
7 Karen *will speak / won't speak* to Paul unless he apologises.
8 If someone *phones / is going to phone*, don't tell them I'm here.
9 You can do anything *if / unless* you try hard enough.
10 Will I have to bring anything if I *come / will come* to the party?

c Complete the sentences with the verbs in brackets and a conditional form. Use *will* where possible.

1 You ____'ll feel____ (feel) bad if you ____drink____ (drink) too much coffee.
2 If you _____ (not want) to watch the film, we _____ (do) something else instead.
3 He _____ (not make) any money unless he _____ (start) selling more products.
4 If you _____ (not finish) tonight, you _____ (not have) the weekend free.
5 If you _____ (feel) like going out later, call me.
6 Unless it _____ (be) really cold, we _____ (try) to run tomorrow morning.
7 You _____ (not get) there on time if you _____ (not take) the train.
8 If you _____ (not be) ready in five minutes, we _____ (leave) without you.

d ▶ Now go back to p.60

Vocabulary Focus

1A Communication

a ▶️1.3 Listen to the words in **bold**. What do you think they mean?

1 You **argue** with someone when you *agree / don't agree* about something.
2 You **complain** when you're *happy / not happy* about something.
3 You **encourage** someone when you say *good / bad* things about what they want to do.
4 If you **persuade** someone, you make them *agree / forget* to do something.
5 If you **insist** on something, you say that something *must happen / might happen*.
6 You **greet** someone when they *arrive at / leave* a place.

b ▶️1.4 <u>Underline</u> the correct words in **a**. Then listen and check.

c 💬 Describe what's happening in pictures 1–4 using the words in **a**.

d 💬 Choose three of these topics to talk about.

- a time when you complained about something in a shop or restaurant
- a time when you insisted on doing something
- a time when you argued about something unimportant
- a time when you encouraged someone who was having problems
- a time when someone persuaded you to do something you didn't want

e ▶ Now go back to p.8

1B Extreme adjectives

a ▶1.12 Listen to the extreme adjectives in the box. <u>Underline</u> the stressed syllable in each word.

---

awful /'ɔːfəl/   boiling /'bɔɪlɪŋ/   brilliant /'brɪlɪənt/   delicious /də'lɪʃəs/   enormous /ɪn'ɔːməs/
filthy /'fɪlθiː/   freezing /'friːzɪŋ/   furious /'fjuːrɪəs/   miserable /'mɪzərəbəl/   tiny /'taɪni/

---

b ▶1.13 Complete the sentences with the extreme adjectives in **a**. Then listen and check.
1   Their house is _enormous_! It's got 12 bedrooms.
2   **A** Was it hot?
     B Yes, it was absolutely _boiling_
3   Why do you look so _miserable_? I've never seen you looking so sad.
4   We had a _brilliant_ holiday. The hotel, the weather, the town – it was all really good.
5   The food was absolutely _awful_. I'm not going there again!
6   I was _furious_ when I found out he'd read my private diary!
7   The picture's _tiny_ – I can't see it. Can you make it a bit bigger?
8   **A** It's _freezing_! Why didn't I bring a coat?
     B Here, you can borrow my jacket.
9   Your T-shirt's _filthy_! Put it in the washing machine.
10 That cake is _delicious_! Could I have some more, please?

c 💬 Think of an example of each of the things below. Then work in small groups and compare your answers. Are any of your answers the same?

- someone who earns an enormous amount of money
- something that makes you furious
- a time you felt absolutely miserable
- an awful film or TV show
- something that tastes delicious
- a brilliant website

d 💬 Use extreme adjectives to describe pictures 1–4.

①

③

②

④

e ▶ Now go back to p.13.

5A Environmental issues

a Match the words in the box with definitions 1–8.

local /ˈləʊkəl/   destroy /dɪˈstrɔɪ/   natural /ˈnætʃrəl/   species /ˈspiʃiːz/
survive /səˈvaɪv/   limit /ˈlɪmɪt/   endangered /ɪnˈdeɪndʒəd/   creature /ˈkriːtʃə/

1 found in nature, and not made by people
2 from a small area, especially of a country
3 to control something so that it doesn't become bigger
4 a type of animal or plant
5 to continue living
6 to damage something so badly that it can't be used
7 anything that lives (but is not a plant)
8 used to describe an animal or plant which might disappear because there are not many alive

b ▶2.3 Complete the texts with the correct form of the words in **a**. Sometimes there is more than one possible answer. Then listen and check your answers.

This is my favourite animal – the orang-utan. Unfortunately, this great ape is ¹_____ . It's terrible that people are cutting down the trees in the area where it lives. If we're not careful, its home will be completely ²_____ . Fortunately, there are several conservation projects working to save this beautiful ³_____ .

The ice in the Arctic is melting. Some people say that the melting ice is ⁴_____ – that human beings are not causing climate change. But we need to do something about it, and fast. The weather is getting stranger. Some scientists think that many ⁵_____ will not be able to ⁶_____ if the temperature changes too much.

Pollution is a big problem here. The air is often like a dirty grey fog. You can hardly see what's in front of you! A lot of people are getting ill. The government needs to ⁷_____ the number of cars and factories, but we can't do anything without the support of the ⁸_____ people. The problem is, everyone wants to drive!

c Make notes on your opinions and feelings about one of these topics.

• a favourite animal, plant or natural place
• an environmental problem where you live
• an environmental problem affecting the planet

d 💬 Take turns to talk about your topic.

e ▶ Now go back to p.56.

5B The natural world

a ▶2.12 Match the words in the box with photos 1–8. Then listen and check.

| bay /beɪ/ cave /keɪv/ coast /kəʊst/ desert /'dezət/ rainforest /'reɪnfɒrɪst/ stream /striːm/ valley /'væli/ waterfall /'wɔːtəfɔːl/ |

b ▶2.13 <u>Underline</u> the correct words. Then listen and check.

1 A *park* / *national park* is a very large area of natural beauty for use by the public.
2 A *river* / *stream* is a long (and often large) area of water that flows into the sea.
3 There are five *oceans* / *seas* in the world: the Pacific, the Atlantic, the Indian, the Arctic and the Southern.
4 A *forest* / *rainforest* is an area of land in a tropical region, where many trees and plants grow together.
5 A *sea* / *lake* is a large area of water with land all around it.

c 💬 Take turns to describe the animals or plants you can see in photos 1–6 below. Say where they live.

d ▶ Now turn to p.61

Audioscripts

Unit 1

▶ 1.7

Four generations – and they all prefer communicating in different ways. There are sure to be misunderstandings and other problems, right? Well, there don't have to be.

OK, so I'm a Millennial – I was born in 1990 – and so being able to connect with people is really important to me. I'm constantly trying to learn, grow and change. And, for me, fast on-screen communication is the best way to do this. I love the way that the internet puts you in touch with all kinds of people you wouldn't meet in everyday life.

Generation X, on the other hand, uses communication to build relationships and develop ideas. This sounds pretty good, but they express their feelings and opinions directly, and aren't afraid to say or write how they feel. My boss is Generation X, and she definitely has an opinion on everything!

And, of course, at home I spend time with Baby Boomers and Veterans. My dad is a typical Baby Boomer. They have a lot in common with Generation X – they can be quite direct about what they think. I don't always agree with his opinions, but I do appreciate his honesty – usually! And Baby Boomers definitely prefer face-to-face communication. My dad's really not very good with emails, social networking or anything like that.

My grandparents are in the generation called Veterans. For them, communication is something that keeps people together and traditions alive. Both Veterans and Baby Boomers take time to talk things over that matter to their job or family, but are not that interested in chatting about personal goals and development.

Understanding these different communication styles is really important for improving our relationships, both at work and at home.

So, for example, one really big difference between us Millennials and the other three generations is that we expect people to tell us – gently – how we're doing. So, I used to get a bit annoyed with my boss for not giving me enough feedback about how things are going at work. But then I realised that other generations don't necessarily notice this difference, so I learnt not to be upset if older people didn't praise me all the time, and I also learnt to ask for help if I needed it.

Similarly, some of us Millennials find it difficult when people criticise us or disagree with us. Generation X and Baby Boomers will tell you clearly if they don't like something. Don't take it personally – although that's often easier said than done!

On a practical level, it can help to use different communication styles with different generations. Pick up the phone, write emails, and make time for face-to-face conversation. When you do, pay attention to your writing style. You might think an informal style is friendly, but to an older person it can seem rude.

Finally, understand that communication differences across generations do exist. So talk about them – with people of all ages. This can open the door to other conversations. You can learn a lot by hearing older people's experiences, and in turn you might be able to teach them about life in the modern world.

▶ 1.10

1 A Are you OK, James?
B No, I'm not. I'm absolutely exhausted! I've been speaking Spanish all day!
2 C Hi, Linda. Are you learning Russian?
D I'm trying to, but this book's useless! It teaches you how to say 'my uncle's black trousers', but not how to say 'hello'!
3 E Hey, guess what? I've just read about this girl, and she's only 10 but she's fluent in several different languages.
F That's fantastic. I can only speak one language – English.
4 G Listen, Olivier: squirrel.
H Squi… Squill … It's impossible! I'll never get it right!
G No, it's not impossible, just difficult. You need to practise. Try again. Listen: Squirrel.
H Squi…rrel…
G Well done!

▶ 1.14 **PART 1**

RACHEL Really? Oh, no … the bookshop?! Are you sure? Oh, thanks for letting me know. Yes, see you soon, Jo. Bye.

BECKY Excuse me?
R Oh, sorry! I thought you were just looking.
B Um, I want something for a friend's wife. I'm going there for dinner.
R OK. What sort of flowers does she like?
B Oh, I don't know. I haven't met her yet.
R Right, well, in my opinion, roses are always a good option.
B Um, aren't they a bit romantic?
R Yes, I know what you mean. I guess something like tulips might be better.
B Yes, they're lovely. How much are they? … How much are the tulips?
R Oh, they're … sorry.
B It's OK. I'll try somewhere else. Thank you.
R Hello? Yes. Yes, it is.

▶ 1.15 **PART 2**

MARK Rachel? You OK?
RACHEL Oh, I'm sorry, love. I'm just a bit worried. Jo phoned today and said that the old bookshop is going to be turned into another florist's.
M The bookshop on the corner? I didn't know they'd sold it.
R Me neither. What am I going to do? It's hard enough already to make money, but I think it's going to be impossible with another florist's in the same street.
M Yeah. Was Jo sure about this?
R I don't know. She seemed pretty certain.
M Well, if you ask me, it's not worth worrying about until we know for sure.
R I know, but I can't help it – it's on my mind. I was even rude to a customer today.
M Really? That's not like you. What happened?
R Well, I wasn't exactly rude, just not very helpful.
M Hey, don't worry about it. Let's just forget about work. Personally, I need a relaxing evening!
R Me too!
M Anyway, Tom and Becky will be here in a minute. I think we should check on the food.
R Yes. I don't want anything else to go wrong today. So, what's Becky like?
M That'll be them now!

▶ 1.21 **PART 3**

MARK Hi! Come in! Hello. Come on in. Rachel, this is Tom and Becky.
TOM Hi, Rachel. Good to meet you.

RACHEL Hi, Tom.

BECKY Hi, Rachel. I think we've met before!

R I'm so sorry about earlier! I had something on my mind.

B Don't worry. Um, I was going to bring you some flowers, but I couldn't get any!

R Thank you.

▶ **1.22**

MARIA How's your revision going?

GILBERTO Not so good. I think I can remember most of the grammar, but remembering vocabulary's a bit harder, for me anyway.

M Yes, there are a lot of words to remember.

G What about you?

M For me, it is probably the opposite – I find the grammar hard to get my head around, but the vocabulary is a lot easier. I've been testing myself at home and it's OK.

G How do you manage to remember all the words, though? What's your secret?

M Well, it's no secret! I have this kind of system for learning words that seems to make it easy …

G OK, what?

M Well, when I get home from class, I record all the new words I've learnt onto my phone. And then I might do something like go for a run, and I listen to them when I'm running. And I make up these sentences with the words and say them to myself.

G As you're running?

M Yes, as I'm running – I just say the sentences quietly to myself.

G Do you remember what the words mean?

M Most of the time. If I forget, I check in my notebook when I get home from my run. And sometimes I play the words and write them down. I think the most important thing is to keep repeating them. I don't know why, but remembering the sounds of the words is important for me. Like, last week I learnt the word 'shine' – you know, like 'the sun is shining'. And that 'sh' sound at the beginning of the word makes me think of light that's getting brighter and brighter.

G Interesting. But I don't know if it would work for me. I need to see things written down. I need to look at the word.

M Right – my sister's like that too. She uses vocabulary cards. Have you tried that?

G No. How does that work?

M She has these small cards and writes all the new words on a card with a picture, or a definition and an example – sometimes a translation too. It worked really well … for a while.

G For a while? Why? What happened?

M She left all the cards on a train.

G Oh, yes. That's probably what I would do!

M I felt so sorry for her – after all that work.

G It sounds like a good idea, but it sounds like you have to be quite organised to have a card system.

M Yes, that's true.

G And, to be honest, I think I'm maybe too lazy to write all those cards and keep them with me wherever I go!

Unit 2

▶ **1.29**

You've got good grades and you've been to lots of interviews, but no one's offered you a job yet. Why? Is it because your knowledge and practical skills aren't right for the job?

Well, according to one careers expert, Nancy Maynard, it's probably because you just haven't got the 'likeability factor'. Likeability is the ability to work well with people. It isn't something you can learn easily at school, but employers want it and they're quick to see it in candidates at interview.

Without likeability, Maynard believes, good grades and practical skills are worth very little. In the first 18 months in a job, most of an employee's success is linked to their likeability, not to how well he or she does the job. Likeability is much more important than other abilities, and anyone who's looking for a job should be trying their hardest to improve their own by spending time with other people. Advice for job hunters goes like this: apply for the jobs that you want, even if you haven't got the right qualifications. If you get an interview, then impress the interviewers with your 'soft skills'. Soft skills are your personal skills – your friendly personality, your positive attitude to work, your ability to communicate with people and your problem-solving skills. It's simple.

Or is it? Is likeability really more important than knowledge and experience? We took to the streets and asked some people for their opinions.

▶ **1.30**

1 People don't realise how important likeability is because employers don't like to talk about it, so they usually give other reasons for not offering someone a job. But let's be honest, if you're paying someone to do a job, you want them to work well with the people around them.

2 Yes, soft skills and likeability are much more important than specific job skills – like being able to use a computer – for the employer and for yourself too. There's no such thing as 'a job for life' any more. Develop your soft skills – be good at working with other people – and you'll always be able to get work.

3 I've been a doctor since I graduated from medical school. I've worked at this hospital for 18 years. My practical skills and my knowledge are all that matters. Without those, I couldn't do my job. I listen to my patients, but I certainly don't believe that I need to be charming and sociable all the time. I've never believed that.

4 I'm afraid it's true and it makes me angry. I'm 23 and I haven't worked since I left college. The only way to develop soft skills is to work with people, but the only way to get work is to have soft skills. It's a no-win situation.

5 When people talk like this, it makes education and hard work sound second best, and that's simply not true. Yes, you need to be able to make a good first impression, but come on, what really matters is that you can offer practical skills and experience to an organisation, not just a friendly face.

▶ **1.33** **PART 1**

RACHEL Oh, hi Becky!

BECKY Oh, hi Rachel.

B Oh no!

R Oh! Oh Becky, I'm so sorry.

B But why? It was me that knocked it over.

R But I distracted you.

B What, by saying hello? Don't worry about it! It was my fault.

R At least let me get you another orange juice!

▶ **1.34** **PART 2**

RACHEL How's the phone?

BECKY Not good. The screen's frozen.

R Oh dear! Have you tried turning it off and on again?

B I was just doing that, but still nothing.

R What about taking the SIM card out and drying it?

B That's worth a try. Thank you. Oh, I hope I haven't lost all my contacts. I haven't saved them anywhere else.

R Oh no, how awful. Could you take it back to the shop?

B Oh, I don't think they'll do anything. I bought it over a year ago.

R Can you claim on your insurance?

B I don't have any. It's just run out. A week ago!

R How annoying! I know, the other day I read about this trick for fixing phones that have got wet.

B Oh yes?

R They said you put the phone in a bag of rice and apparently it dries it out. You could try that.

B That sounds a bit weird.

R I know, but there were lots of comments from people saying that it had worked.

B OK, I'll give it a try. What have I got to lose?

R Exactly, it's cheaper than buying a new phone!

▶ **1.35** **PART 3**

RACHEL Hello. *Fantastic Flowers.*

BECKY Hi Rachel, it's Becky.

R Oh, hi Becky. How are you?

B I'm good and guess what? My phone's working. That rice trick worked.

R That's brilliant! I'm really glad to hear that.

▶ **1.39**

LIN Have you done that presentation yet?

TANIA Yeah, I did it yesterday.

L How did it go?

T Well, you know, the usual thing: I presented my ideas, everyone smiled and thanked me and then said nothing.

L So they didn't even give their opinion?

T No, but I could see they didn't like the idea. The problem with the company I work for is that they're continuing to use the same ideas and aren't thinking enough about new markets. They're not thinking enough about the phone app market at all.

L Isn't that why they employed you?

T That's what I thought. I mean, I've been working there for just over a year now and they haven't said yes to any

of my ideas. When they offered me the job, they said things like, 'Oh yes, we're very interested in your creative thinking and your problem-solving skills', but do they really want to use them? I get the feeling they don't.

L That must be very disappointing.

T I think I've more or less decided. I'm going to look for a new job.

L Really?

T Yeah, it's getting hard to keep having a positive attitude.

L I can understand that. And I thought your app idea was a really good one.

T Thanks. So what do you think about Hong Kong?

L Hong Kong? Why there?

T Well, I'm thinking about making a big change.

L What? Going to live in Hong Kong?

T Yeah, well, you decided to come and live here – maybe I can do the opposite.

L Wow! That's a very big change.

T I want to travel more and I'm really interested in Chinese culture – I'd love to find out more about it.

L Well, yes, everyone says there are plenty of IT jobs in Hong Kong, but it's a bit of a crazy city.

T Well, it could be fun!

Unit 3

▶ **1.45**

CHARLOTTE When people find out I'm a twin, they generally ask the same questions: What's it like? Can you read each other's thoughts? Can people tell you apart? Do you do everything together?

It's true that I often know what Megan is thinking or feeling, but that's because we grew up together and we're very close. We're no different from ordinary sisters.

But if you look at photos of us when we were younger, even I can't say which one is me. We used to look absolutely identical. And Mum says we didn't use to talk much when we were playing together – we seemed to know what each other was thinking.

I guess as we grew up we wanted to create our own unique identities. I remember at school Megan used to dress as differently from me as she could. I went through a phase of wearing lots of black and looking quite messy. So of course, Megan started wearing flowery dresses!

We used to have a lot of arguments as teenagers but now we're really good

friends. We usually speak on the phone two or three times a day, and we get together as often as we can. So, what's it like to have a twin? It's great – you have a best friend for life!

MEGAN Charlotte and I had a wonderful childhood. We did everything together. I had my best friend with me 24/7 and we used to be very close. She had a brilliant imagination and used to invent wonderful stories. Of course, we played the usual twin jokes. At school, we used to swap clothes and confuse the teachers. I'm not sure they even noticed some of the time – we looked so similar that even our parents used to mix us up.

We didn't use to argue much, but in our teenage years we started to grow apart. We were trying to find our own identity, I think, and we each made a different group of friends. Later on, we went to universities in different towns. But it turned out that you can never escape being a twin. After our first year away, we hadn't seen each other for six months. The day we went home, we saw that we'd both cut all our hair off!

These days, I think we have quite different personalities. Charlotte is very kind and caring, but often forgets things and gets lost. I'm a bit more confident and organised. But we still have lots in common – we both love beach holidays, playing football and we both complain about our hair!

▶ **1.49** **PART 1**

PAULA Hi, Mark. Hi, Tom.

MARK Hi, Paula.

TOM Hi!

M We're still meeting at 10, right?

P Yes, we are. We're in meeting room 3, I think. See you in there?

T Yep!

M See you in a minute.

T Coffee?

M Yes, please.

T So, did you have a good weekend?

M It was good, thanks. But you won't believe what I did.

T What?

M Remember I told you my dad wanted a desk for his new office? And I offered to help him find one online?

T Oh yeah?

M Well, I found one. It looked perfect, exactly what I was looking for. It was a fantastic price too.

T Sounds good.

M Exactly, so I ordered it.

T Great!

M And it arrived on Saturday. But, the funny thing is, it was really, really small.

T How small?

M It only came up to my knees!

T Eh?

M It turned out I'd ordered a desk for a child.

T No way!

M Mm-mm! I forgot to check the measurements on the website!

T So, what did you do?

▶ **1.50** **PART 2**

TOM So, what did you do?

MARK Well, I phoned the company to explain, and luckily they agreed to give me a refund.

T Really? That was very good of them.

M Yeah, it was. But anyway, I still had to find a desk. I was looking everywhere, but I couldn't find anything. In the end, Rachel suggested I try one of those freecycling websites.

T Freecycling? What's that?

M It's where people get rid of stuff they don't want any more. I've never heard of it either. But there are a couple of websites for this area. I found the perfect desk straight away – and the best thing is, it's free.

T It's free?

M Yeah, I think the owner doesn't have enough space for it, so he's just giving it away. So all I have to do is go and pick it up.

T Wow! That's good. And you're sure it's the right size this time?

M Ha-ha. Yeah, I double-checked the measurements this time.

P Guys!

M Oh, sorry, Paula! It's my fault. I was just explaining to Tom about my desk mix-up.

▶ **1.53**

BRYAN It's a shame we don't know much about our grandfather, isn't it? Mom used to love talking about him and Grandma. She always used to tell so many interesting stories about them. But I've got no idea where or when they met.

SUSIE Yeah. Well, I know he was born in England.

B Who, Grandad? Yes, I know. And he wanted to go out and see the world, didn't he? That's why he went to train as a chef – so he could get work on a ship.

S What kind of ship?

B Cruise ships. And that was before the war. Some time in the 1930s.

S Oh, right.

B He loved travelling and that was the best way to see the world if you didn't have a lot of money back then.

S So, how did he meet Gran? She was a nurse, wasn't she? And how did they both end up in Canada?

B I … I don't know. I guess we'll have to do some research!

Unit 4
▶ **1.54**

PRESENTER That was Rimsky-Korsakov's *Flight of the Bumblebee*, a piece which was recently performed to a live audience on TV by a six-year-old boy called Tsung Tsung. Tsung Tsung could play the piano when he was three. At the age of five, an internet clip with him at the piano made him famous. Now, he says, he wants to be able to play like Mozart. Our question today is: Do we have to start young to succeed? We've all heard about kids like Tsung Tsung, bright kids who have a particular ability in, say, music, maths or science. But do they grow up to be successful adults? And if you're over 30 and you haven't achieved your goals yet, is it too late? Ed Bickley's been looking into it for us. Ed, what have you found out?

ED OK, well, clearly some talented children go on to do very well as adults. Take Lionel Messi. He started playing football on the street at the age of five. Soon, he was playing against much older boys – and they couldn't get the ball off him. He was so good that he was able to join the Barcelona junior team when he was 11, and achieved international success at 20. Now he's one of the greatest players in the world!

P A real success story!

E Yes. But what's surprising is that most of these talented children when they grow up don't actually achieve much more than other adults. A recent study followed a group of talented children from 1974 until now. Less than 5% managed to become very successful adults.

P That does seem surprising.

E And now for the good news! If you haven't achieved your goals by the time you're 30, don't give up! Plenty of people have found success much later in life. British fashion designer Vivienne Westwood's first job was in teaching. She always wanted to be a designer, but her successful fashion career didn't begin until she was 30 when she started making clothes for a shop in London called *Let it Rock*. Then there's Andrea Bocelli. He's been able to sing well since he was a child, but he didn't become a famous classical singer until he was

36. At 41, his album became the most successful classical album by a solo artist of all time, with 5 million copies sold around the world.

P So to do well at something, we don't have to be good at it at a young age?

E That's right. In most cases, talent develops with experience. You need to practise, make mistakes, get frustrated, learn from your mistakes, practise more … it's hard work. You need a lot of patience, a lot of determination. Confidence and a positive attitude help, too. Say to yourself, 'I can do it!' And just maybe you will! And don't worry if your 10-year-old child can't play the piano. Maybe they'll be able to do it when they're a bit older.

P Ed, you've given us all hope! Thank you very much.

▶ **1.61** **PART 1**

BECKY And these are the photos. You haven't seen the ones of our holiday, have you?

RACHEL No, I haven't. Oh, wow! That's a great photo. That's the hotel you stayed in, isn't it?

B Yes. And there's the beach. It was only a few metres from the hotel.

R Wow, Becky, these are really good.

B Thanks. I enjoyed taking them.

R They're amazing. Actually, can I ask a big favour? You know I'm making a new website, don't you? Well, I need some photos of the shop for it. Do you think you could take them?

B Hmm, I'm not sure. I'm not a real photographer. It's just a hobby.

R But I really love your pictures. Will you do it?

B Well, if you're sure. I'd love to.

R Great!

B So, Mark, Tom told me about your internet shopping mistake. You bought a child's desk instead of an adult one, didn't you?

MARK It was an easy mistake to make – could have happened to anyone! Anyway, it all turned out well in the end. Actually, I'm going to get the desk on Saturday.

B Oh, do you need a hand? I'm sure Tom will help.

TOM Oh yeah? You'll need a bit of muscle!

R It would be great if you could, wouldn't it, Mark?

M Yeah, I was wondering how I was going to move it on my own.

T Why not? But could I ask you a favour in return, Rachel?

R Yes, of course. What?

T I'll tell you later.

RACHEL So, what do you need?

TOM Well, I'm going to ask Becky to marry me.

R Wow, that is great news!

T Thanks, but I wondered if you could come with me to buy the ring. I've never done this before and I don't know where to start.

R Yes of course I could. Oh, that is brilliant.

B What are you two gossiping about?

T Oh, nothing!

🔊 **1.66** PART 3

MARK Go on. Pull it a bit harder.

TOM I can't, it's too heavy!

M We're almost there. Go on.

T No, it's not going to work.

M All right. Put it down.

T What's it made of?

M Metal.

T Let's do it together, both sides. Ready?

M All right. One, two, three … No, put it down, put it down.

T Let's move it across.

M All right. Ready? One, two, three…

T Job done.

🔊 **1.68**

SHEENA Last year, I had some free time and a bit of money to spend. I'd always wanted to go walking and climbing in the Himalayas, but I didn't want to go on my own and none of my friends wanted to go. So I found a website called *Travel Groups*, where you can contact other people who want to go to the same places as you, and you can join up and go together as a group. Anyway, I found three other people to go with and we all met in Delhi in north India and we travelled together. It worked out really well. I think websites like this are a good idea because lots of people don't want to travel on their own, and it works as long as everyone's reasonably sociable. I'm quite self-confident and I think I'm an extrovert, so I think I'm quite good at getting on with people and making friends.

ALYA I had a few months off after university, so I looked on the internet for volunteer work and found a really good website for last-minute volunteer jobs called the *Volunteer Community Project*. It was good because you can arrange things straight away and they pay your fares, and you get basic accommodation and food. You don't earn money, but you don't really spend much either. I went to London and worked there with young children from problem families. I didn't have any experience, but that doesn't matter. You just need to be able to get on with kids and understand what they need. I never realised before, but actually, it seems like I've got a natural talent for teaching children. So it was a really great experience and now I've decided to train as a primary school teacher.

BRAD I really needed to earn some money and I couldn't get a proper job. Someone told me about this website called *Short Work*, where people offer short jobs for a few days or a couple of weeks that they need doing, like helping out with things or fixing things for people. I'm quite good at things like that, and I know a bit about electricity and plumbing. I found this advert for a family who've got a large house and needed someone to do some basic work on it. So I went along and chatted to them, and they gave me the job. I think they could see that I was quite serious about it and I was determined to work hard. It was really good – I was only there for two weeks, but in that time I managed to clear their garden, mend their garden fence, I painted three rooms for them, and I got their kitchen light working. So not bad for two weeks' work!

Unit 5

🔊 **2.4**

PHIL Are they environmentally friendly in Costa Rica? Do they protect their rainforests and animals?

MASHA Well, yes they do. The government is doing a lot, but it takes quite a long time for forests to recover if they've already been cut down. They'll probably grow back, but not immediately.

P Are you going to work in the rainforests?

M No, no I'm not. I'll be by the sea. I'm going to work on a project that looks after turtles.

P Turtles? That's very cool. But how do you look after turtles, I mean, what do you do?

M Well, to be honest – I don't really know! Tomorrow I'm meeting someone who worked on the project, and she's going to tell me about the kinds of things I'm going to do.

P So, who else works on the project? Just people from overseas or local people too?

M I'm not sure about that either. Perhaps I'll work with local people as well.

P So, you're off to save the world. I think that's great.

M Don't know about saving the world. But I'll definitely be able to save some turtles! And I'm going to make the most of my time in Costa Rica and learn some Spanish too.

P Let me know how things go.

M Sure. Actually, I'm going to keep a blog, so I'll write regular updates on the blog and you can follow that.

P Good idea. I'm sure you'll have a great time.

M Yeah, so am I.

🔊 **2.8**

PRESENTER I visited biologist Andrew Parker to find out more about how the natural world has inspired everyday objects. Andrew, hello! What's this little animal you've got here?

ANDREW It's a thorny dragon lizard from the Australian desert. As you can see, it's quite small, about 20cm long. But it's an amazing animal. You see, what I'm really interested in is what this little creature can teach us about collecting water.

P OK.

A So, as I said, this lizard lives in the desert in Australia. And, as you know, it's an incredibly dry place. But this lizard manages to live there very successfully. And we've discovered one of the reasons for this. If the lizard puts a foot somewhere wet – even just a tiny, tiny bit wet – its skin pulls the water up and over its whole body. When the water reaches the lizard's mouth, it drinks it.

P That's very clever!

A Yes. On the lizard's skin, well, in fact, in the skin, we discovered there's like a system of very, very small pipes. So the skin collects the water and these pipes pull it towards the lizard's mouth.

P That sounds really efficient.

A Well, right, yeah. So, you see, we want to copy that system and use it in a device that collects water. If we are successful, the device will provide water for people who live in very dry environments.

P That's fantastic. And what other ideas have we taken from nature?

A Engineers are doing a lot with robots these days. For example, there's the rescue robot. It's just like a spider because it moves on eight legs. And so it can move very quickly and make itself very small. So these rescue robots will be able to help people who are stuck in small spaces, or who are trapped in buildings, for example, if there's an earthquake.

P So they'll be able to help save lives.

A Exactly. And then we're looking at seashells, which are very strong, but, at the same time, they're very light – they don't weigh much at all. Scientists have discovered that seashells are made of lots of tiny blocks that fit together, but this makes them really hard to break. The plan is to copy this material to make safety equipment such as gloves and helmets.

P So this material will protect people like a shell protects a turtle.

A That's right. And again, this could help save lives.

🔘2.14 PART 1

BECKY Hi!

RACHEL Oh hi, Becky.

B How are you?

R I'm fine, thanks.

B So, are you ready for your photo shoot?

R Ha! I guess so.

B The shop looks great!

R Oh, that's because of Tina. She spent the morning cleaning up!

B Well, she did a great job. So Tina, are you going to be in the photos too?

TINA No! I hate having my photo taken!

B I see! Anyway, if you're ready.

R Make sure you get my good side!

B You look great!

R Thank you! So, how do you want to do this?

B Let me see. I think it would be best if I just take some natural shots of you looking busy with the flowers.

R OK.

B Hmm! That's really good!

R Oh, shall I carry on?

B Yes, that's great. So, why did you become a florist?

R That's a good question. I've always loved flowers, ever since I was a little girl, so it seemed a natural thing for me to do. I think it's really important that you do something that you enjoy.

B Fantastic! Yeah, it must be nice to have a job like yours, the freedom you have, and you can be creative, and you're your own boss.

R You sound like you don't enjoy your job.

B No, not at the moment. Not for a while, actually.

R Really? What's wrong with it?

B Oh, lots of things. For instance, all I seem to do is deal with other people's problems, like issues with their pay or holidays. And I hate being stuck inside an office all day, staring at the clock.

R Oh dear!

B I wish I had a job where I could travel the world, spread my wings, be free!

R Such as?

B I don't know, that's the problem. … Lovely!

R Can I see?

B Sure. Here you go.

R Hmm! That's great.

B Thank you.

R Well, how about becoming a professional photographer? You're really good!

B I don't know. Tina, how about a quick shot of you and Rachel together?

T Do I have to?

B Oh, go on! Just stand by Rachel for a moment.

🔘2.16 PART 2

RACHEL So, look at this. There are loads of photography courses you can do. Photojournalism, for example, or portrait photography.

BECKY Thanks, that's great, but we're meant to be choosing which photos you want for your website.

R OK, but I just think it's something that you should consider.

B Well, maybe. Let's look at the photos for now.

MARK Hey, Becky. These are great!

B Thank you!

R I think this is the best one.

B Rachel, we can't see you in that one!

R OK, let me see. … I think this one.

🔘2.21

LIZ I'm on my way to Lane Cove where between 20 and 30 whales have come ashore and can't get back out to sea again. When I get to Lane Cove, I'm meeting Sam Collins from the Marine Life Service. I'm going to help Sam and a team of local people to try and save these whales.

OK, I've just arrived and talked to Sam. It's quite cold, so I think I'll change into my wetsuit before going down on to the beach to work with other people who've come here to help these whales. So far about 50 people have turned up and more are coming. If more people come, we'll have a chance of succeeding.

So, I'm in a team of four people and we're looking after just one poor whale. Sam says it's female, and what

we've done is we've covered her with wet towels and we're pouring buckets of water over her to keep her cool. We have to be careful where we put the towels. If we cover her blowhole, she won't be able to breathe. Sam says our whale's in good condition and he thinks she'll survive. The tide's coming in soon. I'm going to help dig up sand around the whale to make a hole. When the water comes in, it'll fill up the hole. Better get going …

Yes! Success! The tide came in and our whale floated again. There were about five of us. We pushed and pushed and she fought back a bit, then she took off. What a great feeling! She's swimming back out to sea. I think she's going to be OK.

Phonemic Symbols

Vowel sounds

Short

/ə/	/æ/	/ʊ/	/ɒ/
teach**er**	man	p**u**t	g**o**t

/ɪ/	/i/	/e/	/ʌ/
ch**i**p	happ**y**	m**e**n	but

Long

/ɜː/	/ɑː/	/uː/	/ɔː/	/iː/
shirt	p**a**rt	wh**o**	w**a**lk	ch**ea**p

Diphthongs (two vowel sounds)

/eə/	/ɪə/	/ʊə/	/ɔɪ/	/aɪ/	/eɪ/	/əʊ/	/aʊ/
h**ai**r	n**ear**	t**our**	b**oy**	f**i**ne	late	wind**ow**	n**ow**

Consonants

/p/	/b/	/f/	/v/	/t/	/d/	/k/	/g/	/θ/	/ð/	/tʃ/	/dʒ/
picnic	**b**ook	**f**ace	**v**ery	**t**ime	**d**og	**c**old	**g**o	**th**ink	**th**e	**ch**air	**j**ob

/s/	/z/	/ʃ/	/ʒ/	/m/	/n/	/ŋ/	/h/	/l/	/r/	/w/	/j/
sea	**z**oo	**sh**oe	televi**si**on	**m**e	**n**ow	si**ng**	**h**ot	**l**ate	**r**ed	**w**ent	**y**es

Irregular verbs

Infinitive	Past simple	Past Participle
be	was /wɒz/ / were /wɜː/	been
become	became	become
begin	began	begun
blow	blew /bluː/	blown /bləʊn/
break /breɪk/	broke /brəʊk/	broken /'brəʊkən/
bring /brɪŋ/	brought /brɔːt/	brought /brɔːt/
build /bɪld/	built /bɪlt/	built /bɪlt/
buy /baɪ/	bought /bɔːt/	bought /bɔːt/
catch /kætʃ/	caught /kɔːt/	caught /kɔːt/
choose /tʃuːz/	chose /tʃəʊz/	chosen /'tʃəʊzən/
come	came	come
cost	cost	cost
cut	cut	cut
deal /diəl/	dealt /delt/	dealt /delt/
do	did	done /dʌn/
draw /drɔː/	drew /druː/	drawn /drɔːn/
drink	drank	drunk
drive /draɪv/	drove /drəʊv/	driven /'drɪvən/
eat /iːt/	ate /et/	eaten /'iːtən/
fall	fell	fallen
feel	felt	felt
find /faɪnd/	found /faʊnd/	found /faʊnd/
fly /flaɪ/	flew /fluː/	flown /fləʊn/
forget	forgot	forgotten
get	got	got
give /gɪv/	gave /geɪv/	given /'gɪvən/
go	went	gone /gɒn/
grow	grew /gruː/	grown /grəʊn/
have /hæv/	had /hæd/	had /hæd/
hear /hɪə/	heard /hɜːd/	heard /hɜːd/
hit	hit	hit
hold /həʊld/	held	held
keep	kept	kept
know /nəʊ/	knew /njuː/	known /nəʊn/

Infinitive	Past simple	Past Participle
leave /liːv/	left	left
lend	lent	lent
let	let	let
lose /luːz/	lost	lost
make	made	made
meet	met	met
pay /peɪ/	paid /peɪd/	paid /peɪd/
put	put	put
read /riːd/	read /red/	read /red/
ride /raɪd/	rode /rəʊd/	ridden /'rɪdən/
ring	rang	rung
run	ran	run
sit	sat	sat
say /seɪ/	said /sed/	said /sed/
see	saw /sɔː/	seen
sell	sold /səʊld/	sold /səʊld/
send	sent	sent
set	set	set
sing	sang	sung
sleep	slept	slept
speak /spiːk/	spoke /spəʊk/	spoken /'spəʊkən/
spend	spent	spent
stand	stood /stʊd/	stood /stʊd/
steal /stiːl/	stole /stəʊl/	stolen /'stəʊlən/
swim /swɪm/	swam /swæm/	swum /swʌm/
take /teɪk/	took /tʊk/	taken /'teɪkən/
teach /tiːtʃ/	taught /tɔːt/	taught /tɔːt/
tell	told /təʊld/	told /təʊld/
think	thought /θɔːt/	thought /θɔːt/
throw /θrəʊ/	threw /θruː/	thrown /θrəʊn/
understand	understood /ʌndə'stʊd/	understood /ʌndə'stʊd/
wake /weɪk/	woke /wəʊk/	woken /'wəʊkən/
wear /weə/	wore /wɔː/	worn /wɔːn/
win	won	won
write /raɪt/	wrote /rəʊt/	written /'rɪtən/

Acknowledgements

The publishers would like to thank the following teachers and ELT professionals for the invaluable feedback they have provided during the development of the B1+ Student's Book:

Andre Alipio, Brazil; Peggy Altpekin, Turkey and the Gulf; Natalia Bayrak, Russia; Kate Chomacki, UK; Leonor Corradi, Argentina; Ludmila Gorodetskaya, Russia; Ludmila Kozhevnikova, Russia; Steve Laslett, UK; Rabab Marouf, Syria; Christina Maurer Smolder, Australia; Mariusz Mirecki, Poland; Catherine Morley, Spain; Antonio Mota Cosano, Spain; Julian Oakley, UK; Litany Pires Ribeiro, Brazil; Elena Pro, Spain; Wayne Rimmer, Russia; Ruth Sánchez, Spain; Hilda Zubiria, Peru.

The publishers are grateful to the following contributors:
Gareth Boden: commissioned photography
Leon Chambers: audio recordings
Hilary Luckcock: picture research
Rob Maidment and Sharp Focus Productions: video recordings, video stills
Ann Thomson: commissioned photography

The authors and publishers acknowledge the following sources of copyright material and are grateful for the permissions granted. While every effort has been made, it has not always been possible to identify the sources of all the material used, or to trace all copyright holders. If any omissions are brought to our notice, we will be happy to include the appropriate acknowledgements on reprinting.

The publisher has used its best endeavours to ensure that the URLs for external websites referred to in this book are correct and active at the time of going to press. However, the publisher has no responsibility for the websites and can make no guarantee that a site will remain live or that the content is or will remain appropriate.

The publishers are grateful to the following for permission to reproduce copyright photographs and material:
Key: L = left, C = centre, R = right, T = top, B = bottom
p7: Corbis/Andy Richter/Aurora Photos; p8(main): Alamy/OJO Images Ltd; p8(a): Alamy/ Jochen Tack; p8(b): Alamy/ipm; p8(c): Alamy/VISUM Foto GmbH; p8(d): Getty/Nicolas McComber; p11(a): Superstock/Voisin/Phanie; p11(b): CUP; p11(c): Shutterstock/AVAVA; p11(d): Alamy/Claudia Wiens; p19: Alamy/ViewPictures Ltd; p20: Alamy/Wavebreakmedia Ltd UC4; p21(a): Getty/MichaelDeleon; p21(b): Corbis/Chad Springer/Cultura; p21(c): Corbis/Sonja Pacho; p21(d): Getty/Peter Dazeley; p21(e): Corbis/ Odilon Dimier /PhotoAlto; p21(f): Thinkstock/Goodshot; p22: Getty/Mike Harrington; p23(B): Getty/Mareen Fischinger; p25: Alamy/Viktor Cap; pp28/29: Shutterstock/Lai Ching Yuen; p31: Getty/Erik Dreyer; p32: Shutterstock/Anton Gvozdikov; p33(T): Alamy/AF Archive; p33(B): Corbis/ Britta Pedersen/dpa; p35(a): Alamy/Judith Dzierzawa; p35(b): Getty/ Nancy Ney; p35(c): Corbis/68 / Larsen@Talbert/Ocean; p35(d): Masterfile; p35(e): Alamy/David Wall; p35(f): Getty/Juan Silva; p35(g): Corbis/ Paul Burns/Blend Images; p35(h): Superstock/ age fotostock; pp36/37: Superstock/ Henry Georgi/All Canada Photos; p36(T): Alamy/Janine Wiedel Photolibrary; p37(L): Alamy/MBI; p37(R): Alamy/Image Source; p40(main): Corbis/ClassicStock; p40(L): Getty/George Marks; p40(R): Topfoto/Topfoto. co.uk; p43: Getty/Ghislain & Marie David de Lossy; p44(T): The Guardian/ Graeme Robertson; p44(B): Getty/JB Lacroix; p45(TL): SA Glamour Productions/ Salina Ho; p45(TR): Rex; p45(BL): Rex/Offside; p45(BR): Corbis/Andreas Lander /dpa; p46: Corbis/Kevin Dodge; p47: Random House LLC; p48(L): Alamy/ Dinodia Photos; p48(R): Getty/William Philpott; p49(TL): Alamy/Mandoga Media; p49(TR): Masterfile; p49(BL): Getty /Fred Duval; p52(L): Masterfile/Robert Harding Images, p52(R): Masterfile; pp52/53: Corbis/Vstock/ Tetra Images; p55: Getty/Per-Andre Hoffmann; p56(R)(forest): Whitley Fund For Nature; p56(BL): Alamy/Lou Linwei; p57(T)(logo): Whitley Fund For Nature; p57(TR): Whitley Fund For Nature; p57(T)(inset): Alamy/imageBroker; p57(CL): Whitley Fund For Nature; p57(CL)(inset): Whitley Fund For Nature; p57(BL): Alamy/F1online digitale Bildagentur GmbH; p57(BR): Whitley Fund For Nature; p57(BR)(inset): Whitley Fund For Nature; p58(T): Alamy/Kevin Schafer; p58(T)(inset): Alamy/Adrian Hepworth; p58(B): Shutterstock/Juice Team; p59(T)(a): Alamy/Stocksnapper; p59(T)(b): Getty/Anita Stizzoli; p59(1): Getty/Peter Walton Photography; p59(2): Shutterstock/v voe; p59(3): Shutterstock/zcw; p59(B)(a): Getty / AFP; p59(B)(b): Shutterstock/Sergey Skleznev; p59(B)(c): Shutterstock/ violetkaipa; p60(T): Shutterstock/Svetlana Yudina; p60(B): Shutterstock/ Shane Gross; p61(TL): Alamy/ Westend61GmbH; p61(TC): Alamy/Alaska Stock; p61(TR): Alamy/blickwinkel; p61(CL): Corbis/Paul van Hoof/ Buten-beeld/Minden Pictures; p61(CR): Alamy/Juniors Bildarchiv GmbH; p61(BL): Corbis/Stephen Dalton/Minden Pictures; p61(BR): Rex/Image Broker; p64(T): Alamy/World Pictures; p64(B): Rex/Jay Town/Newspix; p65: Rex/FLPA; p154(T): Shutterstock/Pu Su Lan; p154(C): Alamy/Global Warming Images; p154(B): Alamy/Tips Images/Tips Italia Srl a socio unico;

p155(R)(1): Shutterstock/ alslutsky; p155(R)(2): Getty/ Visuals Unlimited. Inc; p155(R)(3): Alamy/Images&Stories; p155(R)(4): Rex/Image Broker; p155(R)(5): Masterfile/Minden Pictures; p155(R)(6): Shutterstock/Cathy Keifer.

Commissioned photography by Gareth Boden: pp10(T,B), 16(all), 28.

We are grateful to Barratt Developments plc and Neide's Deli Cafe for their help with the commissioned photography.

Front cover photograph by Alamy/imageBROKER.

The publishers would like to thank the following illustrators: Beatrice Bencivenni, Mark Bird, Mark Duffin, Jo Goodberry, Mark (KJA Artists), Jerome Mireault, Gavin Reece, Gregory Roberts, Sean (KJA Artists), David Semple, Sean Sims, Marie-Eve-Tremblay.

Corpus Development of this publication has made use of the Cambridge English Corpus (CEC). The CEC is a computer database of contemporary spoken and written English, which currently stands at over one billion words. It includes British English, American English and other varieties of English. It also includes the Cambridge Learner Corpus, developed in collaboration with the University of Cambridge ESOL Examinations. Cambridge University Press has built up the CEC to provide evidence about language use that helps to produce better language teaching materials.

English Profile This product is informed by the English Vocabulary Profile, built as part of English Profile, a collaborative programme designed to enhance the learning, teaching and assessment of English worldwide. Its main funding partners are Cambridge University Press and Cambridge ESOL and its aim is to create a 'profile' for English linked to the Common European Framework of Reference for Languages (CEFR). English Profile outcomes, such as the English Vocabulary Profile, will provide detailed information about the language that learners can be expected to demonstrate at each CEFR level, offering a clear benchmark for learners' proficiency. For more information, please visit www.englishprofile.org

CALD The Cambridge Advanced Learner's Dictionary is the world's most widely used dictionary for learners of English. Including all the words and phrases that learners are likely to come across, it also has easy-to-understand definitions and example sentences to show how the word is used in context. The Cambridge Advanced Learner's Dictionary is available online at dictionary. cambridge.org. © Cambridge University Press, Third Edition, 2008 reproduced with permission.

This page is intentionally left blank

This page is intentionally left blank

This page is intentionally left blank

This page is intentionally left blank

This page is intentionally left blank

Cambridge English

EMPOWER

Combo A
WORKBOOK
WITH ANSWERS

B1+

Peter Anderson

Contents

Unit 1 Talk			Page
1A Keeping in touch	**Grammar** Subject and object questions **Vocabulary** Communication		4
1B I'm using an app for learning English	**Grammar** Present simple and continuous **Vocabulary** Gradable and extreme adjectives		5
1C Well, if you ask me …	**Everyday English** Giving and responding to opinions	**Pronunciation** Word groups	6
1D Different ways of learning	**Reading** A guide	**Writing skills** Introducing a purpose; Referring pronouns **Writing** A guide	7
Reading and listening extension	**Reading** An introduction to a textbook	**Listening** A conversation about a website	8
Review and extension	WORDPOWER *yourself*		9
Unit 2 Modern life			
2A They've just offered me the job	**Grammar** Present perfect simple and past simple **Vocabulary** Work	**Pronunciation** Present perfect simple and past simple	10
2B I've been playing on my phone all morning	**Grammar** Present perfect simple and continuous **Vocabulary** Technology		11
2C Could you take it back to the shop?	**Everyday English** Making suggestions	**Pronunciation** Sentence stress	12
2D I'm going to look for a new job	**Reading** An email from a friend	**Writing skills** Adding new information **Writing** An email to a friend	13
Reading and listening extension	**Reading** A summer camp website	**Listening** A job interview	14
Review and extension	WORDPOWER *look*		15
Unit 3 Relationships			
3A I was working at a café when we met	**Grammar** Narrative tenses **Vocabulary** Relationships	**Pronunciation** Linking	16
3B We used to get together every year	**Grammar** *used to, usually* **Vocabulary** Family; Multi-word verbs		17
3C You won't believe what I did!	**Everyday English** Telling a story	**Pronunciation** Stress in word groups	18
3D He wanted to see the world	**Reading** An email about a family member	**Writing skills** Describing time **Writing** A biography	19
Reading and listening extension	**Reading** A story	**Listening** A conversation between two students	20
Review and extension	WORDPOWER *have*		21

Unit 4 Personality			
4A	I could sing quite well when I was younger	**Grammar** Modals and phrases of ability **Vocabulary** Ability	22
4B	Are you an introvert?	**Grammar** Articles **Vocabulary** -ed / -ing adjectives; Personality adjectives	23
4C	Do you need a hand?	**Everyday English** Question tags; Offering and asking for help	**Pronunciation** Intonation in question tags	24
4D	No experience needed	**Reading** Adverts	**Writing skills** The language of adverts **Writing** An advert for summer camp coaches	25
Reading and listening extension		**Reading** A book review	**Listening** A presentation	26
Review and extension		WORDPOWER *so* and *such*	27

Unit 5 The natural world			
5A	People will care more about the environment	**Grammar** Future forms **Vocabulary** Environmental issues	**Pronunciation** Sound and spelling: *a*	28
5B	If you go to the beach, you can see dolphins	**Grammar** Zero and first conditional **Vocabulary** The natural world		29
5C	Why did you become a florist?	**Everyday English** Reasons, results and examples; Giving yourself time to think	**Pronunciation** Voiced and unvoiced consonants	30
5D	Looking after the environment	**Reading** An essay	**Writing** An essay	31
Reading and listening extension		**Reading** A student's essay	**Listening** The introduction to a lecture	32
Review and extension		WORDPOWER *problem*	33
Vox pop video			64
Audioscripts			72
Answer key			77

1A Keeping in touch

1 GRAMMAR
Subject and object questions

a <u>Underline</u> the correct words to complete the questions.

1 Who *did he write* / <u>*wrote*</u> the play *Romeo and Juliet?*
2 Which tooth *does it hurt* / *hurts* when I touch it?
3 What *did it happen* / *happened* after the police arrived?
4 Which football match *did they watch* / *watched* on TV last night?
5 Which book *did you talk* / *talked* about in your English class?
6 Who *did he talk* / *talked* to at the party last night?
7 Which student *did she get* / *got* the highest marks in the test?
8 Who *did you vote* / *voted* for at the last election?

b Put the words in the correct order to make questions.

1 you / who / that / gave / book / your birthday / for ?
<u>Who gave you that book for your birthday?</u>

2 parents / to / your / which / did / restaurant / go ?
_____

3 Harrison Ford / of / happens / the end / at / the film / what / to ?
_____

4 did / you and / about / friends / your / talk / what ?
_____

5 like / your / first / mobile phone / was / what ?
_____

6 his / about / was / what / presentation ?
_____

7 married / twice / film / got / year / star / last / which ?
_____

8 who / you / to / did / cinema / the / with / go ?
_____

2 VOCABULARY Communication

a Complete the sentences with the words in the box.

> presentation   interviewed   expressing   in public
> opinions   joke   ~~face-to-face~~   in touch

1 I prefer having _face-to-face_ meetings with my colleagues, rather than talking to them on the phone.
2 She used her laptop to give an extremely clear _____ of her project in class.
3 Our teacher always tells a _____ at the beginning of each lesson. Sometimes they're quite funny; sometimes they're terrible.
4 Although I left the country fifteen years ago, I still keep _____ with some of my old friends.
5 The politician was _____ by a journalist from *The Times*.
6 He isn't very good at _____ his feelings. He's rather shy so I never know if he's happy or not.
7 She doesn't usually say much in meetings. I don't think she likes speaking _____.
8 David's a very direct person. He always gives his _____ about my paintings.

b <u>Underline</u> the correct words to complete the sentences.

1 I <u>*complained*</u> / *argued* / *persuaded* to the waiter that my food wasn't hot enough.
2 I said I would take a taxi to the airport but they *complained* / *insisted* / *kept* on driving me in their car.
3 We were *argued* / *encouraged* / *greeted* at the airport by the Minister of Tourism.
4 He *argued* / *expressed* / *persuaded* her to lend him the £500 he needed to buy a new TV.
5 My father *argued* / *encouraged* / *expressed* me to apply for the job although I had very little experience in that area.
6 My husband and I always *argue* / *complain* / *insist* about where to go on holiday. I prefer the beach while he prefers the mountains.
7 The babysitter *argued* / *complained* / *persuaded* the children to go to bed at 9 o'clock.
8 Our teacher *complained* / *encouraged* / *persuaded* us to read English and American newspapers online.

1B I'm using an app for learning English

1 GRAMMAR
Present simple and continuous

a Match 1–8 with a–h to make sentences and questions.

1 $\boxed{g}$ They play
2 $\boxed{}$ He's thinking
3 $\boxed{}$ She's going
4 $\boxed{}$ I'm having
5 $\boxed{}$ He thinks
6 $\boxed{}$ We go
7 $\boxed{}$ I have
8 $\boxed{}$ They're playing

a a yoga class on Monday evenings.
b to school on Saturday mornings in my country.
c tennis in the park. Why don't you go and join them?
d about all the things he needs to do before his holiday.
e my dinner now so can I call you back in ten minutes?
f that his children will live until they are 100 years old.
g chess with their grandad every Sunday after lunch.
h to work by bike at the moment because she wants to get fit.

b Complete the conversation with the present simple or present continuous form of the verbs in brackets. Use contractions where possible.

ARTHUR ¹*Is Emma doing* (Emma, do) well at school these days?

PAT Yes, she is.

ARTHUR ²_____ (she, study) languages, like her brother?

PAT Yes, she ³_____ (learn) French and Spanish.

ARTHUR Really? ⁴_____ (she, want) to become an interpreter?

PAT She ⁵_____ (not, know) yet. She ⁶_____ (be) only 14, after all.

ARTHUR Yes, that's true. And what about sport? ⁷_____ (she, play) a lot of sport at school?

PAT Yes, she ⁸_____ (love) all sports. She ⁹_____ (be) particularly good at basketball. In fact, she ¹⁰_____ (play) for the school team in a match today.

ARTHUR Really? Great!

PAT Hold on … er, my phone ¹¹_____ (ring) …

ARTHUR Who is it?

PAT It's my husband. Sorry, I must go – he ¹²_____ (wait) for me in the car.

ARTHUR OK, bye!

2 VOCABULARY
Gradable and extreme adjectives

a Match 1–8 with a–h to make sentences.

1 $\boxed{f}$ I hate swimming in the North Sea because
2 $\boxed{}$ I thought the book was brilliant, probably the best detective story
3 $\boxed{}$ After we'd walked 25 km
4 $\boxed{}$ They gave him such an enormous portion of spaghetti that
5 $\boxed{}$ Lots of tourists had just left their rubbish behind them so
6 $\boxed{}$ I asked her to open the window because
7 $\boxed{}$ If you're late for his class again
8 $\boxed{}$ We all thought the play was awful so

a I felt absolutely exhausted.
b the beach was absolutely filthy.
c even he couldn't finish it.
d it was boiling in there.
e I've ever read.
f the water's always freezing.
g we left the theatre at the interval.
h he'll be furious!

b Complete the sentences with the words in the box.

| tiny | impossible | ~~fantastic~~ | delicious |
| miserable | freezing | useless | filthy |

1 We had a ___*fantastic*___ holiday in Bali. The weather was lovely, the hotel was perfect and the beaches were beautiful.
2 The weather was _____ when I was in Moscow last week – minus 15° during the day!
3 He's renting a _____ flat in the centre of Paris – it's only got one room!
4 The children looked so _____ when their pet rabbit died.
5 He spoke so quickly it was _____ to understand what he was saying.
6 Nobody had cleaned the kitchen for months. It was absolutely _____.
7 Thanks for a lovely dinner. The seafood risotto was absolutely _____. You must give me the recipe.
8 My football team are completely _____. We lost our last match 6 – 0.

1 USEFUL LANGUAGE
Giving and responding to opinions

a Complete the exchanges with the words in the box.

guess   sure   see   concerned   mean   opinion   ~~ask~~   think

1 **A** Well, if you _____ask_____ me, Tanya Davies would be the best person for the job.
   B Actually, I don't agree. As far as I'm _____, Luke Adams would be better.
2 **A** Well, I _____ you could take the shoes back to the shop.
   B I'm not so _____ about that. I've already worn them.
3 **A** I _____ it's going to be difficult to make enough money to survive.
   B Yes, I _____ where you're coming from. Maybe we should find a cheaper office?
4 **A** Well, in my _____, Italian is easier than French.
   B I know what you _____. I think it's easier to pronounce.

b ▶1.1 Listen and check.

c Underline the correct words to complete the sentences.

1 **A** It *comes* / *means* / *seems* to me that their coffee is better than ours.
   B Yes, I know exactly what you *mean* / *opinion* / *think*. It's really smooth, isn't it?
2 **A** As far as *I'm concerned* / *I guess* / *my opinion*, I think it makes sense to take the train to Paris.
   B I'm not so *mean* / *right* / *sure* about that. It takes nearly three hours.
3 **A** I *mean* / *sure* / *think* Germany will probably win the football World Cup.
   B Yes, I think that's *mean* / *right* / *sure*. They've got the best team.
4 **A** Well, in my *ask* / *guess* / *opinion*, we need to find another business partner in Spain.
   B Yes, I see *what* / *where* / *why* you're coming from. Maybe a company based in Madrid this time?

d ▶1.2 Listen and check.

2 PRONUNCIATION
Word groups

a ▶1.3 Listen to the exchanges and underline the word you hear before each speaker pauses.

1 **A** Guess what, Tony? I've just read about this girl, and she's only ten but she's fluent in several different languages.
   B That's fantastic. I can only speak one language – English.
2 **A** Hi, Linda. Are you learning Russian?
   B I'm trying to! But this book's useless! It teaches you how to say 'my uncle's black trousers' but not how to say 'hello'!

1D Skills for Writing
Different ways of learning

1 READING

a Read the text and tick (✓) the best ending for the sentence.

If you want to be a good photographer, …
a ☐ you shouldn't take lots of photos.
b ☐ you shouldn't use your smartphone.
c ☐ you don't need to study the manual.
d ☐ you should always take your camera with you when you go out.

b Read the text again. Are the sentences true or false?

1 With a digital camera or smartphone it is easier to take good photos than 20 years ago.
2 You shouldn't use automatic mode when you start using a new camera.
3 It is better not to take many photos when you are learning how to use a camera.
4 Your family and friends will be more relaxed if you take lots of photos.
5 It is easy to take good photos of people using the flash on your camera.

2 WRITING SKILLS Introducing a purpose; Referring pronouns

a Underline the correct words to complete the sentences.

1 *For improving / Improving / To improve* your listening skills, it's a good idea to watch films in English.
2 You should write a sentence that includes the new word *in order / to / so that* you can remember it more easily.
3 It's better to use a monolingual dictionary. *These / This / Those* will help you to start thinking in English.
4 Some people prefer to write the new words on cards with the translation. *That / These / This* technique will help you to remember what the word means and how it is spelt.
5 There are lots of things you can do *in order / so / that* to become a better language learner.
6 Why don't you practise repeating the questions that you hear on the DVD-ROM *so / that / to* you learn the correct intonation?

3 WRITING

a Read the notes. Write a guide on how to be a better cook.

Notes for 'How to improve your cookery skills'

1) Introduction: How to become a good cook
   • Try new dishes. Practise.
   • Don't repeat same dishes all the time.
2) Learn new dishes
   • Buy recipe books.
   • Test on family/close friends first. Larger groups later.
   • Try new recipes 2–3 times a week.
   • Ask family/friends for honest opinions. Make improvements.
3) Watch TV cookery programmes
   • Easy way to follow recipe. Watch & download recipes from website.
4) Share recipes
   • Enjoyed a good meal? Ask for recipe. Will discover new dishes & improve.

Read article   Edit   Comment

How to take better photos

These days it is much easier to become a good photographer because of the big improvements in camera technology over the past 20 years. In order to take good photos you need to have a good digital camera or a smartphone with a good camera.

Make sure you read the manual carefully before you start using your camera. This will help you to understand the most important functions, such as how to use the flash and the zoom. Putting the camera in automatic mode is a good way to make sure you don't make too many mistakes while you are still unfamiliar with how your camera works.

It is a good idea to take your camera with you at all times so that you are always ready to take a photo whenever you see something interesting. Try to take as many photos as possible. This will help you to get better at using your camera and will result in better photos. Remember the saying 'Practice makes perfect'. The more you practise taking photos, the better you will become.

If you take lots of photos of your family and friends, in the end they will forget about the camera and feel more relaxed when you take photos of them. This will help you to take photos that look more natural and less posed.

To get the best photos of people you need to be outdoors, as the light outside is much better. It is extremely difficult to take attractive photos of people indoors using flash, so it is always better to be outside when you photograph people.

7

UNIT 1
Reading and listening extension

1 READING

a Read part of an introduction to a textbook for students. Are the sentences true or false?

The writer of this textbook believes that …

1 teachers in many countries expect their students to speak perfect English.
2 her book is for students who want to improve their English in a short time.
3 phrases that seem to be similar can sometimes communicate opposite meanings.
4 students may sound rude in English if they do not learn to speak the language perfectly.
5 we can understand someone more easily when we think about the culture that they come from.

b Read the text again. Match the words in bold in 1–7 with the things they refer to in a–g.

1 [e] By **this**, they mean that …
2 [ ] … **that** might seem strange
3 [ ] … someone gives **them** a present.
4 [ ] Why did you get me **this**?
5 [ ] Why is **this**?
6 [ ] And in fact, **this** phrase (or something like **it**) …
7 [ ] … different cultures say **them** in different ways …

a A birthday present.
b Ideas which are similar to each other.
c People from English-speaking countries.
d Saying *Oh, you didn't need to get me anything!*
e Speaking English perfectly.
f *Why did you get me this?*
g Why one phrase is rude but the other one is polite.

c Write a short email to the students in your class about learning English. Your email should:

- introduce yourself (your name, where you come from)
- explain why you are learning English
- describe where you have learned English in the past
- say what you hope to learn on this course.

Use the phrases below to help you.

Hi! My name's … and I'm from …
I'm learning English because I *want to … / need to … / am going to …*
I have been learning English *for* + [AMOUNT OF TIME] / *since* + [POINT IN TIME]
I started learning English *at school / when I was* + [AGE]
On this course, I really want to improve my …

A Beginner's Guide to
INTERCULTURAL COMMUNICATION

A personal goal for many students is to be able to speak English perfectly. By **this**, they mean that they would like to be able to tell a joke or feel completely confident in a face-to-face conversation with a group of native speakers. Any student can achieve this goal (and many do) but it takes many, *many* years of study.

If just the thought of all those years of study makes you feel exhausted, then the book you are now holding in your hands may be for you. *A Beginner's Guide to Intercultural Communication* has been written to help students who are learning English answer the question 'What are the best ways to communicate in a foreign language?'

But first of all let's think about what communication actually means. In our first language, we know that we have to choose our words very carefully. For example, I'm from Australia so when someone gives me a birthday present, I might say:

Oh, you didn't need to get me anything!

If you are not a native English speaker, **that** might seem strange. But many English speakers feel it is polite to say this when someone gives **them** a present. However, the same speakers would find it quite rude to say:

*Why did you get me **this**?*

Why is **this**? After all, the meaning of both phrases is quite similar. And in fact, **this** phrase (or something like **it**) is quite common in a number of European languages. The answer is simple – whether something seems to be rude or polite depends on culture. To communicate successfully in a foreign language, we need to remember that people are usually trying to say the same things but we also need to remember that different cultures say **them** in different ways – and that is what intercultural communication is all about.

2 LISTENING

a ⏵**1.4** Listen to a conversation between Bridget and Joe and tick (✓) the correct answers.

1 What is the main topic of their conversation?
  a ☐ the subject Bridget studies at university
  b ☐ a holiday that Bridget has had
  c ☐ a website that Bridget is creating

2 Bridget is feeling very tired because she has …
  a ☐ been writing something in a foreign language.
  b ☐ had a lot of essays to write for university.
  c ☐ just returned from a holiday in Mexico.

3 Bridget wants Joe to help her to …
  a ☐ check her grammar and spelling.
  b ☐ design a website.
  c ☐ improve her Spanish.

4 Bridget shows Joe a photo of a place in …
  a ☐ Egypt.
  b ☐ Mexico.
  c ☐ Singapore.

b Listen again. Underline the correct words to complete the sentences.

1 Bridget has *just started* / *almost finished* / *stopped working* on her website.
2 At her university, Bridget is a student in the *French and Spanish* / *Latin American studies* / *Culture and Politics* department.
3 Bridget's website is for students at her own university and also for students *all around the world* / *in Colombia* / *in Mexico*.
4 *A professor* / *Another student* / *Nobody else* has helped Bridget to write the information she needs for her website.
5 Chichen Itza is the name of *a building* / *a city* / *a university* they can see in her photo.
6 Joe thinks the photo of Chichen Itza is *absolutely perfect* / *the wrong size* / *too old-fashioned* for Bridget's website.

c Write a conversation between two people planning a website for your English class. Think about these questions:

  • what information students need (e.g. homework, vocabulary)
  • how the information will be organised
  • who will create the website.

◉ Review and extension

1 GRAMMAR

Correct the sentences.

1 What time started the football match?
  What time did the football match start?
2 My brother isn't liking coffee.
3 How was your holiday in Spain like?
4 Look at Tom – he wears his new shoes.
5 Who did take you to the station?
6 Can you repeat that? I'm not understanding.

2 VOCABULARY

Correct the sentences.

1 You've just walked 20 kilometres – you must be exausted.
  You've just walked 20 kilometres – you must be exhausted.
2 When we were young my brother and I used to discuss all the time, but now we've become good friends.
3 It's imposible to sleep because my neighbours are having a party.
4 I haven't rested in touch with many of my old school friends.
5 That cake was delicius but there was only a tiny piece left!
6 My dad is very funny. He loves making jokes about his time in the army.

3 WORDPOWER *yourself*

Complete the sentences with the verbs in the box.

| enjoy | help | ~~hurt~~ | do | teach | look after |

1 Hello, Grandma. I'm sorry you fell over while you were shopping. It's lucky you didn't ___*hurt*___ yourself.
2 _____ yourself to a hot drink. There's some fresh coffee and tea in the kitchen.
3 Have a great time at the party! _____ yourself.
4 You don't need to go to classes to learn a foreign language. You can _____ yourself using books and a DVD.
5 Make sure you _____ yourself while I'm away. Eat plenty of food and get enough sleep.
6 You don't need to pay someone to paint your bedroom. It isn't hard. You can _____ it yourself.

2A They've just offered me the job

1 GRAMMAR Present perfect simple and past simple

a Underline the correct words to complete the exchanges.

1 **A** How long *were you* / <u>*have you been*</u> at your present company?
 B *I worked* / *I've worked* for them since 2012.

2 **A** *Did you ever arrive* / *Have you ever arrived* late for a job interview?
 B Yes, last month, because of a delay on the train. *I arrived* / *I've arrived* there two hours late!

3 **A** *Did she ever work* / *Has she ever worked* in another country?
 B Yes, *she spent* / *she's spent* nine months in our Madrid office in 2008.

4 **A** *Matt applied* / *Matt's applied* for 20 jobs since January.
 B Yes and he *didn't have* / *hasn't had* any interviews yet.

5 **A** *Did you meet* / *Have you met* your new boss yet?
 B Yes, *I met* / *I've met* her for the first time yesterday.

b Complete the conversation with the present perfect or past simple form of the verbs in brackets. Use contractions where possible.

A ¹<u>Have you worked</u> (you, work) for a television company before?

B Yes, ²I _____ (work) for three different companies since I finished university. Immediately after university I ³_____ (get) a job with MTV.

A OK, so can you tell us something about your job at MTV?

B Yes, of course. What would you like to know?

A How long ⁴_____ (you, stay) at MTV?

B I ⁵_____ (stay) there for five years, from 2006 to 2011.

A Five years? And what ⁶_____ (you, like) most about the job?

B I really ⁷_____ (enjoy) being in charge of a team. It ⁸_____ (give) me some useful experience of managing other people.

A And now you're working at the BBC. So how long ⁹_____ (you, be) with the BBC?

B I ¹⁰_____ (be) in my current job for two years.

A So how much experience ¹¹_____ (you, have) of children's TV since you ¹²_____ (join) the BBC?

B I ¹³_____ (be) the editor of *The Magic Garden* for the last nine months.

2 VOCABULARY Work

a Match 1–8 with a–h to make sentences.

1 [e] Steve and Kevin both applied for
2 [ ] We've invited four of the candidates for
3 [ ] At conferences, I try to meet lots of people. It's good to have
4 [ ] She's a manager now and she's in charge of
5 [ ] Honda are one of the biggest employers in the region, with
6 [ ] He's studying photography at university and he'd like to have
7 [ ] I've been a teacher for 20 years so I've got a lot of
8 [ ] I've got good problem-solving

a a career in television or films.
b business contacts from other organisations.
c a second interview next Monday and Tuesday.
d experience in education.
e the job but only Kevin was invited for an interview.
f a team of five sales representatives.
g skills, so I can usually find a solution when things go wrong.
h over 2,000 employees in their new car factory.

b Complete the sentences with the words in the box.

grades   apply   charge   experience
~~career~~   team   interview   CV

1 My uncle had a long ___<u>career</u>___ in the army.
2 Philip has just been promoted. He's now in _____ of the marketing department at work.
3 I work in a _____ of five people.
4 They've invited me for an _____ next week.
5 When you write a _____, it's best to put all the information on a maximum of two pages.
6 I have fifteen years' _____ in hotel management.
7 My brother got excellent _____ at school.
8 Why don't you _____ for a job as a journalist?

3 PRONUNCIATION Present perfect simple and past simple

a ▶ 2.1 Listen to the sentences. Which sentence do you hear? Tick (✓) the correct box.

1 a [✓] I applied for lots of jobs.
 b [ ] I've applied for lots of jobs.

2 a [ ] We worked very hard today.
 b [ ] We've worked very hard today.

3 a [ ] I learned a lot in this job.
 b [ ] I've learnt a lot in this job.

4 a [ ] They offered me more money.
 b [ ] They've offered me more money.

5 a [ ] You had a fantastic career at the BBC.
 b [ ] You've had a fantastic career at the BBC.

2B I've been playing on my phone all morning

1 GRAMMAR Present perfect simple and continuous

a Complete the sentences with the present perfect continuous form of the verbs in the box. Use contractions where possible.

cry   learn   go   post   wait   read   cook   ~~play~~

1 I feel exhausted because I *'ve been playing* tennis all afternoon.
2 We _____ at the station for half an hour but my dad's train hasn't arrived yet.
3 She _____ a lot of messages on Facebook lately.
4 My eyes feel really tired. I _____ all day.
5 Dad _____ for hours. He's made an enormous meal.
6 You look really upset. _____ you _____?
7 My kids _____ Spanish for four years and now they can understand nearly everything.
8 How long _____ Neil _____ out with his girlfriend?

b Underline the correct verb forms to complete the sentences and questions.

1 *Dan's been using* / *Dan's used* his phone a lot recently to take photos of his children.
2 *I've been installing* / *I've installed* the new program and it's working perfectly.
3 Have you *been turning off* / *turned off* your phone? The film's starting now.
4 My computer *hasn't been working* / *hasn't worked* properly recently. I think something's wrong.
5 *You've been playing* / *You've played* that computer game all afternoon. Can you stop for five minutes, please?
6 How long have you *been waiting* / *waited* for your computer to install that weather app?
7 *I've been having* / *I've had* this tablet for three years and it still works perfectly.
8 *We've been trying* / *We've tried* to call Fiona on her mobile phone all day but she's not answering.

2 VOCABULARY Technology

a Underline the correct words to complete the sentences.

1 You can *download* / *upload* ebooks onto your tablet and then read them while you're on holiday.
2 Your *password* / *browser* should be a combination of letters, numbers and other characters.
3 Please help us to save energy by turning *on* / *off* your computer when you leave the office.
4 I've just found an amazing new *icon* / *app* which translates pop songs from English to Portuguese.
5 You can *share* / *delete* your photos with your family and friends on our new photo management website.
6 I think I *pressed* / *deleted* your email by mistake so could you send it to me again?
7 If you *click* / *type* on this button, it opens the program.
8 Why don't you *upload* / *download* a more recent profile photo on your homepage?
9 You're *clicking* / *typing* the wrong letters because the CAPS LOCK button is on.
10 When you enter the system, you need to enter your unique *username* / *icon*, which in your case is johnsmith.

b Complete the crossword puzzle.

	¹			²
³C	L	I	⁴C	K
	⁶			⁵
⁷			⁸	

→ Across

3 To visit our website, please ____*click*____ on this link.
6 If you _____ this app, we'll be able to use our phones to have video calls.
7 To surf the Internet, you need to have a _____ such as Internet Explorer or Google Chrome.
8 To log onto your account, you have to _____ your username and password.

↓ Down

1 We'd love to see your photos from the party. Can you _____ them onto Facebook so we can all see them?
2 It's quicker to send a text _____ to your friends than to send them an email.
4 If you are in a café with wi-fi, you can _____ your laptop or tablet to the Internet.
5 If you don't recognise the sender of an email, you should _____ it as it might be dangerous.

1 USEFUL LANGUAGE
Making suggestions

a <u>Underline</u> the correct words to complete the sentences.

1 Could you *ask* / *asking* your brother to help you?
2 Oh, really? That's a *dear* / *shame*.
3 How about *take* / *taking* it back to the shop where you bought it?
4 I'm really *brilliant* / *glad* to hear that.
5 Why don't you try *talk* / *talking* to your boss about it?
6 Let's *take* / *taking* it to the garage.
7 Oh dear. How *annoy* / *annoying*!
8 Shall we *ask* / *asking* his girlfriend what kind of music he likes?

b ▶ **2.2** Listen and check.

c Complete the words.

GARY	I'm moving to a new flat next week but I don't know how to move all my things. Look at all these boxes!
KAREN	How about ¹*just__* hiring a car?
GARY	No, that's too expensive.
KAREN	²W_____ about ordering a taxi?
GARY	That's ³w_____ a try but there are a lot of things here. We might need three trips in a taxi. That's not going to be cheap.
KAREN	No, it isn't. Have you ⁴t_____ asking a friend to drive you?
GARY	I'll ⁵g_____ it a try but all my friends are students. Nobody has a car.
KAREN	Oh, I know! Susie's mum has a flower shop and they have a van. You could get all your things in it and she could drive you to the new flat. ⁶S_____ I ask her to help?
GARY	That's a great ⁷i_____!
KAREN	Cool! Hey, ⁸I_____ invite her for dinner tonight and we can ask her then.
GARY	Sure. Why ⁹n_____?
KAREN	Great. ¹⁰C_____ you go to the supermarket and get some food, and I'll call her now?
GARY	OK. Thanks, Karen.
KAREN	No problem, Gary. You know what they say. Two heads are better than one!

d Put the conversation in the correct order.

- ☐ **B** Oh, no. How awful!
- ☐ **B** That's brilliant! I'm so pleased!
- ☐ **A** OK … No, it isn't in there …
- ☐ **A** Oh, listen – it's ringing! It's behind that cushion on the sofa!
- ☐ **A** I've been looking for it everywhere. I'm sure I had it when I got home.
- ☐ **A** That's a great idea. I'll give it a try. Can I borrow your phone for a minute?
- ☐ **B** OK, so it isn't in your bag. Have you tried phoning your number from another phone?
- ☒ **A** I've lost my phone!
- ☐ **B** What about checking in your bag?
- ☐ **B** Yes, sure. Here you are.

e ▶ **2.3** Listen and check.

2 PRONUNCIATION Sentence stress

a ▶ **2.4** Listen to the sentences and <u>underline</u> the stressed syllables.

1 Barbara's just <u>bought</u> a new <u>car</u> and it <u>won't</u> <u>start</u>!
2 My boss has been criticising my work recently.
3 My neighbours had a party last night so I didn't sleep very well.
4 My computer's been running very slowly since I installed that new program.

1 READING

a Read the text and tick (✓) the correct answer.

a ☐ Francesca has found a job with an advertising agency in London.
b ☐ Francesca is going to join a rock band in London.
c ☐ Francesca is going to begin her new job in London in April.
d ☐ Francesca is going to work in a hotel in the centre of London.

| Inbox | 📁 | 🗑 | ✉ |

Hi Anna

I'm sorry I didn't reply to your last email straightaway but I've been very busy for the last two weeks.

I've been travelling from Manchester to London most days for job interviews. I've had interviews with some major advertising agencies and marketing companies and it's been great to make so many business contacts in London.

You'll never believe this, but Outreach Marketing have just emailed me to offer me a job in their offices in Covent Garden. The job sounds brilliant! They want me to be in charge of a team that helps to promote some well-known pop stars and rock bands. And what's really amazing is that they also want me to find new singers and bands that we could promote in the future.

They've made me a fantastic job offer. Apart from giving me a really good salary they're also going to give me a company car. But the best thing is that they've agreed to pay for me to stay in a hotel in Central London for a month while I look for a flat to rent. Besides going to lots of free concerts, I'll also be able to visit all the museums and art galleries I've read about. I've accepted the offer and am going to start my new job at the beginning of April. I can't wait!

Everyone says that London's a fantastic city so I'm really looking forward to living there. We must get together before I leave, so why don't we meet up for coffee in the next two or three weeks? Let me know a day that suits you.

Best wishes

Francesca

b Read the text again. Are the sentences true or false?

1 Francesca has been to London several times in the last two weeks.
2 Francesca didn't meet any important people in London.
3 Francesca is going to be a manager in a marketing company.
4 Outreach Marketing aren't interested in promoting new singers or bands.
5 Francesca has already found a flat to rent in London.
6 Francesca thinks that it will be nice to live in London.

2 WRITING SKILLS
Adding new information

a Match 1–6 with a–f to make sentences.

1 ☐ f Besides its wonderful beaches,
2 ☐ In addition to my teaching experience in the UK,
3 ☐ I've worked as a pilot for an American airline
4 ☐ Besides agreeing to pay for four flights back to the UK each year
5 ☐ I have excellent technical qualifications.
6 ☐ Apart from paying me a higher salary they're

a apart from Flexi Airlines.
b In addition, I speak three languages fluently.
c they've also agreed to pay for my family to fly to Dubai once a year.
d also going to give me a company car.
e I've also worked in a primary school in South Africa for two years.
f Sicily also has lots of interesting historical sites.

3 WRITING

a Read the notes. Write an email to Martina.

Notes for email to Martina

1) Apology for not replying sooner.
2) Wrote new book. Sent to London publishing companies. Been offered contract.
3) Asked to make changes. More interesting for young people. Will work with editor.
4) Will pay me a lot of money. Can stop teaching & spend all my time writing.
5) Best part -- going to New York. First trip to USA. Meeting American editors & Hollywood film producers. Might make it into film.
6) Dinner together next week? New Italian restaurant in centre. Want to try?

UNIT 2
Reading and listening extension

1 READING

a Read the text and tick (✓) the correct answers.

1 Where might you see a text like this?
   a ☐ in a book of short stories
   b ☐ in a university textbook
   c ☐ on a university website

2 What is the main purpose of this text?
   a ☐ to explain how to program a robot dog
   b ☐ to give people facts about the camp
   c ☐ to persuade students to come to the camp

3 What is the main purpose of the student stories?
   a ☐ to show that students can have fun while they learn
   b ☐ to show that the camp can help your future career
   c ☐ to show that the camp leaders are helpful

4 When did Dan and Kristen write their student stories?
   a ☐ before the camp
   b ☐ during the camp
   c ☐ after the camp

b Read the text again and tick (✓) the correct answers.

Who ...	Dan	Kristen	Neither Dan nor Kristen
1 has been to the camp before?		✓	
2 says the camp is not the same as their normal education?			
3 felt unhappy at the beginning of the camp?			
4 is going to university soon?			
5 says they have improved their problem-solving skills?			
6 surprises people in their hometown with their knowledge of computers?			
7 was told about the camp at their school?			
8 prefers camp because they do not enjoy their normal school?			
9 has a busy social life in their hometown?			
10 mentions something they have been making at the camp?			

c Write a 'student story' for a course you are taking. Include the following:
- how you felt about the course before you began
- how you feel about the course now
- what kind of things you have been doing (or did) on the course
- why you think other people might enjoy the course.

COMPUTER CAMP

ABOUT

The first Computer Camp at the Central Scotland University (CSU) was in 2004. Since then, we have given more than 4,000 students a wonderful opportunity to improve their knowledge of computers and computer languages. The camp is for any student aged between 14 and 18 who wants to learn and have lots of fun at the same time.

STUDENT STORIES

Dan Austin from Glasgow, 15

This is my first time, so I didn't know what to expect. I've been having a really amazing time though and I really want to come back again. It's completely different from school and that's something I really like about the camp.

I've always got the highest marks in everything at my high school, and especially in maths. It was my maths teacher who told me about the camp. She persuaded my dad that it could help me get a career in computers. I suppose that must be true and I'm pretty sure that's why my dad let me come here, but for me I just enjoy it.

This week, I've been working on a program that can control the lights in a building. It's been really cool and I love working with kids who are just like me.

Kristen Berg from Aberdeen, 18

I've been coming to the CSU Computer Camp since I was 13 so this is my fifth time here. There's no doubt about it – this is one of the coolest things you can do in the summer holidays.

A lot of people back in Aberdeen are really surprised that I know so much about computers. They don't expect me to know anything about them because I'm a girl with long blonde hair and I love music, dancing and going out with friends. Every camp has been great and I've learned so much here. In fact, I'm starting a degree in Computer Science this October in Edinburgh.

2 LISTENING

a ▶ **2.5** Listen to part of a job interview. Put the topics from the interview in the order that you hear them.

☐ a practical skill someone has learned at work
☐ high school education
☐ an ability the employers think is useful
☐ work experience
☐ a qualification from university
☐ the place where one speaker was born
☐ 1 how the interview will be organised

b Listen to the interview again and tick (✓) the correct answers.

1 Carlos came to the interview …
   a ☐ by car.   b ☐ by plane.   c ✓ by train.

2 How old is Carlos?
   a ☐ 23   b ☐ 24   c ☐ 25

3 Where did Carlos study Computer Science?
   a ☐ in Spain   b ☐ in the UK   c ☐ in the US

4 How many languages does Carlos speak?
   a ☐ 2   b ☐ 3   c ☐ 4

5 When Carlos says he is 'a people person' he means that …
   a ☐ he can work with other people easily.
   b ☐ he has a specialist knowledge of people.
   c ☐ his family come from different countries.

6 What does Carlos do in his current job?
   a ☐ He creates apps for mobile phones.
   b ☐ He sells mobile phones.
   c ☐ He teaches computer languages.

c Look at the job advert below. Write a conversation between two people. Person A is interviewing Person B for the job of team leader. Use these questions to help you:
   • Can you tell us about yourself? (name, age, work/study)
   • What experience do you have that would be helpful for this job?
   • Why do you think you would be a good team leader? (Person B gives reasons)

TEAM LEADER FOR INTERNATIONAL YOUTH SUMMER CAMP

Every year, the Central Scotland University (CSU) provides an International Youth Summer Camp for 600 children aged 12–14 from countries all around the world. The purpose of the camp is to:
• develop self-confidence and creative thinking
• teach problem-solving skills
• give opportunities to practice practical skills with technology
• let them have fun!
We are looking for people to be team leaders. Team leaders must:
• speak English and at least one other language
• have a positive attitude to work
• have knowledge about a sport, a skill or a hobby that will help students learn self-confidence, creative thinking, problem-solving or practical skills.

◉ Review and extension

1 GRAMMAR

Correct the sentences. Use contractions where possible.

1 Did you ever go to Australia?
   Have you ever been to Australia?
2 I can't talk to Julia because she's spoken on the phone all day.
3 I've been to Portugal on holiday three years ago.
4 I've been knowing Jack for about five years.
5 His train was late this morning so he just arrived.
6 Last night she has gone to the party with her sister.
7 He works as a taxi driver since 2008.
8 She's got red eyes because she's cried.

2 VOCABULARY

Correct the sentences.

1 She's the manager of a game of five sales representatives.
   She's the manager of a team of five sales representatives.
2 Please turn out your phones as the film is about to start.
3 Can you give me your password so I can connect to Internet?
4 I've got a lot of experiences of managing people.
5 My brother just sent me a text massage to say he'll be late.
6 Sarah applied the job at the hospital but she didn't get it.
7 The English keyboard is different to the one in my language so I keep making mistakes when I press.
8 My brother has just got a new work with a large bank in London.

3 WORDPOWER *look*

Underline the correct words to complete the sentences.

1 I think we're lost. Let's look *after / at / out* the map so we can see where we are.
2 I looked *after / at / up* my friend's dog while she was away on holiday last week.
3 Can I help you? Yes, we're looking *after / for / out* a hotel.
4 Why don't you look *at / out / up* the phone number of the restaurant on the Internet?
5 I'm really looking *after / for / forward* to meeting you.
6 Shall we look *after / around / out* the old town to see if there are any nice places to eat?
7 Look *at / for / out*! There's an old lady crossing the road!

◔ REVIEW YOUR PROGRESS

Look again at Review your progress on p.30 of the Student's Book. How well can you do these things now?
3 = very well   2 = well   1 = not so well

I CAN ...

talk about experiences of work and training	☐
talk about technology	☐
make and respond to suggestions	☐
write an email giving news.	☐

3A I was working at a café when we met

1 GRAMMAR Narrative tenses

a Underline the correct words to complete the sentences.

1 By the time we *were getting* / *had got* / *got* to the park, it *had started* / *started* / *was starting* snowing heavily so we *were making* / *made* / *had made* a snowman.

2 While he *cleaned* / *had cleaned* / *was cleaning* the window above the door, he *had fallen* / *fell* / *was falling* off the chair and *broke* / *was breaking* / *had broken* his leg.

3 By the time it *stopped* / *had stopped* / *was stopping* raining, it *was* / *was being* / *had been* too late to go to the beach.

4 When the two police officers *were ringing* / *rang* / *had rung* my doorbell, I *was having* / *had* / *had had* dinner.

5 Barbara *was meeting* / *met* / *had met* him in 2010 while she *was working* / *worked* / *had worked* in Berlin.

6 When I *was seeing* / *had seen* / *saw* Mario yesterday, he *looked* / *was looking* / *had looked* sad because his pet rabbit *escaped* / *had escaped* / *was escaping* the day before.

7 They *talked* / *were talking* / *had talked* about the accident when the ambulance *had arrived* / *was arriving* / *arrived*.

b Complete the sentences with the past simple, the past continuous or the past perfect forms of the verbs in brackets.

1 He ____met____ (meet) his girlfriend while they _____ (study) together at Oxford University.

2 We _____ (leave) Barcelona on Monday morning and by Wednesday evening we _____ (cycle) 275 kilometres.

3 By the time the police _____ (arrive), the bank robbers _____ (escape) in their car.

4 This morning she _____ (ride) her bike around the lake and _____ (take) photos of the birds.

5 She _____ (hear) the fireworks while she _____ (watch) a film on TV.

6 The car _____ (crash) into the tree while they _____ (cross) the road.

7 The restaurant _____ (close) by the time we _____ (get) there.

8 Ibrahim _____ (call) me while he _____ (wait) for his flight.

2 VOCABULARY Relationships

a Match 1–6 with a–f to make sentences and questions.

1 [d] I've always had a good
2 [ ] They come from the same
3 [ ] I think that he's really funny – he's got a great
4 [ ] They have a lot of shared
5 [ ] Who do you get
6 [ ] I have quite a few things

a on best with – your brother or your sister?
b in common with Jack. For example, we both like rap music.
c background. Both of their families were farmers in Wales.
d relationship with both of my parents.
e interests. They're both mad about football and photography.
f sense of humour even when things go wrong.

b Complete the sentences with the words in the box.

relatives	~~touch~~	friendship
support	stranger	humour

1 It's easy to keep in _____touch_____ with your family when you go on a business trip – you can send emails and texts and talk to them via Skype.

2 Our _____ is really important to us. We've known each other since we were five years old.

3 When he came back to his home town, he felt like a complete _____. All of his friends had moved to London so he didn't know anyone.

4 Louise gave me a lot of _____ when I got divorced. She really helped me during a very difficult time in my life.

5 I have some _____ in both Montreal and Quebec because two of my uncles moved to Canada in the 1980s.

6 He's got a fantastic sense of _____. He's always telling us jokes and making us laugh.

3 PRONUNCIATION Linking

a ▶ 3.1 Listen to the sentences. Underline the linked words where one word ends in a consonant sound and the next word starts with a vowel sound.

1 Mark and Tania got to know <u>each other</u> when they <u>worked in</u> Spain.
2 They've got lots of shared interests.
3 He gets on very well with his aunt.
4 I'm not very good at keeping in touch with old friends.
5 What does she have in common with her American cousin?

3B We used to get together every year

1 GRAMMAR *used to, usually*

a Underline the correct words to complete the sentences.

1 Our family <u>*usually get together*</u> / *used to get together* on Sundays. It's nice to keep in touch with everyone.
2 These days I *usually walk* / *used to walk* to work – it's much healthier.
3 When I was seven, my parents *usually send* / *used to send* me to stay with my grandparents in Scotland for six weeks.
4 *Do you usually get* / *Did you used to get* on well with your teachers when you were at primary school?
5 She *doesn't usually like* / *didn't use to like* tea or coffee when she was little.
6 When I was a little girl I *usually hang out* / *used to hang out* with my cousin and her friends a lot.
7 As I was an only child, I *didn't use to have* / *don't usually have* a brother or sister to play with during the holidays.
8 *Did you used to take* / *Do you usually take* the bus to work when it rains?

b Complete the article with the verbs in the box and the correct form of *used to* or the present simple.

---
drive   live   go   sit   eat

Before Jason won the lottery two years ago, he ¹<u>*used to live*</u> in a small flat next to the train station. Now he ²_____ in an enormous house with a swimming pool and a tennis court. Jason ³_____ a 15-year-old car but these days he ⁴_____ a brand new Ferrari. Before winning the lottery he hardly ever ⁵_____ on holiday but nowadays he usually ⁶_____ on holiday to places like Bali or the Caribbean. On hot summer days Jason ⁷_____ in the park but these days he usually ⁸_____ by the swimming pool in his enormous garden. When Jason didn't have much money he ⁹_____ in restaurants very often but now he usually ¹⁰_____ in expensive restaurants three or four times a week.

2 VOCABULARY Family

a Complete the sentences with the words in the box.

---
niece   childhood   ~~elder~~   only
nephew   eldest   middle   generations
---

1 Pauline is my _____*elder*_____ sister. She was born two years before me.
2 My brother's son's birthday is next week. I've just bought him a card that says, 'Happy birthday, _____!'
3 I had a very happy _____. My parents spent a lot of time with us and we used to laugh all the time.
4 Jane's two years older than me and Joe's one year younger so I'm the _____ child.
5 It wasn't much fun being an _____ child. I never had any brothers or sisters to play with.
6 I've got two brothers and Nick is the _____. He's 26, Mike is 20 and I'm 23.
7 My sister's just had a new baby girl, so now I've got a _____.
8 There will be four _____ of our family at the wedding! My great-grandfather will be there too!

3 VOCABULARY Multi-word verbs

a Match 1–8 with a–h to make sentences.

1 [f] When I was a teenager I used to hang
2 [ ] John's got a great sense of humour. I think he takes
3 [ ] After I left home, my parents started to grow
4 [ ] In *The Jungle Book*, Mowgli was brought
5 [ ] When Megan felt lonely she used to ring
6 [ ] I've got an identical twin and some people have always mixed us
7 [ ] All the students from my old class get
8 [ ] Most people think that I'm English, but in fact I grew

a up her mother for a chat.
b up by a family of wolves. It's an incredible story.
c up in Ireland and then came to live in London after university.
d together every two or three years for a reunion party.
e after his grandad, who was always telling jokes.
f out with my elder brother and his friends.
g apart and two years later they got divorced.
h up. They can't tell the difference between us.

3C Everyday English
You won't believe what I did!

1 USEFUL LANGUAGE
Telling a story

a Complete the sentences with the words in the box.

> matters   turned   anyway   end
> won't   guess   ~~thing~~   funny

1 The best ___thing___ is that my new flat is air conditioned.
2 _____, we still hadn't found a hotel for my grandparents.
3 In the _____, we bought him a computer game.
4 It _____ out that he had never played golf in his life.
5 You'll never _____ what Sarah said to David.
6 The _____ thing was that he didn't know she was joking.
7 You _____ believe what he bought her for her birthday. A snake!
8 To make _____ worse, the water was too cold to have a shower.

b ▶ 3.2 Listen and check.

c Put the words in the correct order to make sentences.
1 guess / you'll / happened / the / what / party / never / at .
  You'll never guess what happened at the party.
2 best / got / pool / thing / that / the / it's / swimming / a / is .
  _____
3 Maggie / we still / find / had / to / a / anyway, / for / present .
  _____
4 heavily / worse, / make / raining / to / it / matters / started .
  _____
5 did / you / believe / Saturday / I / on / what / won't .
  _____
6 funny / the / what / realise / thing / was / she / that / didn't / happened / had .
  _____
7 in / us / end, / the / he / the / to drive / to / station / agrood .
  _____
8 ticket / it / out / had / that / turned / train / she / her / lost .
  _____

d ▶ 3.3 Listen and check.

2 PRONUNCIATION
Stress in word groups

a ▶ 3.4 Listen to the sentences and <u>underline</u> the words before the speakers pause.
1 But, <u>anyway</u>, the train was still at the <u>station</u> and we got on just as the doors were closing.
2 In the end, we went to a little restaurant near the station, where we had a lovely meal.
3 To make matters worse, the waiter dropped the bottle of wine and it ruined my new white dress.
4 On top of that, when she eventually got to the airport they told her that her flight was nearly two hours late.
5 Anyway, in the end I found a lovely flat in the centre, and the best thing is that it's only 800 euros a month!

b Listen to the sentences again and <u>underline</u> the stressed syllables.
1 But, <u>anyway</u>, the train was still at the <u>station</u> and we got on just as the doors were <u>closing</u>.
2 In the end, we went to a little restaurant near the station, where we had a lovely meal.
3 To make matters worse, the waiter dropped the bottle of wine and it ruined my new white dress.
4 On top of that, when she eventually got to the airport they told her that her flight was nearly two hours late.
5 Anyway, in the end I found a lovely flat in the centre, and the best thing is that it's only eight hundred euros a month!

3D Skills for Writing
He wanted to see the world

1 READING

a Read the email and tick (✓) the correct answer.

a ☐ Jack played professional football in the 1960s.
b ☐ Jack played for Newcastle United for five years.
c ☐ Jack joined Newcastle United in 1953.
d ☐ Jack scored 100 goals for the factory team.

b Read the email again. Are the sentences true or false?

1 Paolo and Carla's uncle used to be a professional footballer.
2 When Jack was 16 he played for Newcastle United.
3 Jack was still playing professional football in the 1960s.
4 Jack and Giulia got married two years after they met.
5 Jack and Giulia died in 1992.

2 WRITING SKILLS Describing time

a Match 1–6 with a–f to make sentences.

1 ☐f She lived in Buenos Aires for
2 ☐ He continued studying until he was 22. Meanwhile,
3 ☐ He visited the Grand Canyon during
4 ☐ Uncle Julian was a major in the army from 1986
5 ☐ She worked as a receptionist over
6 ☐ My parents met a long time ago while

a his first business trip to the USA.
b his twin brother was working in the family's shoe factory.
c they were both teaching English in Indonesia.
d the summer holidays when it was particularly busy.
e until his retirement a few years ago.
f seven years before moving to England.

3 WRITING

a Read the notes. Imagine your grandfather was James Cooper. Write his biography.

Mail

Hi Carla

I've been talking to Dad about our family history and I've found out some interesting things about his brother Giacomo, our Uncle Jack. Well, apparently, he was a professional footballer for a few years in the 1950s!

Jack left school at 16 in 1948 and worked in a car factory in Newcastle for five years. While he was working there, he used to play football every Saturday for the factory team. One day some men came to watch him from Newcastle United. They offered him a contract so in 1953 Jack left the car factory and became a professional footballer. Apparently, he played for Newcastle United from 1953 until 1959 and scored over 100 goals for them. However, he broke his leg badly in 1959 and had to give up playing professional football.

After that, he got a job as a sports teacher at a local secondary school and that's where he met his wife, Auntie Giulia. She was an Art teacher. They fell in love and got married two years later, in 1961. Our cousins Luigi and Anna were born in 1962 and 1964. As you know, we left Great Britain and came to live here in Australia in 1965, so it was quite difficult for Dad and Uncle Jack to keep in touch after that.

Meanwhile, in 1969 Uncle Jack and Auntie Giulia opened an Italian restaurant called La Forchetta in the centre of Newcastle. During the 1970s and 1980s this was the most popular Italian restaurant in Newcastle. Sadly, in 1992 Uncle Jack was killed in a car crash and Auntie Giulia decided to sell the restaurant.

When I travel to the UK on business later this year, I'm planning to meet our cousins, Luigi and Anna.

Hope to see you soon

Paolo

Notes for biography of James Cooper (Grandad)

Introduction: James Cooper (Grandad). My sister and I very fond of him. Remember lunch with grandparents every Sunday when young. Always made us laugh – lots of jokes and funny stories.

Life story:
1928 Born London. Very happy childhood. 1 brother & 2 sisters.
1936 Family moved to Montreal. Stayed there 10 years. Spoke English and French.
1946–1952 Studied medicine at Cambridge University, UK.
1952 Graduated from Cambridge.
1953–1962 Worked in different hospitals in UK.
1962–1975 Job in hospital in San Francisco. Met Elspeth Clark (Grandma).
1964 Married Elspeth.
1965 My mother born. No other children.
1975–1980 Job in Johannesburg, South Africa. Friendship with famous heart surgeon Christiaan Barnard.
1988 Retired aged 60.
2000 Died aged 72. Miss him very much.

UNIT 3
Reading and listening extension

1 READING

a Read the text and tick (✓) the correct answers.

1 This text comes from …
   a ☐ a newspaper article.
   b ☐ a novel.
   c ☐ an essay.

2 Which of these adjectives best describes the text?
   a ☐ amusing   b ☐ romantic   c ☐ strange

3 What is the best way to describe what happens in this text?
   a ☐ A student cannot complete an essay because of a noise outside her room.
   b ☐ A student is trying to complete an essay when something unusual happens.
   c ☐ A student is waiting for her friends to ring her up but they come to her house instead.

4 In the text, what is compared to 'a busy teacher'?
   a ☐ a clock   b ☐ a computer   c ☐ a drawer

5 In the text, what is compared to 'a dog's nose'?
   a ☐ the curtains   b ☐ the rain   c ☐ the streets

b The order of the events in the story is different from the order that the events happened. Read the text again and put the events in the order they happened.

☐ Jen started writing her essay.
☐ It stopped raining.
☐ Jen had a big shock.
☐ A voice called Jen's name.
1 It started raining.
☐ Jen heard a noise outside.
☐ The group hid from Jen.
☐ Jen turned her computer on.

c Write a short story that begins with this sentence: *I had just arrived at the cinema when Larissa called.*

Jen sighed heavily. She hadn't done anything for at least ten minutes. She looked at the clock and the clock looked back at her. It was like a busy teacher: 'tick', 'tick', 'tick' … It ticked every second and the seconds became minutes. Jen sighed again, even more heavily this time.

'You're no friend of mine,' she said, picking up the noisy clock. She walked to the other side of her bedroom, opened a drawer, threw the clock in and closed it again. Jen went back to her computer to do some more sighing. None of her friends were online and she had at least another 500 words to write.

Suddenly, there was a noise from outside. Jen went over to the window, opened the curtains just a centimetre and put one eye very carefully to the gap. It had been raining that day and the streets were as cold, black and wet as a dog's nose. She couldn't see very clearly, but she could hear them.

There was a group of maybe seven or eight figures all hanging out together. She checked her phone – no one had sent her a text in the last five minutes. She looked at the computer – everyone she knew was still offline. So who were they?

The laughing and shouting from outside had become much louder so Jen went to the curtains for another look. As soon as she opened the curtains, everything went quiet.

'That's strange,' she thought. The whole group had disappeared. She listened more carefully but there was only silence.

'JEN! JEN!! WE CAN *SEE* YOU, JEN!!!' eight voices shouted at once.

There was a feeling like someone had poured a glass of ice-water into her stomach and suddenly she was jumping away from the curtains, her hand over her mouth.

'JEEEeennnn …' came a single voice, 'JEEEeennnn …'

Jen froze. Whose voice was it? Was it someone she knew? A stranger? Who could it be? There was only one way to find out …

2 LISTENING

a ▶ **3.5** Listen to part of a conversation between two students at a university. Are the sentences true or false?

1 Education is the main topic of the conversation.
2 The conversation is a friendly chat.
3 One of the speakers is from Africa.
4 The speakers have not met before.
5 One speaker describes his/her family.
6 Relationships are the main topic of the conversation.
7 The conversation is an interview.
8 One speaker is a professional sportsperson.

b Listen to the conversation again and tick (✓) the correct answers

1 What is Ben studying at university?
  a ☐ Economics
  b ☐ Physics
  c ☐ Politics

2 How old is Ben?
  a ☐ 24
  b ☐ 28
  c ☐ 32

3 Rosie is surprised that Ben …
  a ☐ has a girlfriend.
  b ☐ is already married.
  c ☐ is not in a relationship.

4 How many sisters does Ben have?
  a ☐ 3
  b ☐ 5
  c ☐ 6

5 Ben believes he is confident because …
  a ☐ he has always been good at sport.
  b ☐ his family looked after him.
  c ☐ there are so many women in his family.

6 Why did Ben not like Zippy when they first met?
  a ☐ Because Zippy did not understand Ben's sense of humour.
  b ☐ Because Zippy was a better football player than Ben.
  c ☐ Because Zippy's sister had an argument with Ben.

c Write a conversation between two people discussing family and friendship. Use these questions to help you:
- How would you describe your childhood?
- Do you keep in touch with friends you made at school?
- How important is a sense of humour in friendship?
- What other things are important in a good friendship?

⊙ Review and extension

1 GRAMMAR

Correct the sentences.

1 He phoned me while I got ready to go out.
  He phoned me while I was getting ready to go out.
2 I use to have long hair when I was a little girl.
3 He played football when he fell over and hurt his ankle.
4 When he got to his house he was angry because someone broke his window.
5 I got to the station five minutes late this morning and, unfortunately, my normal train already left.
6 After the film we were going to the café for a drink.
7 Did you used to play football when you were at school?
8 I didn't used to like English when I was at school.

2 VOCABULARY

Correct the sentences.

1 I've never had a very good relation with my sister.
  I've never had a very good relationship with my sister.
2 Joanne's mother died when she was three so she was grown up by her grandparents.
3 I got knowing Jasmine really well when we went travelling around South America together.
4 All my relatives met together at my dad's birthday party.
5 I don't have any brothers or sisters so I'm a lonely child.
6 She doesn't go on very well with her two brothers.
7 We share a lot of the same interestings, for example literature.
8 My little brother's very calm and patient, so he looks after his mother because she's like that too.

3 WORDPOWER *have*

Complete the sentences with the words in the box.

idea	~~lesson~~	go	look	time	lunch

1 My son has a piano ___lesson___ every Monday after school.
2 We had a great _____ at Debbie's party.
3 I felt really hungry so I had _____ at 12 o'clock.
4 I had no _____ they had got divorced.
5 Are those your holiday photos? Can I have a _____?
6 Do you want to have a _____ on my skateboard?

↻ REVIEW YOUR PROGRESS

Look again at Review your progress on p.42 of the Student's Book. How well can you do these things now?
3 = very well   2 = well   1 = not so well

I CAN …

talk about a friendship	☐
talk about families	☐
tell a story	☐
write about someone's life.	☐

4A I could sing quite well when I was younger

1 GRAMMAR
Modals and phrases of ability

a Underline the correct words to complete the sentences.

1 He *wasn't able to* / *won't be able to* / *hasn't been able to* practise with the band since he started his new job.
2 Your sister speaks English really well. *Could you* / *Can you* / *Have you been able to* speak it as well as her?
3 By the time he was seven, *he can* / *he could* / *he's been able to* speak four languages fluently.
4 The banks are all closed now, but, don't worry; *you'll be able to* / *you could* / *you were able to* change some money tomorrow morning.
5 He missed the last bus but, fortunately, he *could* / *can* / *was able to* find a taxi to take him back to the hotel.
6 I *can't* / *couldn't* / *haven't been able to* find where your street was, so in the end I asked a policeman.
7 Before she goes abroad on holiday, she tries to learn some of the language, as she likes *being able to* / *can* / *will be able to* say a few words to the people she meets.
8 She looked everywhere in her apartment but she *can't* / *won't be able to* / *didn't manage to* find her car keys.

b Match 1–6 with a–f to make sentences.

1 [b] Tomorrow the weather will definitely be better, so you
2 [ ] Even when he was a child, Pablo Picasso
3 [ ] I've
4 [ ] He spoke very slowly so we
5 [ ] I'm learning Greek because I want to
6 [ ] We looked everywhere but in the end, we didn't

a be able to speak to my wife's family in their language.
b will be able to go to the beach.
c were able to understand him easily.
d been able to ride a bike since I was three years old.
e manage to find a hotel room.
f could draw really well.

2 VOCABULARY Ability

a Underline the correct word to complete the sentences.

1 To run 20 marathons in less than a month was an incredible *success* / *achievement* / *attitude*.
2 She has the *ability* / *success* / *achievement* to learn languages very quickly.
3 Jenny has a really positive attitude *at* / *towards* / *to* her studies. She works really hard.
4 I am *brilliant* / *confident* / *determined* to get a grade A in the exam.
5 They were one of the most *successful* / *determined* / *confident* bands of the 1960s. They sold millions of records.
6 Unfortunately, he *succeeded in* / *achieved* / *gave up* studying languages when he was 14 so his English isn't very good.

b Complete the crossword puzzle.

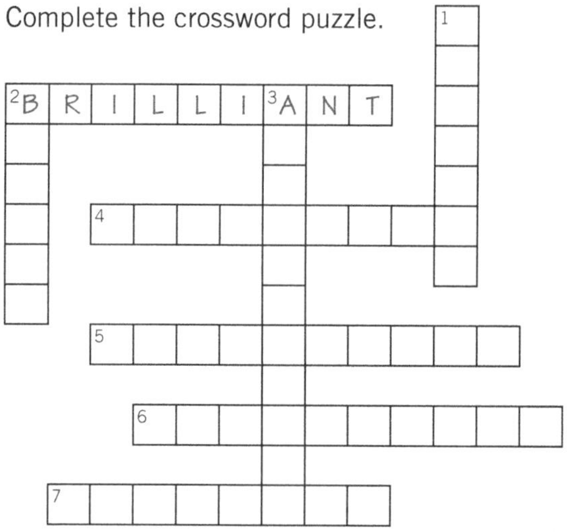

²B	R	I	L	L	I	³A	N	T	

(crossword grid with across clues 2, 4, 5, 6, 7 and down clues 1, 2, 3)

→ Across

2 He was absolutely b rilliant_____ at chess. He could beat his father when he was only seven.
4 Rafael Nadal is an extremely c_____ tennis player – he expects to win every game he plays.
5 He was easily the most s_____ manager in the history of this football club. He won the championship eight times.
6 Although she felt extremely tired, she was d_____ to finish the marathon so she continued running.
7 Roger Federer is probably the most t_____ tennis player of his generation.

↓ Down

1 He had a great sense of humour and he loved telling jokes. He always had the a_____ to make people laugh.
2 She was extremely b_____ – probably the most intelligent student I've ever taught.
3 In the 1960s, NASA's greatest a_____ was to land a spacecraft on the moon.

4B Are you an introvert?

1 GRAMMAR Articles

a Complete the sentences with *a*, *an*, *the* or *Ø* (zero article).

1 On _____Ø_____ Saturday we went to _____ best Chinese restaurant in _____ London.
2 Do you know if there's _____ bank near here where I can buy _____ dollars?
3 I don't go to _____ school on _____ Saturdays.
4 Sometimes it's difficult to find _____ doctor when you live in _____ countryside.
5 **A** I saw _____ Italian film on TV last night. It was called *Cinema Paradiso*.
  B Really? What did you think of _____ film?
6 I think _____ Spanish people are very friendly.
7 I eat _____ fish two or three times _____ week.
8 Venice is one of _____ most beautiful cities in _____ world.

b Correct the sentences.

1 He's working as translator in UK.
  He's working as a translator in the UK.
2 I usually go to gym three times the week.
  _____
3 Is there supermarket opposite a bus stop near your house?
  _____
4 She usually goes to the school on Number 75 bus.
  _____
5 I often listen to radio before I go to the bed.
  _____
6 The British pop groups are very popular in USA.
  _____
7 There isn't the underground station near my hotel, so I'll have to take taxi.
  _____
8 Usain Bolt was fastest man in world at Olympic Games in 2012.
  _____

2 VOCABULARY *-ed/-ing* adjectives

a Underline the correct adjectives to complete the sentences.

1 I watched a *fascinating* / *fascinated* documentary about tigers on TV last night.
2 I was so *boring* / *bored* during his lecture that I nearly fell asleep.
3 That was one of the most *terrifying* / *terrified* horror films I've ever seen.
4 I'm looking forward to doing nothing when I go on holiday next week. It's going to be so *relaxing* / *relaxed*.
5 The children were really *disappointing* / *disappointed* when Uncle Paul didn't bring them a present.
6 This cloudy, wet weather is so *depressing* / *depressed*. There hasn't been any sunshine for weeks!
7 I'm not really *interesting* / *interested* in modern art.
8 If you aren't completely *satisfying* / *satisfied* with the service, you shouldn't leave the waiter a tip.

3 VOCABULARY Personality adjectives

a Complete the sentences with the words in the box.

sensitive talkative introvert shy
~~active~~ serious extrovert sociable

1 Bill and Philip are really ___active___. In their free time they always go running or swimming or they play football. They never seem to relax.
2 My brother's an _____. He likes spending time with other people and he's very good at making new friends.
3 Sarah's extremely _____. You have to be very careful with what you say to her, as she gets upset very easily.
4 Amanda's rather _____. She doesn't like meeting new people and she hates going to parties where she doesn't know anyone.
5 I think Joe's very _____. He has a lot of friends and he really enjoys meeting new people.
6 My sister is so _____. She often chats to her friends on the phone for hours!
7 Charles has very few friends and spends most of his time by himself. I think he's an _____.
8 James is a _____ student. He works very hard all the time and he rarely goes out with friends.

4C Everyday English
Do you need a hand?

1 USEFUL LANGUAGE Question tags

a Match 1–9 with a–i to make questions.

1 [h] You don't smoke any more,
2 [ ] It's a lovely day today,
3 [ ] Tom isn't going to ask her to marry him,
4 [ ] You haven't been waiting long for me,
5 [ ] She'd already bought him a present,
6 [ ] They'll phone us when they get to the airport,
7 [ ] The twins both got good grades in their exams,
8 [ ] Andrew speaks five languages fluently,
9 [ ] You don't want any rice, Jim,

a doesn't he?
b didn't they?
c have you?
d won't they?
e isn't it?
f is he?
g hadn't she?
h do you?
i do you?

b ▶4.1 Listen and check.

2 CONVERSATION SKILLS
Offering and asking for help

a Complete the exchanges with the words in the box.

| favour   need   return   could   how |
| something   ask   ~~wondered~~   help   hand |

1 **A** I __wondered__ if you could do me a favour?
  B Sure, _____ can I help you?
  A Do you think you _____ cut the grass in my garden for me?
  B Yes, of course. No problem.

2 **A** I've got a lot of things to get ready for the party tomorrow night.
  B Is there _____ I can do?
  A Yes, there is, actually. Can you give me a _____ with the shopping?
  B Yes, that's fine. Could I ask you a favour in _____?
  A Go ahead!
  B Could you lend me your black trousers for tomorrow?
  A No problem. I'll just get them for you.

3 **A** Could I ask you a _____, Ben?
  B Of course, what do you _____?
  A Could you _____ me move my desk into the other office?
  B Actually, I've got a bad back. Can you _____ someone else?

b ▶4.2 Listen and check.

3 PRONUNCIATION
Intonation in question tags

a ▶4.3 Listen to the sentences. Does the intonation go up ↗ or down ↘? Tick (✓) the correct answer.

	↗	↘
1 You've been to Cairo before, haven't you?	✓	
2 Jack's really good at tennis, isn't he?		
3 They've got four children, haven't they?		
4 This is the best beach in Thailand, isn't it?		
5 You're glad you left London, aren't you?		
6 You didn't go to Canada last year, did you?		

4D Skills for Writing
No experience needed

1 READING

a Read both adverts and tick (✓) the correct answer.

1 If you want to go on the adventure holiday in the Atlas Mountains, you …
   a ☐ have to be good at riding camels.
   b ☐ have to be under 30.
   c ☐ need to have a good bike.
   d ☐ mustn't be an introvert or a shy person.

2 If you want to be a volunteer English teacher, you should …
   a ☐ have a lot of experience of teaching.
   b ☐ be able to work well with children.
   c ☐ be able to speak another language very well.
   d ☐ have your own car.

Volunteer English teachers needed – 6 hours a week

Duties include teaching English to schoolchildren with a low level of English in local primary schools and to adults from all over the world that have come to work in the UK.

No qualifications or previous teaching experience needed. Volunteers will be required to attend a training programme. Candidates should be enthusiastic and outgoing and be good at working with children and adults. Candidates should be educated to degree level, have good English language skills and some experience of learning a foreign language.

Please complete the attached online application form. One of our coordinators will get in touch with you to discuss potential opportunities. Reasonable travel expenses reimbursed.

b Read the adverts again. Are the sentences true or false?

1 There will be eight people in the group that goes on the holiday to the Atlas Mountains.
2 They aren't planning to go walking in the mountains every day of the trip.
3 The people who go on this trip don't need to have any previous experience of walking in mountains.
4 The adults that are learning English come from lots of different countries.
5 New teachers don't need to receive any training.
6 It is better if new teachers have previously studied another language.

2 WRITING SKILLS
The language of adverts

a Match sentences 1–8 with the reduced expressions a–h.

1 [g] Candidates don't need to pay for a place to stay.
2 ☐ Candidates must be able to drive a car.
3 ☐ We will need to see your references from your previous jobs.
4 ☐ We're looking for someone with a university degree.
5 ☐ It doesn't matter if you've never done this job before.
6 ☐ The candidate needs to have previous classroom experience.
7 ☐ Candidates should be able to speak French.
8 ☐ We will train the successful applicant to do the job.

Trekking in the Atlas Mountains

We're looking for three or four people to join us on a 2-week adventure holiday in Morocco. We're meeting up in Marrakech on 27 April and spending 10 days walking and camping in the Atlas Mountains.

We're planning to climb Mount Toubkal, the highest mountain in North Africa, visit Berber villages and travel through a section of the Sahara Desert. We're also planning to go horse-riding and mountain-biking and we may also get the chance to ride a few camels! We'll spend the last 2–3 days exploring the fabulous city of Marrakech.

Ideally, you should be in your twenties or thirties with an outgoing personality and a sense of adventure. You should be good at getting on well with people and making friends easily. You should be very fit and have some experience of walking with a backpack in mountainous areas.

If this sounds like the trip for you, email us at the address below and we'll get back to you as soon as possible.

Jake, Suzie and Gary

3 WRITING

a Read the notes. Write an advert for summer camp coaches.

Notes for summer camp coaches advert

Camp for children 5–12 years.

Duties: Organise indoor/outdoor activities. Get kids ready in morning. Help at meal & bed times. Entertain during free time.

Person requirements: Energetic, enthusiastic, sense of adventure, sense of humour & positive attitude. Good at sports & art, etc. Must love working with children & work well with others in a team. 18 or over. University students/graduates preferred.

No experience required. Two-day training course.

Online application form & CV to Human Resources Dept. HRD will contact applicants for interviews.

a No previous experience needed.
b University graduate preferred.
c Teaching experience required.
d Full training programme provided.
e French-speaker preferred.
f Good references required.
g Accommodation provided.
h Driving licence required.

1 READING

a Read the text and tick (✓) the correct answers.

1 Where might you usually see this kind of text?
   a ☐ in a newspaper
   b ☐ in an email from a friend
   c ☐ on the back of a book

2 According to the reviewer, 'self-help' books …
   a ☐ are usually very expensive
   b ☐ have a large number of readers
   c ☐ help readers earn more money

3 Where did Burkeman go to collect information for the book?
   a ☐ capital cities in Europe
   b ☐ countries in North and South America
   c ☐ many different places

4 The reviewer enjoys a description of …
   a ☐ a family party
   b ☐ a funeral in a small town
   c ☐ a traditional festival

b Read the text again. Are the sentences true or false?

1 The phrase 'worth their weight in gold' in the first paragraph means 'valuable'.
2 Burkeman's book *The Antidote* is a typical example of a 'self-help' book.
3 Burkeman did not expect to find happiness in some of the places he visited.
4 Burkeman discovers that life is more difficult for people when they have a lot of money.
5 Burkeman says we cannot understand happiness unless we also have bad experiences.
6 People are often happy and enjoy themselves during the Day of the Dead.
7 Although there are some good parts, the reviewer does not recommend this book.

c Write a review of a non-fiction book you have enjoyed reading. Include the following:
   • the name of the author and the title of the book
   • a paragraph describing the general topic of the book
   • a paragraph describing the main ideas in the book
   • a paragraph describing the best part(s) of the book
   • a recommendation which explains why other people should read the book.

BOOK Reviews

THE ANTIDOTE: HAPPINESS FOR PEOPLE WHO CAN'T STAND POSITIVE THINKING

by Oliver Burkeman

Is your life disappointing? Does that make you feel depressed? If you answered 'yes' to those two questions, what can you do to find happiness? The answers to these questions can be worth their weight in gold – last year, people spent almost $11 billion on 'self-help' books. These books promise to make us more confident, more sociable and more successful. They tell us that all we really need to find love and achieve our goals is a positive attitude.

If you are amused by promises like these, then Oliver Burkeman's book *The Antidote* might just be for you. Burkeman has travelled the world in search of happiness and he has found it in some very unusual places. For example, he meets poor people in Africa who seem to be happier than some wealthy people he knows in London. For Burkeman, this shows us that people who do not own very much cannot worry about losing it. In other words, having a lot of things can add a lot of stress to our lives. Of course he is not saying that poor people in Africa have an easy life. Instead, Burkeman uses this example to talk about 'negative paths'.

A 'negative path' is important for a satisfying life. He suggests that we need to remind ourselves that bad things happen and that we should learn to live with them. True happiness – if it exists – must include both positive and negative experiences. A complete life should be one that knows hate as well as love and illness as well as health.

In my favourite part of the book, Burkeman takes us to a small village in Mexico on the Day of the Dead. The Day of the Dead is a festival that celebrates everyone who has died. However, it is not a sad festival at all, but a colourful party for friends and family. According to Burkeman, we need events like this to remember why we should be happy more often. *The Antidote* is an interesting book that has the ability to make you feel that happiness really is possible.

2 LISTENING

a ▶**4.4** Listen to an expert in advertising tell a story during a talk to university students and tick (✓) the correct answers.

1 Where did the story take place?
   a ☐ in England   b ☐ in Germany   c ☐ in Russia

2 Why did Frederick want people to start eating potatoes?
   a ☐ because they were cheap and easy to grow
   b ☐ because they were the solution to a problem
   c ☐ because they were very popular with the people

3 Frederick was surprised that the people …
   a ☐ did not know how to grow potatoes.
   b ☐ gave the potatoes to their animals.
   c ☐ said they could not eat the potatoes.

4 According to the speaker, the story can teach us something about …
   a ☐ food.   b ☐ history.   c ☐ psychology.

b Listen again and correct the information in the sentences. Use the words in the box to help you. You do not need all the words.

> animal   be successful   bread   business   hungry
> meat   psychology   soldier   steal   ~~talented~~

1 Frederick II is sometimes called Frederick the Great because he was so tall.
   Frederick II is sometimes called Frederick the Great
   because he was so talented.

2 Cheese was the most important part of most people's diet.
   _____

3 Frederick thought that if people had potatoes, they would not be angry any more.
   _____

4 People in Kolberg said their children could not eat potatoes.
   _____

5 People understood that potatoes were valuable when they saw the gates around Frederick's garden.
   _____

6 People began eating potatoes from Frederick's garden.
   _____

7 Frederick's plan did not work.
   _____

8 Frederick's plan was an example of good farming.
   _____

c Think of a story about a famous person or event in your country. Use these questions to make notes:
   • Does the story teach a lesson?
     (For example, can the story help people become more patient / more confident / healthier?)
   • Who are the main characters in the story?
   • What happens?
   Write the story.

⊙ Review and extension

1 GRAMMAR

Correct the sentences.

1 I've could speak English since I was seven years old.
   I've been able to speak English since I was seven years old.

2 When she goes to cinema she doesn't like seeing the horror films.

3 Will you can help me with my Maths homework this evening?

4 I love watching the documentaries about the whales.

5 She would like to can play the piano as well as her sister.

6 He usually gets to the work at about 8.30 in summer.

7 We weren't able find the restaurant so we went to the pizzeria instead.

8 It's one of best shopping websites on Internet.

2 VOCABULARY

Correct the sentences.

1 He has very positive attitude towards his studies.
   He has a very positive attitude towards his studies.

2 We had a very relax holiday in the South of France.

3 The film was so bored that I nearly fell asleep.

4 My uncle was a very succesful businessman in the 1960s.

5 My sister doesn't want to watch the match because she isn't very interesting in sport.

6 I thought that documentary about the environment was rather depressed.

3 WORDPOWER *so and such*

Complete the sentences with the words in the box.

> so far   such   ~~such a~~   and so on   so tired   or so

1 He's __such a__ brilliant musician!

2 He's been fishing for six hours and _____ he hasn't caught any fish.

3 It's a short book – no more than 100 pages _____.

4 To make a cake you'll need all the usual things – sugar, flour, butter _____.

5 It will be _____ fun at the party on Saturday, won't it?

6 I was _____ that I fell asleep on the train.

◔ REVIEW YOUR PROGRESS

Look again at Review your progress on p.54 of the Student's Book. How well can you do these things now?
3 = very well   2 = well   1 = not so well

I CAN …

describe people and their abilities	☐
describe feelings	☐
offer and ask for help	☐
write an informal online advert.	☐

1 GRAMMAR Future forms

a Match 1–8 with a–h to make sentences and questions.

1 [f] Jack really hates his job, so he's going to
2 [ ] Don't worry – this year I promise I won't
3 [ ] At 1 o'clock I'm
4 [ ] Brian's been studying very hard, so I'm sure he
5 [ ] I probably won't
6 [ ] What a lovely day! Shall we
7 [ ] Look at those dark clouds. I think it's
8 [ ] Your train doesn't get here until 11.30, so shall I

a meeting Susie for lunch at Café Classic.
b 'll get good grades in his exams.
c meet you at the station in my car?
d going to rain. Let's stay inside.
e go to the beach this afternoon?
f start looking for a new one in September.
g forget your birthday!
h see her today, as she usually visits her grandparents on Sundays.

b Correct the sentences.

1 **A** Will we go out for a pizza tonight?
Shall we go out for a pizza tonight?
B Yes, good idea. I'm phoning the pizzeria to book a table.

2 **A** What time shall your brother arrive?

B This evening. I drive to the station to meet him at 6.30.

3 Hello, John. The traffic's really bad in the centre. We're being about 20 minutes late.

4 In my opinion the next president of the USA shall be a Republican.

5 Will I help you bring in the shopping from the car?

6 **A** What time shall you have your hair cut this afternoon?

B I've made an appointment for 3 o'clock.

7 I don't think Brazil is winning the football match tomorrow.

8 **A** What are Ricky's plans for the future?
B I don't know. Perhaps he's getting a job in that new hotel at the beach.

2 VOCABULARY Environmental issues

a Match 1–5 with a–e to make sentences.

1 [a] People should be able to recycle
2 [ ] Air pollution has seriously damaged
3 [ ] The environmental group are trying to prevent
4 [ ] Around 1,500 pandas survive
5 [ ] Environmental organisations are trying to save

a more than 50% of their household rubbish.
b the Siberian tiger from extinction.
c in the mountains of Western China.
d the destruction of the rainforest in Puerto Rico.
e the outside of the pyramids near Cairo.

b Complete the sentences with the words in the box.

wildlife   conservation   environmentally   pollution
climate   destroyed   ~~environment~~   endangered

1 We have to protect the _environment_ for future generations.
2 Scientists are very worried about _____ change.
3 The _____ caused by cars and lorries is affecting air quality in the city centre.
4 The hybrid car is the most _____ friendly car.
5 Large areas of the Amazon Rainforest are _____ by farmers every year.
6 The black rhino is an _____ species. There are very few animals left in the wild.
7 There is incredible _____ in Kenya, including lions, elephants and giraffes.
8 I'm working on a _____ project at the moment to protect and preserve rare plants.

3 PRONUNCIATION
Sound and spelling: *a*

a How is the underlined letter *a* pronounced in each word in the box? Complete the table with the words.

pl<u>a</u>nt   <u>a</u>broad   s<u>a</u>ve   <u>a</u>long   d<u>a</u>m   d<u>a</u>nger   n<u>a</u>ture
p<u>a</u>rk   loc<u>a</u>l   gorill<u>a</u>   m<u>a</u>mmal   educ<u>a</u>tion   <u>a</u>fter
<u>a</u>nimal   br<u>a</u>nch   ch<u>a</u>rity

Sound 1 /eɪ/ (e.g. *paper*)	Sound 2 /ɑː/ (e.g. *glass*)	Sound 3 /æ/ (e.g. *and*)	Sound 4 /ə/ (e.g. *climate*)

b ▶ **5.1** Listen and check.

5B If you go to the beach, you can see dolphins

1 GRAMMAR Zero and first conditional

a Put the words in the correct order to make sentences.

1 going / offer me / to London / I'm / the job, / if / move / they / to .
   If they offer me the job, I'm going to move to London.

2 when / at / plane / we'll / Glasgow Airport / phone / lands / our / you .
   _____

3 tigers, / if / extinct / we / they'll / stop hunting / don't / 20 years' time / be / in .
   _____

4 too / the / when / cold, / south / birds / gets / weather / fly / the .
   _____

5 new laptop / my / a / help him / I / the house / dad / buy me / if / paint / will .
   _____

6 or an / you / later, / apple / if / feel hungry / have / a banana .
   _____

7 11 o'clock / the / be there / with / train / problem / unless / at / a / i'll / there's .
   _____

8 take / the / soon, / a / I'm / unless / going to / comes / taxi / bus .
   _____

b ▶**5.2** Listen and check.

c <u>Underline</u> the correct words to complete the sentences.

1 If they *win* / *will win* / *are winning* the match tomorrow, *they're* / *they'll be* / *they were* champions.

2 If you *will see* / *see* / *don't see* Kate tomorrow, *give* / *you'll give* / *you're going to give* her an invitation to the party.

3 When the chameleon *will go* / *goes* / *is going to go* into a different environment, its skin *will change* / *is going to change* / *changes* colour.

4 *Unless* / *If* / *When* it stops raining soon, we *couldn't* / *can't* / *won't be able to* go to the beach this afternoon.

5 *You will open* / *Open* / *You're going to open* the window if you *feel* / *will feel* / *don't feel* too hot.

6 If *she's going to miss* / *she'll miss* / *she misses* the last train this evening, she *had to* / *will have to* / *has to* come tomorrow instead.

7 When the sun *will go* / *goes* / *is going to go* behind the clouds, it *usually feels* / *will usually feel* / *usually felt* much colder.

8 He *can't* / *won't be able to* / *couldn't* find your house unless you *will send* / *are going to send* / *send* him a map.

2 VOCABULARY The natural world

a Look at the animals and label the pictures. Use the words in the box.

petal	scales	paws	tail	branch
web	fur	~~skin~~	feathers	

1 ___skin___   2 _____   3 _____

4 _____   5 _____   6 _____

7 _____   8 _____   9 _____

b Complete the crossword puzzle.

```
¹N A T I O N A L P A ²R K S
                         R
    ³                    
⁴                    ⁵
              ⁶
⁷
                    ⁸
          ⁹
```

→ **Across**

1 One of the most famous _____ _____ in the USA is Yosemite in California.

4 I'd love to have a house by the _____. It would be lovely to go for a walk on a beach every day.

5 There are five _____ in the world – the Pacific, the Atlantic, the Indian, the Arctic and the Southern Antarctic.

7 The largest _____ in Africa is the Sahara.

9 The highest _____ in the world are the Angel Falls in Venezuela.

↓ **Down**

2 Large areas of the Amazon _____ are destroyed every year.

3 The largest _____ in the world is Superior, on the border between Canada and the USA.

6 _____ are usually much smaller than rivers.

8 In 1940 four French teenagers discovered prehistoric paintings in an underground _____ in Lascaux in the south-west of France.

1 USEFUL LANGUAGE
Reasons, results and examples

a Complete the sentences with the words in the box.

like	as a result	due to	because of
for instance	~~because~~	such as	since	so

1 Alice doesn't enjoy her current job __because__ she often has to work until 8 pm.
2 There are lots of things I can offer this company, _____ my talent for creating attractive websites and my experience of management.
3 It took me over an hour to get to work this morning _____ a serious accident on the motorway.
4 **A** There are some things I don't like about my job.
   B _____?
   A Well, _____, I don't like having to drive 50 km to work every day.
5 Tom didn't get on with his new boss _____ he decided to apply for a job with another company.
6 _____ there weren't any meeting rooms free at 11 o'clock, they had to hold the meeting in his office.
7 I had to stay late at work yesterday. _____, I didn't get home until nine o'clock.
8 My train arrived 45 minutes late this morning _____ the bad weather in Scotland.

b ▶ **5.3** Listen and check.

2 CONVERSATION SKILLS
Giving yourself time to think

a Complete the sentences with the words in the box.

second	well	sure	~~see~~	question

1 **A** So how old is your father now?
   B Let me ____see____. I think he'll be 62 in June.
2 **A** So what skills can you bring to this job?
   B _____, to begin with, I've got excellent computer skills.
3 **A** So why do you want to leave your current job?
   B That's a good _____. The main reason is that I need a new challenge.
4 **A** What time does their plane arrive at Heathrow Airport?
   B Just a _____. I'll check on their website.

b ▶ **5.4** Listen and check.

3 PRONUNCIATION
Voiced and unvoiced consonants

a ▶ **5.5** Listen to the pairs of words. Tick (✓) the words you hear.

1	☐ paw		✓	bore
2	☐ pear		☐	bear
3	☐ cap		☐	cab
4	☐ plume		☐	bloom
5	☐ cup		☐	cub

1 READING

a Read the essay and <u>underline</u> the correct phrases to complete the text.

b Read the essay again and tick (✓) the correct answer.

In the writer's opinion …

a ☐ petrol cars are more efficient than electric cars.
b ☐ diesel cars are more environmentally friendly than electric cars.
c ☐ electric cars are better now than a few years ago.
d ☐ people should buy petrol cars in the future.

c Are the sentences true or false?

1 Electric cars are more expensive now than they were a few years ago.
2 Electric cars do not cause problems for the environment.
3 Some people become stressed due to the noise caused by traffic.
4 It costs the same to operate electric cars and petrol cars.
5 You can easily recharge your electric car at home.

Electric cars are the future

If you are thinking of buying a new car soon, perhaps you should consider getting an electric car. In the last few years electric cars have become more efficient and they're now much cheaper to buy. So why should we switch to electric cars?

[1]*In conclusion / First of all / Finally*, air pollution in our cities has become a serious problem over the past 50 years or so. Electric cars do not produce any CO_2 emissions and as a result they don't pollute the atmosphere. If we drive electric cars, this will significantly improve the quality of the air we breathe.

[2]*Firstly / Finally / Secondly*, electric cars are quieter than cars which use petrol or diesel. Today's cars and lorries cause a lot of noise pollution and this can make people feel very stressed.

[3]*Secondly / Finally / First of all*, they are cheaper to operate than conventional cars. The price of petrol is extremely high and the cost per kilometre of an electric car is much lower than a petrol or diesel car. In addition, it is more convenient to recharge your electric car at home than to drive to a petrol station to re-fuel.

[4]*In conclusion / First of all / In addition*, I would say that if we really care about the environment we should all consider buying electric cars. They have improved a great deal in recent years and they will definitely be the vehicle of the future.

2 WRITING

a Read the notes. Write an essay about the advantages of solar panels.

Notes for essay about solar panels

Spend too much on electricity? Solar panels may be the solution.

1) Efficient and good for environment. No pollution, e.g. no carbon dioxide or other gases. If plenty of sunshine, can generate all electricity for the home.

2) Not cheap to buy, but will save money on electricity bills in long term & energy companies buy extra electricity produced. Result: may actually make money.

3) Can increase value of house. People pay higher price to save money on electricity.

4) Conclusion. A good idea. Environmentally friendly & cheap electricity.

UNIT 5
Reading and listening extension

1 READING

a Read the student's essay. Match the paragraphs A–D with functions 1–6. There are two extra functions you do not need.

☐ Paragraph A   ☐ Paragraph C
☐ Paragraph B   ☐ Paragraph D

1 To describe the consequences of climate change
2 To describe weather problems
3 To give the student's own opinion
4 To introduce the main topic and explain the purpose of the essay
5 To show why climate change might be true
6 To show why climate change might not be true

b Read the essay again and tick (✓) the correct answer.

1 According to environmental scientists, …
   a ☐ forest fires and snow have changed the world's climate.
   b ☐ pollution has created problems all around the world.
   c ☐ it is not possible to protect the environment from climate change.

2 The writer explains that the purpose of her essay is …
   a ☐ to consider two different opinions about climate change.
   b ☐ to prove that climate change does not really exist.
   c ☐ to prove that environmental scientists are telling the truth.

3 Why did scientists change their minds in the 1970s?
   a ☐ because the weather changed unexpectedly
   b ☐ because they could not predict changes in the weather
   c ☐ because world temperatures had increased

4 The writer's main purpose in paragraph B is to show …
   a ☐ how the world's weather changed after World War II.
   b ☐ that scientists often disagree with each other.
   c ☐ why some people might not believe in climate change.

5 According to the writer, why is it difficult to predict the weather?
   a ☐ Environmental scientists do not have the correct equipment.
   b ☐ The environment never stays the same for very long.
   c ☐ There are not enough scientists to make accurate predictions.

6 The writer's main purpose in paragraph C is to show …
   a ☐ how difficult it can be to make accurate predictions.
   b ☐ why scientists are wrong about climate change.
   c ☐ why we should believe environmental scientists.

7 According to the writer, …
   a ☐ it is not possible to protect the environment from pollution.
   b ☐ terrible weather proves that climate change exists.
   c ☐ we should not trust the predictions of environmental scientists.

'There is no such thing as climate change. Environmental scientists have been lying to us.' Discuss.

A All around the world, we hear stories of terrible weather becoming even worse. For instance, while forests in Australia are on fire, fields in Egypt are covered in snow. Environmental scientists explain that events such as these are due to climate change. They say that if we cannot protect the environment from pollution, we will definitely destroy the Earth, and everything and everyone that lives on it. Despite this, there are still many people who say that scientists have been lying to us and there is no such thing as climate change. This essay will look at both sides of the argument to see who is telling the truth.

B First of all, it is necessary to remember that scientific opinion has changed many times since the end of the Second World War. For example, in the 1950s, average temperatures in many countries seemed to be rising. Some of the world's best scientists said that this proved that the world was becoming hotter. However, in the early 1970s the world began to freeze. Many countries had the worst winters they had ever known. As a result, scientists made new predictions: the world was not becoming hotter, but much colder. After the freezing winters of the 1970s, world temperatures began to rise again in the 1980s and 1990s. Scientists changed their predictions again and decided that the world was now becoming too hot.

C Some people have said that these examples prove that climate change does not exist. And it is true that scientists have made mistakes. However, I don't believe this means that they are wrong about climate change. Even with advanced technology, it is very difficult to make predictions about the future of weather. The environment is very complex. It consists of billions of creatures and we should also remember that natural environments such as jungles, deserts and mountains are also alive. Therefore it is hard for environmental scientists to make accurate predictions about the weather because all living things change all the time. So although scientific predictions can sometimes be wrong, it does not mean that climate change is not real.

D In conclusion, environmental scientists have not invented climate change. They have made mistakes but the important point is not whether the world is becoming hotter or colder but that the climate is becoming worse. We have an opportunity to prevent climate change and take action.

c Write an essay. Read the question below. Then use the Internet to find ideas, facts and information which agree and disagree with the statement. Decide whether you agree or disagree with the statement in the question.

> 'Climate change is natural – sometimes the earth's temperature is hot, other times it is cold. Climate change is not a consequence of pollution.' Discuss.

2 LISTENING

a ⏵ **5.6** Listen to the introduction of a lecture. Then put these parts of the introduction in the correct order.

- ☐ He describes a result of not looking after the environment.
- ☐ He explains how the talk will be organised.
- ☐ He explains why local problems are important.
- ☐ He gives the title of his talk.
- ☐ 1 He uses a story to explain a main idea of the lecture.

b Listen again. Are the sentences true or false?

1 The writer Theodore Dalrymple sees many different kinds of rubbish in the streets.
2 The lecturer says that people need to understand that the environment includes towns and cities.
3 The lecturer says people must save the environment before they make their streets clean and tidy.
4 The lecturer explains that we need to invent more environmentally friendly methods of clearing up rubbish.
5 The talk will include a description of how we can change people's ideas.
6 The lecturer believes that people must make small changes before they can make bigger ones.

c Write a letter to a newspaper about a problem with your local environment. For example:

There's too much rubbish in the local parks.

Remember to include:
- the consequences of not doing anything about the problem
- solutions to the problem
- why some people may disagree with your ideas
- what you say to the people who disagree with your solution.

⊙ Review and extension

1 GRAMMAR

Correct the sentences.

1 What time will we meet outside the cinema?
   What time shall we meet outside the cinema?
2 If he'll arrive before 2.00, we'll take him to that Italian restaurant for lunch.
3 Wait! I help you do the shopping if you like.
4 Unless it will rain this afternoon, we play golf.
5 I can't come with you because I will play tennis with Joe this afternoon. We meet at the tennis club at 3.00.
6 When they will win the next game, they'll win the gold medal.

2 VOCABULARY

Correct the sentences.

1 We must do everything we can to protect the nature.
   We must do everything we can to protect the environment.
2 There are fantastic beaches on the cost near Rio de Janeiro.
3 It hardly ever rains in the dessert.
4 Air dirt is a serious problem in big cities like Tokyo.
5 The leafs of that tree are as big as my hand.
6 She's working on a very important project to safe endangered species from extinction.

3 WORDPOWER *problem*

Complete the sentences with the words in the box. You might need to change the verb form.

cause	tackle	be aware of	face	fix	~~solve~~

1 The IT Department ___*solved*___ the problem with my computer immediately.
2 I'm sure the mechanic will _____ your car.
3 Sometimes it _____ problems on your computer if you install a new program while other programs are open.
4 The government has just launched a new campaign to try to _____ obesity among teenagers.
5 These days most people _____ the problem of deforestation in the Amazon Rainforest.
6 My baseball team are _____ a big problem after losing their last five matches.

⟳ REVIEW YOUR PROGRESS

Look again at Review your progress on p.66 of the Student's Book. How well can you do these things now?
3 = very well   2 = well   1 = not so well

I CAN ...

talk about the future	☐
talk about *if* and *when*	☐
give reasons, results and examples	☐
write a discussion essay.	☐

Vox pop video

Unit 1: Talk

1a ◀ **What do you talk about when you're with your friends?**

a Watch video 1a. Match 1–3 with a–c to make sentences.

1 [c] When she's with her friends, Jo usually talks about
2 [ ] When she's with her friends, Lauren usually talks about
3 [ ] When she's with her friends, Rachel usually talks about

a their boyfriends, husbands and holiday plans.
b their partners and other friends.
c going to museums, exhibitions and holidays.

1b ◀ **What do you talk about when you're with your family?**

b Watch video 1b. <u>Underline</u> the correct words to complete the sentences.

1 Jo *sometimes* / *rarely* / *always* discusses serious topics with her mother.
2 Rachel usually talks to her family about *friends* / *other family members* / *people in the news*.
3 Lauren has more interesting conversations with her *mother* / *brother* / *father*.

1c ◀ **What language are you best at apart from your own?**

c Watch video 1c and tick (✓) the correct answers.

1 Jo lived in Spain for _____.
   a [ ] 6 months
   b [✓] 12 months
   c [ ] 18 months
2 Now Jo's Spanish is _____ when she lived in Spain.
   a [ ] the same as
   b [ ] better than
   c [ ] not as good as
3 Rachel had the opportunity to practise her French when she was _____.
   a [ ] living in France
   b [ ] at school
   c [ ] at university
4 Rachel doesn't get the chance to speak _____ very often.
   a [ ] other languages
   b [ ] Spanish
   c [ ] French
5 Lauren speaks Spanish _____.
   a [ ] perfectly
   b [ ] badly
   c [ ] quite well
6 Lauren thinks it's hard to understand young people because they _____.
   a [ ] don't speak clearly
   b [ ] speak very quickly
   c [ ] have a strange accent

d Watch video 1c again. <u>Underline</u> the correct words to complete the sentences.

1 Jo wants more *Spanish lessons* / *Spanish friends* / *trips to Spain*.
2 Rachel *speaks several languages* / *only speaks English and French* / *speaks some German*.
3 Lauren doesn't know a lot of *formal Spanish* / *Spanish grammar* / *colloquial Spanish*.

Unit 2: Modern life

2a ◀ Which app do you use most?

a Watch video 2a. Match 1–4 with a–d to make sentences.

1 [c] James uses his favourite app to
2 [ ] Eugenia uses her favourite app to
3 [ ] Brian uses his favourite app to
4 [ ] Guy uses his favourite app to

a keep in touch with friends.
b avoid getting lost.
c send photos and messages.
d listen to music.

b Watch video 2a again and tick (✓) the correct answers.

1 James usually saves _____ photos.
  a [ ] all his
  b [ ] cool
  c [✓] funny

2 Eugenia thinks her app _____.
  a [ ] is difficult to use
  b [ ] is essential
  c [ ] is a lot of fun

3 Brian _____ his smartphone.
  a [ ] is obsessed with
  b [ ] plays games on
  c [ ] sometimes can't find

4 Guy uses his app to _____.
  a [ ] organise things
  b [ ] share videos with other people
  c [ ] stay in touch with his family

2b ◀ How many times have you been on social networking sites in the last week?

c Watch video 2b and tick (✓) the correct answers.

1 James mainly uses _____.
  a [ ] Instagram
  b [✓] Twitter
  c [ ] Facebook

2 Eugenia uses social networking sites to keep in touch with friends _____.
  a [ ] in her country
  b [ ] at university
  c [ ] in different countries

3 Brian goes on social networking sites _____ a day.
  a [ ] 7 – 13 times
  b [ ] 14 – 16 times
  c [ ] 17 times or more

4 Guy goes on social networking sites _____.
  a [ ] every day
  b [ ] every 2 days
  c [ ] 4 times a week

2c ◀ What do you like or dislike about social networking?

d Watch video 2c. Match 1–4 with a–d to make sentences.

1 [c] James likes
2 [ ] Eugenia talks about
3 [ ] Brian mentions
4 [ ] Guy discusses

a online bullying.
b the pressure to be friends with people online.
c free social media.
d living in another country.

e Watch video 2c again. Underline the correct words to complete the sentences.

1 James doesn't like the fact that *your friends* / *your family* / *companies* can have lots of information about you.
2 Eugenia likes the fact it's easy to keep in touch with her friends who live in *Cambridge* / *London* / *Chicago*.
3 Brian thinks that using text to communicate is *better than* / *very different from* / *not as good as* speaking to them in person.
4 Guy thinks that with social networking it's *fun* / *hard* / *easy* to organise things with friends.

Unit 3: Relationships

3a ◀ How did you first meet your best friend?

a Watch video 3a. Match 1–4 with a–d to make sentences.

1 [d] Heather met her best friend
2 [ ] Hannah met her best friend
3 [ ] Richard met his best friend
4 [ ] Maddy met her best friend

a when they were at nursery school together.
b when they were both working in Germany.
c through her family.
d when they worked for the same company.

3b ◀ How often do you see each other?

b Watch video 3b. Match 1–4 with a–d to make sentences.

1 [c] Heather and her best friend
2 [ ] Hannah and her best friend
3 [ ] Richard and his best friend
4 [ ] Maddy and her best friend

a see each other every day at school.
b talk on the phone together every two months.
c don't talk to each other on Skype.
d see each other every three weeks.

c Watch video 3b again. <u>Underline</u> the correct words to complete the sentences.

1 Heather and her best friend meet *every week / every couple of months / once a year*.
2 Hannah usually meets her best friend at *her house / school / a local café*.
3 Richard doesn't often see his best friend because *he doesn't have time / he lives a long way away / they don't have the same hobbies*.
4 Maddy and her best friend *are in the same class / live in the same house / play on the same team*.

3c◀ What do you do together?

d Watch video 3c and tick (✓) the correct answers.

1 Heather enjoys _____ with her friend.
  a ☐ dancing
  b ☐ laughing
  c ✓ talking
2 Hannah enjoys _____ with her friend.
  a ☐ listening to music
  b ☐ staying at home
  c ☐ going to the park
3 Richard and his friend _____ together.
  a ☐ go to the park
  b ☐ go walking
  c ☐ laugh
4 Maddy and her friend _____ together.
  a ☐ dance a lot
  b ☐ laugh a lot
  c ☐ listen to music

e Watch video 3c again. Match 1–4 with a–d to make sentences.

1 [a] Heather and her best friend
2 ☐ Hannah and her best friend
3 ☐ Richard and his best friend
4 ☐ Maddy and her best friend

a like to have lunch together.
b are like family.
c go walking around together.
d like to complain about modern life.

Unit 4: Personality

4a◀ Can you tell me about something you're very good at?

a Watch video 4a. Match 1–4 with a–d to make sentences.

1 [c] Who is very good at martial arts?
2 ☐ Who can draw very well?
3 ☐ Who has stopped doing a sport because of an injury?
4 ☐ Who doesn't usually get lost when visiting a new place?

a Ollie
b Margaret
c Chris
d John

b Watch video 4a again and tick (✓) the correct answers.

1 Ollie stopped rowing because _____.
  a ☐ he lost lots of competitions
  b ✓ he had an injury
  c ☐ his friends stopped doing it
2 Margaret _____ takes a map with her when she goes to a new place.
  a ☐ always
  b ☐ hardly ever
  c ☐ usually
3 Chris has a hobby from _____.
  a ☐ China
  b ☐ Russia
  c ☐ the USA
4 When he was younger, John was good at _____.
  a ☐ acting
  b ☐ playing an instrument
  c ☐ sports

4b ◀ **Can you tell me about something you're not very good at?**

c Watch video 4b. <u>Underline</u> the correct words to complete the sentences.

1 Ollie isn't very good at *maths* / <u>*French*</u> / *sport*.
2 Margaret thinks speaking *in meetings* / *in public* / *to strangers* is difficult.
3 Chris isn't very good at *sport* / *spelling* / *languages*.
4 John doesn't think enough about what he *eats* / *says* / *wears*.

4c ◀ **What do you think is the most important skill to have?**

d Watch video 4c. Match 1–4 with a–d to make sentences.

1 [c] Ollie thinks that it's important to be able to
2 [ ] Margaret thinks that it's important to be able to
3 [ ] Chris thinks that it's important to be able to
4 [ ] John thinks that it's important to be able to

a communicate effectively.
b listen to other people.
c interact with other people.
d hold a good conversation.

Unit 5: The natural world

5a ◀ **Is pollution a problem where you live?**

a Watch video 5a. <u>Underline</u> the correct words to complete the sentences.

1 Where Anna lives the *sea* / <u>*river*</u> / *streets* used to be very polluted.
2 Where Anna lives people leave a lot of litter *in the park* / *on the beach* / *in the street*.
3 Where Matt lives the *land* / *river* / *air* is quite polluted.
4 Martina thinks that *the rivers are* / *the air is* / *the roads are* cleaner in the countryside.
5 Martina says that in London the pollution is mainly caused by *cars and lorries* / *people* / *aeroplanes*.
6 Lauren says that there *is a lot of* / *isn't very much* / *isn't any* pollution in Cambridge.

b Watch video 5a again and tick (✓) the correct answers.

1 Anna mentions _____ in her local area.
  a [ ] the trees and plants
  b [ ] the weather
  c [✓] the wildlife
2 Matt mentions local _____.
  a [ ] farmers
  b [ ] politicians
  c [ ] shops

3 Martina says the road near her house makes her home _____.
  a [ ] dangerous
  b [ ] dirty
  c [ ] noisy
4 Lauren says that there are a lot of _____ in Cambridge.
  a [ ] bikes
  b [ ] cars
  c [ ] trains

5b ◀ **What can people do to help the environment?**

c Watch video 5b. Match 1–4 with a–d to make sentences.

1 [c] Anna thinks that
2 [ ] Matt thinks that
3 [ ] Martina thinks that
4 [ ] Lauren thinks that

a people shouldn't travel short distances by plane.
b more people should cycle to work.
c more children should walk to school.
d people should try and recycle their old clothes.

d Watch video 5b again. <u>Underline</u> the correct words to complete the sentences.

1 Anna says her husband should <u>*be more organised*</u> / *cycle more often* / *recycle more*.
2 Matt does not mention *recycling* / *travelling by plane* / *saving water*.
3 Martina feels *bad about* / *proud of* / *satisfied with* what she does to help the environment.
4 Lauren mentions recycling *glass* / *metals* / *paper*.

5c ◀ **How do you think the climate will change in the next hundred years?**

e Watch video 5c. Match 1–4 with a–d to make sentences.

1 [c] Anna thinks that
2 [ ] Matt thinks that
3 [ ] Martina thinks that
4 [ ] Lauren thinks that

a in the UK the weather will never be extremely hot.
b average temperatures in the UK will be higher.
c our summers will be warmer and our winters will be cooler.
d sea levels will be higher and it will be warmer.

This page is intentionally left blank

Audioscripts

Unit 1

▶ **1.1**

1 **A** Well, if you ask me, Tanya Davies would be the best person for the job.
   B Actually, I don't agree. As far as I'm concerned, Luke Adams would be better.
2 **A** Well, I guess you could take the shoes back to the shop.
   B I'm not so sure about that. I've already worn them.
3 **A** I think it's going to be difficult to make enough money to survive.
   B Yes, I see where you're coming from. Maybe we should find a cheaper office?
4 **A** Well, in my opinion, Italian is easier than French.
   B I know what you mean. I think it's easier to pronounce.

▶ **1.2**

1 **A** It seems to me that their coffee is better than ours.
   B Yes, I know exactly what you mean. It's really smooth, isn't it?
2 **A** As far as I'm concerned, I think it makes sense to take the train to Paris.
   B I'm not so sure about that. It takes nearly three hours.
3 **A** I think Germany will probably win the football World Cup.
   B Yes, I think that's right. They've got the best team.
4 **A** Well, in my opinion, we need to find another business partner in Spain.
   B Yes, I see where you're coming from. Maybe a company based in Madrid this time?

▶ **1.3**

1 **A** Guess what, Tony? I've just read about this girl, and she's only ten but she's fluent in several different languages.
   B That's fantastic. I can only speak one language – English.
2 **A** Hi, Linda. Are you learning Russian?
   B I'm trying to! But this book's useless! It teaches you how to say 'my uncle's black trousers' but not how to say 'hello'!

▶ **1.4**

JOE So, Bridget, are you going to tell me about your website? Are you working on it at the moment?
BRIDGET Yes, it's almost ready, but it isn't finished just yet.
J And who's it for?
B Well, you remember what I'm studying, don't you?
J Yes, uh, well. You're studying French or Spanish or something, aren't you?
B Well, sort of. I'm in the Latin American studies department so yes I learn Spanish but I also study history, culture, politics – all that kind of thing.
J Oh right. So the website is for the Latin American studies students?
B Yes, but not just for them. It's also for students of Spanish and for students from the World History department too. They're all going to use it. And all the information on it has to be in Spanish as well as English so that I can keep in touch with all the students I met at UNAM.
J UNAM?
B Oh, that's the name of the university in Mexico where I was studying.
J Oh, I see. So, are you writing everything in Spanish as well as English?
B Yes, I'm completely exhausted!
J I'm not surprised! That sounds like an absolutely enormous job!
B Well, I'm not doing everything on my own. There's a Colombian girl, Monica, she's helping me to check my grammar and spelling and stuff.

J Oh, OK. So what can I do to help?
B Well, I'm not very good at web design so would you have any time to look at it for me? I need someone to check that everything on the website is working properly.
J Well, I'm a little busy …
B You have to help me, Joe! You're my only hope!
J OK, OK. I'll help you!
B Wonderful! So, I've chosen the main photo for the website. But I thought maybe I could ask your opinion?
J Sure, let's have a look.
B Great. It's here on my iPad.
J Wow! This is great! Where's this place?
B It's called Chichen Itza.
J Is that the name of the pyramid in the middle of the photo?
B No, Chichen Itza's the name of the ancient city. The pyramid … I can't remember what the name of the pyramid is.
J Well anyway, it's a great photo for your website. It's got history, and culture and it just looks really cool.
B Great! So, when can you help me with the design of the website? Do you have any time …

Unit 2

▶ **2.1**

1 I applied for lots of jobs.
2 We've worked very hard today.
3 I've learnt a lot in this job.
4 They offered me more money.
5 You've had a fantastic career at the BBC.

▶ **2.2**

1 Could you ask your brother to help you?
2 Oh, really? That's a shame.
3 How about taking it back to the shop where you bought it?
4 I'm really glad to hear that.
5 Why don't you try talking to your boss about it?
6 Let's take it to the garage.
7 Oh dear. How annoying!
8 Shall we ask his girlfriend what kind of music he likes?

▶ **2.3**

A I've lost my phone!
B Oh, no. How awful!
A I've been looking for it everywhere. I'm sure I had it when I got home.
B What about checking in your bag?
A OK … No, it isn't in there …
B ok, so it isn't in your bag. Have you tried phoning your number from another phone?
A That's a great idea. I'll give it a try. Can I borrow your phone for a minute?
B Yes, sure. Here you are.
A Oh, listen – it's ringing! It's behind that cushion on the sofa!
B That's brilliant! I'm so pleased!

▶ **2.4**

1 Barbara's just bought a new car and it won't start!
2 My boss has been criticising my work recently.
3 My neighbours had a party last night so I didn't sleep very well.
4 My computer's been running very slowly since I installed that new program.

▶ **2.5**

DIANE So, Carlos, how was your journey this morning? Did you drive or …?
CARLOS Oh, it was fine thank you. I came by train from London.
D I see. Right, well, let's start, shall we? To begin with I'll ask you a few questions about your CV and your education, your work experience and so on and then Steven is going to talk to you about the job. OK? Any questions so far?

C No, no, everything is fine so far, thank you.
D Great! OK, so can you tell me a little bit about yourself?
C Yes, of course. So, I'm 23 years old and I have just recently completed a university course in Computer Science. And that was in London, where I've been living for the last three, in fact, almost four years now. Before coming to England I was at school in Spain.
D Ah yes, that's right, I see from your CV that you went to high school in Madrid.
C Yes. Although, I was actually born in San Francisco. But when I was 14 I moved to Spain to live with my grandparents, who are from Madrid.
D Ah, so you are a Spanish speaker, then?
C Yes. And as well as English and Spanish I also speak German. That's because of my father. He's an engineer from Düsseldorf.
D I see. That's very impressive. As you may already know, this company has offices in several different European countries so we're keen to find people who can speak at least one other language as well as English.
C Well, that's good. I'd like the chance to use my languages.
D OK, now, in your opinion, why should this organisation choose you for this job?
C That's a very good question. Well, first of all I'm a people person. I'm very friendly and so I have a real ability to work in a team. Specialist knowledge is important, but you also need to be able to explain ideas simply and clearly. And that's something that I think I've learned in the job I do now. And I think it's been a good experience for this job.
D And why's that, may I ask? We don't really meet any customers in this job.
C True. But I soon learned that the best way to sell a phone wasn't to talk about all the technical things – it was to show people the apps! I discovered that I could sell more phones if I used clear and simple language to explain how to use them. So for almost three years now, I've been staying up to date on all the most popular apps and selling more phones than anyone else.
D Very interesting. OK, now, …

Unit 3

▶ **3.1**

1 Mark and Tania got to know each other when they worked in Spain.
2 They've got lots of shared interests.
3 He gets on very well with his aunt.
4 I'm not very good at keeping in touch with old friends.
5 What does she have in common with her American cousin?

▶ **3.2**

1 The best thing is that my new flat is air conditioned.
2 Anyway, we still hadn't found a hotel for my grandparents.
3 In the end, we bought him a computer game.
4 It turned out that he had never played golf in his life.
5 You'll never guess what Sarah said to David.
6 The funny thing was that he didn't know she was joking.
7 You won't believe what he bought her for her birthday. A snake!
8 To make matters worse, the water was too cold to have a shower.

▶ **3.3**

1 You'll never guess what happened at the party.
2 The best thing is that it's got a swimming pool.
3 Anyway, we still had to find a present for Maggie.
4 To make matters worse, it started raining heavily.

5 You won't believe what I did on Saturday.
6 The funny thing was that she didn't realise what had happened.
7 In the end, he agreed to drive us to the station.
8 It turned out that she lost her train ticket.

▶ 3.4

1 But, anyway, the train was still at the station and we got on just as the doors were closing.
2 In the end, we went to a little restaurant near the station, where we had a lovely meal.
3 To make matters worse, the waiter dropped the bottle of wine and it ruined my new white dress.
4 On top of that, when she eventually got to the airport they told her that her flight was nearly two hours late.
5 Anyway, in the end I found a lovely flat in the centre, and the best thing is that it's only eight hundred euros a month!

▶ 3.5

ROSIE Hi there! Hi, my name's Rosie Cameron and I'm a student here at the university. Do you have a few minutes?

BEN Oh, uh, sure. What do you need?

R Well, I'm doing a questionnaire on family and friendship, so would it be OK to ask you some questions?

B Sure, no problem.

R Great! Thank you so much! OK, so can you tell me your name and what you do?

B Sure. My name's Ben. Ben Boole. And I'm a second-year politics student.

R Well, hello Ben! Oh I've said that already, haven't I? OK, so you're male – obviously – and your age group is 18 to 24?

B A bit older, actually. I'm 28. So you need to tick the 25 to 32 box.

R Twenty-eight. Great, thanks. OK, so first question. Are you in a relationship?

B No, I'm single at the moment.

R No way!

B What?

R Nothing! Sorry – not married, no girlfriend – OK, next question! When you meet people for the first time, do you find it easy to make friends with them?

B Yes, I think so. I'm not shy. In fact, I think I'm generally quite confident.

R OK, and how would you describe your childhood?

B Really happy. Um, I grew up in quite a big family: there was my mum and dad, of course, but I've also got five older sisters.

R Wow, so you're the youngest of six children, then?

B Yeah, that's right. But I also lived with two of my grandparents – my mum's mum and dad.

R So there were three generations and ten people living in the same house, then? Wow.

B Yes. Basically, I was brought up in a house full of women. My grandmother, my mum, and my elder sisters. I think that's why I'm quite confident now. Because I had so much support when I was growing up, I mean.

R How cool! OK, do you keep in touch with friends you made at school?

B Yes, I've got a friend called 'Zippy'. Actually, his real name's Sipho, Sipho Zulu. His dad's from Zimbabwe. But everyone calls him Zippy.

R And did you get on with Zippy straight away?

B No! Actually, that was the funny thing. Before we met, I'd been the best football player in the whole school.

R Oh, I'm sure you were.

B Sorry?

R Nothing!

B Uh, so anyway Zippy was such a good player that I really hated him at first.

R So how did you become friends?

B Well, we eventually discovered that we had lots of things in common. He's also the youngest child in a big family and he also only has older sisters. And we definitely share the same sense of humour.

R How important is a sense of humour in friendship?

B Oh, really important! I mean …

Unit 4

▶ 4.1

1 You don't smoke any more, do you?
2 It's a lovely day today, isn't it?
3 Tom isn't going to ask her to marry him, is he?
4 You haven't been waiting long for me, have you?
5 She'd already bought him a present, hadn't she?
6 They'll phone us when they get to the airport, won't they?
7 The twins both got good grades in their exams, didn't they?
8 Andrew speaks five languages fluently, doesn't he?
9 You don't want any rice, Jim, do you?

▶ 4.2

1 **A** I wondered if you could do me a favour?
   B Sure, how can I help you?
   A Do you think you could cut the grass in my garden for me?
   B Yes, of course. No problem.
2 **A** I've got a lot of things to get ready for the party tomorrow night.
   B Is there something I can do?
   A Yes, there is, actually. Can you give me a hand with the shopping?
   B Yes, that's fine. Could I ask you a favour in return?
   A Go ahead!
   B Could you lend me your black trousers for tomorrow?
   A No problem. I'll just get them for you.
3 **A** Could I ask you a favour, Ben?
   B Of course, what do you need?
   A Could you help me move my desk into the other office?
   B Actually, I've got a bad back. Can you ask someone else?

▶ 4.3

1 You've been to Cairo before, haven't you?
2 Jack's really good at tennis, isn't he?
3 They've got four children, haven't they?
4 This is the best beach in Thailand, isn't it?
5 You're glad you left London, aren't you?
6 You didn't go to Canada last year, did you?

▶ 4.4

Thank you, thank you. OK! So my talk tonight is called 'Psychology in Advertising', but I'm going to start with a little story.

In the 18th century, Germany was divided into lots of different countries and one of these was called Prussia, and the king there was called Frederick the Second. Now this particular king was a really very talented man. In fact, he was so brilliant that he is still known as Frederick the Great.

OK, so at that time, the 1770s, hardly anyone in Prussia ate potatoes, because the main meal for almost everyone was bread. But there was a problem with bread: in those days, sometimes the wheat didn't grow very well, or it grew but then it died before people could make bread from it. And every time that happened, people, especially poor people, would have nothing to eat.

So when Frederick heard about the potato, he thought 'A-ha! Perfect! If the people can grow these potatoes as well as bread, then no one will ever be hungry again!'

Frederick was so satisfied with this idea that he immediately ordered everyone in the country to start growing potatoes. But to his surprise, they refused. They simply would not touch these potatoes. The people of Kolberg sent Frederick a letter, telling him that potatoes were so disgusting that even their animals couldn't eat them.

Now Frederick was a very intelligent man, and although there were no psychologists in 1774, he certainly had a talent for understanding the psychology of his people. So he soon came up with a very interesting plan.

First, he planted potatoes in a big field, which he called the 'Royal Potato Garden'. Next, because it was not just any potato garden, but the Royal Potato Garden, he sent soldiers to guard it.

As soon as people saw the garden and the soldiers, they started asking each other 'What could be in that field that is worth so much?' And of course, as soon as they found out that the field was full of potatoes, they all wanted some. It was not long afterwards that people started going to the field at night to steal potatoes. Frederick, of course, had expected this to happen. In fact, he had even given secret instructions to his soldiers to pretend that they had not seen the potato thieves and actually let them steal the potatoes, because that was what Frederick had wanted to happen.

There is an important lesson here for people about psychology in advertising.

When Frederick told people they would never be hungry again if they ate potatoes – they were not interested. When Frederick ordered them to grow potatoes – they refused. But when people believed that they were not allowed to eat potatoes, and that they were only eaten by kings and queens, then they immediately wanted to have them. And that's good psychology.

Unit 5

▶ 5.1

/eɪ/: save, danger, education, nature
/ɑː/: plant, park, after, branch
/æ/: charity, animal, mammal, dam
/ə/: local, abroad, gorilla, along

▶ 5.2

1 If they offer me the job, I'm going to move to London.
2 We'll phone you when our plane lands at Glasgow Airport.
3 If we don't stop hunting tigers, they'll be extinct in 20 years' time.
4 When the weather gets too cold, the birds fly south.
5 My dad will buy me a new laptop if I help him paint the house.
6 If you feel hungry later, have a banana or an apple.
7 I'll be there at 11 o'clock unless there's a problem with the train.
8 Unless the bus comes soon, I'm going to take a taxi.

▶ 5.3

1 Alice doesn't enjoy her current job because she often has to work until 8 pm.
2 There are lots of things I can offer this company, like my talent for creating attractive websites and my experience of management.
3 It took me over an hour to get to work this morning due to a serious accident on the motorway.
4 **A** There are some things I don't like about my job.
   B Such as?
   A Well, for instance, I don't like having to drive 50 km to work every day.
5 Tom didn't get on with his new boss so he decided to apply for a job with another company.
6 Since there weren't any meeting rooms free at 11 o'clock, they had to hold the meeting in his office.
7 I had to stay late at work yesterday. As a result, I didn't get home until nine o'clock.
8 My train arrived 45 minutes late this morning because of the bad weather in Scotland.

▶ 5.4

1 **A** So how old is your father now?
   B Let me see. I think he'll be 62 in June.
2 **A** So what skills can you bring to this job?
   B Well, to begin with, I've got excellent computer skills.
3 **A** So why do you want to leave your current job?
   B That's a good question. The main reason is that I need a new challenge.
4 **A** What time does their plane arrive at Heathrow Airport?
   B Just a second. I'll check on their website.

▶ 5.5

1 bore   4 bloom
2 pear   5 cup
3 cap

Thank you, thank you. So, I'd like to begin today
with something that the British writer, Theodore
Dalrymple, once said.

Walking through the streets of the city where he lives,
he starts to notice piles of rubbish everywhere he
looks. And not just any rubbish, but the rubbish left
behind by people who have bought food. And not just
any food, but fast food, junk food.

Seeing all this, he asks himself: What did it mean?
All this litter? At the very least, it suggested that an
Englishman's street is his dining room … as well as
his dustbin.

I wanted to share this with you because – well, partly
because it is true, of course. Anyone who lives or
has lived in a modern British city will recognise that
description. But I have another reason for sharing
that story with you and that is that I want you to
understand that pollution is not just something that
happens to the natural environment or even to the
wildlife that lives in it. It happens here, where we live.
As I will explain during this talk, we cannot expect to
improve the natural world if we do not first improve
the condition of our own streets and cities. How can
we expect to protect the environment from pollution
when our own streets are full of rubbish?

In other words, we need to clean our own streets before
we can even dream about preventing pollution in the
rainforests of the Amazon, or the seas and oceans.
And it is important to understand that the damage that
we do to the world is not just 'out there'. It is here, and
with us, all of the time. And we also need to remember
that when we do damage to our environment we are
actually doing damage to ourselves.

So my talk today is called 'Save yourself!' and my
message is simple: we have to help ourselves before
we can hope to help wildlife or the environment.

My talk is going to be in three parts. First of all, I will
say some more about the problem of rubbish in the
local areas where we live. It is now possible for us to
manage our rubbish in a way that is environmentally
friendly – but we don't. So in this part of my talk, I'm
going to be asking 'Why not? Why, when it is possible
to be more environmentally friendly, do most people
seem not to care?'.

Next, I will discuss the problem of people. There are
currently seven billion of us in the world and that
is almost twice the number of people living in the
world 50 years ago. For this reason, I will suggest
that we need to change people's minds and I will also
describe some ways of doing this. Ways that I think, I
hope, will be successful in the future.

Finally, I will show how protecting your local area
is the first step to protecting the planet for future
generations of children.

Answer key

Unit 1

1A

1

a 2 hurts 3 happened 4 did they watch 5 did you talk 6 did he talk 7 got 8 did you vote

b 2 Which restaurant did your parents go to?
3 What happens to Harrison Ford at the end of the film?
4 What did you and your friends talk about?
5 What was your first mobile phone like?
6 What was his presentation about?
7 Which film star got married twice last year?
8 Who did you go to the cinema with?

2

a 2 presentation 3 joke 4 in touch 5 interviewed 6 expressing 7 in public 8 opinions

b 2 insisted 3 greeted 4 persuaded 5 encouraged 6 argue 7 persuaded 8 encouraged

1B

1

a 2 d 3 h 4 e 5 f 6 b 7 a 8 c

b 2 Is she studying 3 's learning 4 Does she want 5 doesn't know 6 's 7 Does she play 8 loves 9 is 10 's playing 11 's ringing 12 's waiting

2

a 2 e 3 a 4 c 5 b 6 d 7 h 8 g

b 2 freezing 3 tiny 4 miserable 5 impossible 6 filthy 7 delicious 8 useless

1C

1

a 1 **B** concerned 2 **A** guess **B** sure 3 **A** think **B** see 4 **A** opinion **B** mean

c 1 **B** mean 2 **A** I'm concerned **B** sure 3 **A** think **B** right 4 **A** opinion **B** where

2

a 1 **A** Guess what, Tony? I've just read about this girl, and she's only ten but she's fluent in several different languages.
B That's fantastic. I can only speak one language – English.
2 **A** Hi, Linda. Are you learning Russian?
B I'm trying to! But this book's useless! It teaches you how to say 'my uncle's black trousers' but not how to say 'hello'!

1D

1

a d

b True: 1, 4; False: 2, 3, 5

2

a 2 so that 3 This 4 This 5 in order 6 so

3

a **Suggested answer:**
How to improve your cookery skills

In order to become a good cook, the most important thing is to try new dishes and practise often. Most people usually cook the same dishes all the time. This means that they don't have the opportunity to improve their cookery skills by learning to cook new things.

It's a good idea to buy a few good recipe books so that you can learn how to cook some new dishes for the first time. At first, it's best to try cooking these new dishes for your family or one or two close friends only. This will make sure that you can cook them successfully before you cook them for a larger group of people at a dinner party. To become a confident cook, you should try cooking new recipes two or three times a week. Why not ask your family or friends to tell you what they really think of your food so that you can make it better the next time?

Another good way to improve your cookery skills is to watch cookery programmes on TV. It's usually easier to follow a recipe when someone shows you what to do. First you can watch the TV chef and then you can download the recipe from the TV channel's website.

Finally, each time you enjoy a good dish at a friend's house or at a restaurant, don't be afraid to ask for the recipe. This is the best way to discover new dishes and to become a better cook.

Reading and listening extension

1

a True: 2, 3, 5; False: 1, 4

b 2 d 3 c 4 a 5 g 6 f 7 b

2

a 1 c 2 a 3 b 4 b

b 2 Latin American studies 3 in Mexico 4 Another student 5 a city 6 absolutely perfect

Review and extension

1

2 My brother doesn't like coffee.
3 What was your holiday in Spain like? / How was your holiday in Spain?
4 Look at Tom – he's wearing his new shoes.
5 Who took you to the station?
6 Can you repeat that? I don't understand.

2

2 When we were young my brother and I used to argue all the time, but now we've become good friends.
3 It's impossible to sleep because my neighbours are having a party.
4 I haven't kept in touch with many of my old school friends. / I haven't stayed in touch with many of my old school friends.
5 That cake was delicious but there was only a tiny piece left!
6 My dad is very funny. He loves telling jokes about his time in the army.

3

a 2 Help 3 Enjoy 4 teach 5 look after 6 do

Unit 2

2A

1

a 1 **B** I've worked 2 **A** Have you ever arrived **B** I arrived 3 **A** Has she ever worked **B** she spent 4 **A** Matt's applied **B** hasn't had 5 **A** Have you met **B** I met

b 2 've worked 3 got 4 did you stay 5 stayed 6 did you like 7 enjoyed 8 gave 9 have you been 10 've been 11 have you had 12 joined 13 've been

2

a 2 c 3 b 4 f 5 h 6 a 7 d 8 g

b 2 charge 3 team 4 interview 5 CV 6 experience 7 grades 8 apply

3

2 b 3 b 4 a 5 b

2B

1

a 2 've been waiting 3 's been posting 4 've been reading 5 's been cooking 6 Have, been crying 7 have been learning 8 has, been going

b 2 I've installed 3 turned off 4 hasn't been working 5 You've been playing 6 been waiting 7 I've had 8 We've been trying

2

a 2 password 3 off 4 app 5 share 6 deleted 7 click 8 upload 9 typing 10 username

b Across: 6 install 7 browser 8 type
Down: 1 upload 2 message 4 connect 5 delete

2C

1

a 2 shame 3 taking 4 glad 5 talking 6 take 7 annoying 8 ask

c 2 What 3 worth 4 tried 5 give 6 Shall/Should 7 idea 8 let's 9 not 10 Can/Could

d 2, 10, 5, 9, 3, 7, 6, 1, 4, 8

2

a 2 My <u>boss</u> has been <u>criticising</u> my <u>work</u> recently.
3 My <u>neighbours</u> had a <u>party</u> last <u>night</u> so I <u>didn't sleep</u> very <u>well</u>.
4 My com<u>pu</u>ter's been <u>running</u> very <u>slowly</u> since I in<u>stall</u>ed that new <u>program</u>.

2D

1

a c

b True: 1, 3, 6; False: 2, 4, 5

2

a 2 e 3 a 4 c 5 b 6 d

3

a Suggested answer:

Hi Martina

I'm sorry I haven't been in touch for the past few weeks but I've been incredibly busy.

I think I told you that I've been writing a story. I finished writing it a month ago and decided to send it to some publishing companies in London. Well, you'll never believe this but the editor of one of the biggest companies has just rung to offer me a contract.

They want me to make a few changes to the story so that it is more interesting for young people. I'm going to work closely with one of their editors who will make suggestions for improving the story. Besides helping me to improve the novel they're also going to pay me quite a lot of money. This means I can stop teaching and spend all of my time writing.

But the best thing is that they want me to go to New York to meet their American editors. I've never been to the USA before so I'm really looking forward to it. They think it might be possible to produce an American edition of the book. And what's really amazing is that they think my book could also become a film. Apart from meeting their American editors they also want me to meet some film producers from Hollywood!

What about having dinner together one day next week? There's a new Italian restaurant in the city centre that I'd like to try. Let me know a day that suits you.
Best wishes

Reading and listening extension

1

a 1 c 2 c 3 a 4 b

b 2 Dan 3 Neither 4 Kristen 5 Neither 6 Kristen 7 Dan 8 Neither 9 Kristen 10 Dan

2

a 6, 3, 5, 2, 4, 1

b 2 a 3 b 4 b 5 a 6 b

Review and extension

1

2 I can't talk to Julia because she's been speaking on the phone all day.
3 I went to Portugal on holiday three years ago.
4 I've known Jack for about five years.
5 His train was late this morning so he's just arrived.
6 Last night she went to the party with her sister.
7 He's been working as a taxi driver since 2008.
8 She's got red eyes because she's been crying.

2

2 Please turn off your phones as the film is about to start.
3 Can you give me your password so I can connect to the Internet?
4 I've got a lot of experience of managing people.
5 My brother just sent me a text message to say he'll be late.
6 Sarah applied for the job at the hospital but she didn't get it.
7 The English keyboard is different to the one in my language so I keep making mistakes when I type.
8 My brother has just got a new job with a large bank in London.

3

2 after 3 for 4 up 5 forward 6 interesting 6 around 7 out

Unit 3

3A

1

a 1 had started, made
2 was cleaning, fell, broke
3 had stopped, was
4 rang, was having
5 met, was working
6 saw, looked, had escaped
7 were talking, arrived

b 1 were studying
2 left, had cycled
3 arrived, had escaped
4 rode, took
5 heard, was watching
6 crashed, were crossing
7 had closed, got
8 called, was waiting

2

a 2 c 3 f 4 e 5 a 6 b

b 2 friendship 3 stranger 4 support 5 relatives 6 humour

3

a 2 They've got <u>lots of shared interests</u>.
3 He <u>gets on</u> very well with <u>his aunt</u>.
4 I'm not very <u>good at keeping in</u> touch with friends.
5 What does she <u>have in</u> common with <u>her American</u> cousin?

3B

1

a 2 usually walk
3 used to send
4 Did you used to get
5 didn't use to like
6 used to hang out
7 didn't use to have
8 Do you usually take

b 2 lives
3 used to drive
4 drives
5 used to go
6 goes
7 used to sit
8 sits
9 didn't use to eat
10 eats

2

a 2 nephew 3 childhood 4 middle 5 only 6 eldest 7 niece 8 generations

3

a 2 e 3 g 4 h 5 a 6 h 7 d 8 c

3C

1

a 2 Anyway 3 end 4 turned 5 guess 6 funny 7 won't 8 matters

c 2 The best thing is that it's got a swimming pool.
3 Anyway, we still had to find a present for Maggie.
4 To make matters worse, it started raining heavily.
5 You won't believe what I did on Saturday.
6 The funny thing was that she didn't realise what had happened.
7 In the end, he agreed to drive us to the station.
8 It turned out that she had lost her train ticket.

2

a 2 In the <u>end</u>, we went to a little restaurant near the <u>station</u>, where we had a lovely meal.
3 To make matters <u>worse</u>, the waiter dropped the bottle of <u>wine</u> and it ruined my new white dress.
4 On top of <u>that</u>, when she eventually got to the <u>airport</u> they told her that her flight was nearly two hours late.
5 <u>Anyway</u>, in the <u>end</u> I found a lovely flat in the <u>centre</u>, and the best thing <u>is</u> that it's only eight hundred euros a month!

b 2 In the <u>end</u> we went to a little <u>restaurant</u> near the station where we had a <u>lovely</u> meal.
3 To make matters <u>worse</u>, the waiter dropped the bottle of <u>wine</u> and it <u>ruined</u> my <u>new</u> <u>white</u> dress.
4 On top of <u>that</u>, when she eventually got to the <u>airport</u> they told her that her flight was nearly <u>two</u> hours late.
5 <u>Anyway</u>, in the <u>end</u> I found a lovely flat in the <u>centre</u>, and the <u>best</u> thing is that it's only <u>eight hundred</u> euros a month!

3D

1

a c

b True: 1, 4; False: 2, 3, 5

2

a 2 b 3 a 4 e 5 d 6 c

3

a Suggested answer:

My grandad's name was James Cooper and my sister and I were very fond of him. When we were children we used to go to my grandparents' house every Sunday for lunch. Grandad had a great sense of humour. He used to tell us terrible jokes and funny stories about his travels around the world.

James Cooper was born in London in 1928 and he had a very happy childhood. He had one brother and two sisters and they all got on very well. In 1936, his family moved to Montreal, in Canada, and he lived there for 10 years. He grew up speaking English and French fluently and in 1946 he returned to the UK to study medicine at Cambridge University. He graduated in 1952 and worked as a doctor in different hospitals in the UK from 1953 until 1962.

In 1962, he got a job at a hospital in San Francisco and lived in the USA for the next 13 years. While he was working there, he met Grandma and they got married in 1964. One year later, my mother was born. They didn't have any other children, so she was an only child. When my mother was 10, Grandad was offered a job in South Africa and so they all went to live in South Africa in 1975. They lived there for five years and they then returned to San Francisco in 1980. During their stay in Johannesburg, Grandad became good friends with the famous South African heart surgeon, Christiaan Barnard.

Grandad retired in 1988 and died 12 years later, in 2000. We all miss him very much.

Reading and listening extension

1

a 1 b 2 c 3 b 4 a 5 c

b 4, 2, 7, 8, 1, 5, 6, 3

2

a True: 4, 5, 6, 7; False: 1, 2, 3, 8

b 1 c 2 b 3 c 4 b 5 b 6 b

Review and extension

1

2 I used to have long hair when I was a little girl.
3 He was playing football when he fell over and hurt his ankle.
4 When he got to his house he was angry because someone had broken his window.
5 I got to the station five minutes late this morning and, unfortunately, my normal train had already left.
6 After the film we went to the café for a drink.
7 Did you use to play football when you were at school?
8 I didn't use to like English when I was at school.

2

2 Joanne's mother died when she was three so she was brought up by her grandparents.
3 I got to know Jasmine really well when we went travelling around South America together.
4 All my relatives got together at my dad's birthday party.
5 I don't have any brothers or sisters so I'm an only child.
6 She doesn't get on very well with her two brothers.
7 We share a lot of the same interests, for example literature.
8 My little brother's very calm and patient, so he takes after his mother because she's like that too.

3

2 time 3 lunch 4 idea 5 look 6 go

Unit 4

4A

1

a 2 Can you 3 he could 4 you'll be able to 5 was able to 6 couldn't 7 being able to 8 didn't manage to

b 2 f 3 d 4 c 5 a 6 e

2

a 2 ability 3 towards 4 determined 5 successful 6 gave up

b Across: 4 confident 5 successful 6 determined 7 talented
Down: 1 ability 2 bright 3 achievement

4B

1

a 1 the, Ø 2 a, Ø 3 Ø, Ø 4 a, the 5 an, the 6 Ø 7 Ø, a 8 the, the

b 2 I usually go to the gym three times a week.
3 Is there a supermarket opposite the bus stop near your house?
4 She usually goes to school on the Number 75 bus.
5 I often listen to the radio before I go to bed.
6 British pop groups are very popular in the USA.
7 There isn't an underground station near my hotel, so I'll have to take a taxi.
8 Usain Bolt was the fastest man in the world at the Olympic Games in 2012.

2

a 2 bored 3 terrifying 4 relaxing 5 disappointed 6 depressing 7 interested 8 satisfied

3

a 2 extrovert 3 sensitive 4 shy 5 sociable 6 talkative 7 introvert 8 serious

4C

1

a 2 e 3 f 4 c 5 g 6 d 7 b 8 a 9 i

2

a 1 **B** how **A** could 2 **B** something **A** hand **B** return
3 **A** favour **B** need **A** help **B** ask

3

a 2 ↘ 3 ↘ 4 ↗ 5 ↗ 6 ↘

4D

1

a 1 d 2 b

b True: 2, 4, 6; False: 1, 3, 5

2

a 2 h 3 f 4 b 5 a 6 c 7 e 8 d

3

a Suggested answer:

Summer camp coaches needed

Coaches are needed for a summer camp for children aged 5–12. Duties include organising indoor and outdoor activities for the children, helping them get ready for each day, have their meals and go to bed and entertaining them during their free time.

Candidates should be energetic and enthusiastic with an outgoing personality. A sense of adventure, a sense of humour and a positive attitude are essential. Candidates should be good at sports and ideally have a talent for art. Our summer camp coaches should love working with children and should be able to get on well with all the other members of the team.

Candidates should be aged 18 or over and preferably be university students or graduates. No previous experience is required. All new staff will be required to attend a two-day training course.

Candidates should complete the online application form and include an up-to-date CV. You will be contacted by our Human Resources Department to discuss potential opportunities.

Reading and listening extension

1

a 1 a   2 b   3 c   4 c

b True: 1, 3, 5, 6;   False: 2, 4, 7

2

a 1 b   2 b   3 c   4 c

b Possible answers
2 Bread was the most important part of most people's diet.
3 Frederick thought that if people had potatoes, they would not be hungry any more.
4 People in Kolberg said their animals could not eat potatoes.
5 People understood that potatoes were valuable when they saw the soldiers around Frederick's garden.
6 People began stealing potatoes from Frederick's garden.
7 Frederick's plan was successful.
8 Frederick's plan was an example of good psychology.

Review and extension

1

2 When she goes to the cinema she doesn't like seeing horror films.
3 Will you be able to help me with my maths homework this evening? / Can you help me with my maths homework this evening?
4 I love watching documentaries about whales.
5 She would like to be able to play the piano as well as her sister.
6 He usually gets to work at about 8.30 in the summer.
7 We weren't able to find the restaurant so we went to the pizzeria instead.
8 It's one of the best shopping websites on the Internet.

2

2 We had a very relaxing holiday in the South of France.
3 The film was so boring that I nearly fell asleep.
4 My uncle was a very successful businessman in the 1960s.
5 My sister doesn't want to watch the match because she isn't very interested in sport.
6 I thought that documentary about the environment was rather depressing.

3

2 so far   3 or so   4 and so on   5 such   6 so tired

Unit 5

5A

1

a 2 g   3 a   4 b   5 h   6 e   7 d   8 c

b 1 **B** Yes, good idea. I'll phone the pizzeria to book a table.
2 **A** What time is your brother arriving? / What time is your brother going to arrive? / What time will your brother arrive?
   B This evening. I'll drive to the station to meet him at 6.30. / I'm going to drive to the station to meet him at 6.30.
3 Hello, John. The traffic's really bad in the centre. We'll be about 20 minutes late. / We're going to be about 20 minutes late.
4 In my opinion the next president of the USA will be a Republican. / In my opinion the next president of the USA is going to be a Republican.
5 Shall I help you bring in the shopping from the car?
6 **A** What time are you having your hair cut this afternoon? / What time are you going to have your hair cut this afternoon?
7 I don't think Brazil will win the football match tomorrow. / I don't think Brazil is going to win the football match tomorrow.
8 **B** I don't know. Perhaps he'll get a job in that new hotel at the beach. / Perhaps he's going to get a job in that new hotel at the beach.

2

a 2 e   3 d   4 c   5 b

b 2 climate   3 pollution   4 environmentally   5 destroyed   6 endangered   7 wildlife   8 conservation

3

a /eɪ/: save, danger, education, nature
/ɑː/: plant, park, after, branch
/æ/: charity, animal, mammal, dam
/ə/: local, abroad, gorilla, along

5B

1

a 2 We'll phone you when our plane lands at Glasgow Airport.
3 If we don't stop hunting tigers, they'll be extinct in 20 years' time.
4 When the weather gets too cold, the birds fly south.
5 My dad will buy me a new laptop if I help him paint the house.
6 If you feel hungry later, have a banana or an apple.
7 I'll be there at 11 o'clock unless there's a problem with the train.
8 Unless the bus comes soon, I'm going to take a taxi.

c 1 they'll be   2 see, give   3 goes, changes   4 Unless, won't be able to   5 Open, feel   6 she misses, will have to   7 goes, usually feels   8 won't be able to, send

2

a 2 fur   3 paws   4 feathers   5 tail   6 petal   7 branch   8 web   9 scales

b Across: 4 sea   5 oceans   7 desert   9 waterfalls
Down: 2 rainforest   3 lake   6 streams   8 cave

5C

1

a 2 like   3 due to   4 **B** Such as **A** for instance   5 so   6 Since   7 As a result   8 because of

2

a 2 Well   3 question   4 second

3

a 2 pear   3 cap   4 bloom   5 cup

5D

1

a 1 First of all   2 Secondly   3 Finally   4 In conclusion

b c

c True: 2, 3, 5; False: 1, 4

2

a **Suggested answer:**

Getting our energy from the sun

If you think that you spend too much money on electricity, you might consider buying solar panels for your house. So, what are the advantages of solar panels?

Firstly, solar panels are a very efficient way of producing energy and they are very good for the environment. They don't pollute the atmosphere with carbon dioxide or other harmful gases. If you live somewhere with plenty of sunshine, they will generate all the electricity you need for a family home.

Secondly, although they aren't cheap to buy or install, they will eventually save you a lot of money on your electricity bills. Also, if you produce more electricity than you need, your energy company will pay you for the extra electricity. As a result, you will earn extra money if you have solar panels.

Finally, solar panels can increase the value of your home. If your house has solar panels on the roof, people will usually pay a higher price because they know that they will save money on their electricity bills.

In conclusion, I would say that it is a very good idea to buy solar panels for your house. It is environmentally friendly and it will give you cheaper electricity for many years.

Reading and listening extension

1

a A4 B6 C5 D3

b 1b 2a 3a 4b 5b 6a 7b

2

a 3, 5, 2, 4, 1

b True: 2, 5, 6; False: 1, 3, 4

Review and extension

1

2 If he arrives before 2.00, we'll take him to that Italian restaurant for lunch.
3 Wait! I'll help you do the shopping if you like.
4 Unless it rains this afternoon, we'll play golf.
5 I can't come with you because I'm playing tennis with Joe this afternoon. We're meeting at the tennis club at 3.00.
6 If they win the next game, they'll win the gold medal.

2

2 There are fantastic beaches on the coast near Rio de Janeiro.
3 It hardly ever rains in the desert.
4 Air pollution is a serious problem in big cities like Tokyo.
5 The leaves of that tree are as big as my hand.
6 She's working on a very important project to save endangered species from extinction.

3

2 fix   3 causes   4 tackle   5 are aware of   6 facing

Video exercises

Unit 1

a 2a 3b

b 2 other family members   3 father

c 2c 3b 4a 5c 6b

d 2 speaks several languages   3 colloquial Spanish

Unit 2

a 2b 3d 4a

b 2b 3c 4a

c 2c 3b 4a

d 2d 3a 4b

e 2 Cambridge   3 very different from   4 easy

Unit 3

a 2c 3b 4a

b 2d 3b 4a

c 2 her house   3 he lives a long way away   4 are in the same class

d 2b 3c 4a

e 2c 3d 4b

Unit 4

a 2d 3a 4b

b 2b 3b 4c

c 2 to strangers   3 spelling   4 wears

d 2b 3d 4a

Unit 5

a 2 in the street   3 land   4 the air is   5 cars and lorries   6 isn't very much

b 2a 3b 4a

c 2b 3a 4d

d 2 saving water   3 bad about   4 glass

e 2b 3d 4a

Acknowledgements

The authors and publishers acknowledge the following sources of copyright material and are grateful for the permissions granted. While every effort has been made, it has not always been possible to identify the sources of all the material used, or to trace all copyright holders. If any omissions are brought to our notice, we will be happy to include the appropriate acknowledgements on reprinting and in the next update to the digital edition, as applicable.

The publisher has used its best endeavours to ensure that the URLs for external websites referred to in this book are correct and active at the time of going to press. However, the publisher has no responsibility for the websites and can make no guarantee that a site will remain live or that the content is or will remain appropriate.

The publishers are grateful to the following for permission to reproduce copyright photographs and material:

Key: L = left, C = centre, R = right, T = top, B = bottom

p.4(TR): Shutterstock/ARENA Creative; p.4(BL): Alamy/allesalltag; p.5(TL): Shutterstock/stefanolunardi; p.5(BR): Shutterstock/Christian Knospe; p.6(T): Shutterstock/TATSIANAMA; p.6(BR): Shutterstock/Ruslan Guzov; p.7(BR): Shutterstock/Iakov Filimonov; p.8(CR): Shutterstock/oneinchpunch; p.9(TL): Shutterstock/f9photos; p.10(BL): Shutterstock/wavebreakmedia; p.11(CL): Shutterstock/Galina Barskaya; p.11(TR): Shutterstock/Patryk Kosmider; p.12(B): Shutterstock/OrelPhoto; p.13(TR): Shutterstock/Stephen Coburn; p.14(TR): Shutterstock/wavebreakmedia; p.15(TL): Shutterstock/racorn; p.16(TL): Shutterstock/2xSamara.com; p.16(BR): Shutterstock/BlueOrange Studio; p.17(TL): Alamy/MBI/Stockbroker; p.17(BL): Alamy/OJO Images Ltd/Robert Nicholas; p.17(BR): Alamy/Janine Wiedel Photolibrary/janine wiedel; p.18(B): Shutterstock/Alan49; p.19(BL): Alamy/ClassicStock/H. ARMSTRONG ROBERTS; p.20(B): Shutterstock/Alex Staroseltsev; p.21(TL): Shutterstock/Johnny Habell; p.22(CL): Shutterstock/Pavel L Photo and Video; p.22(T): Alamy/PCN Photography/PCN Black; p.23(CR): Shutterstock/Visionsi; p.23(TL): Alamy/Kumar Sriskandan; p.23(TR): Shutterstock/RubinowaDama; p.24(BR): Alamy/Johner Images; p.24(TR): Shutterstock/Anton Kudclin; p.25(TR): Alamy/Pontino; p.26(BL): Shutterstock/Magiara; p.28(BL): Alamy/Blend Images/Ronnie Kaufman/Larry Hirshowitz; p.28(TR): Alamy/Lou Linwei; p.29(CL): Shutterstock/Stuart Monk; p.29(1): Shutterstock/Matt Gibson; p.29(2): Shutterstock/LoloStock; p.29(3): Shutterstock/LauraDyer; p.29(4): Shutterstock/Panu Ruangjan; p.29(5): Shutterstock/italay; p.29(6): Shutterstock/Olha Insight; p.29(7): Shutterstock/wandee007; p.29(8): Shutterstock/Aleksey Stemmer; p.29(9): Shutterstock/Tiago M Nunes; p.30(BL): Shutterstock/MNBB Studio; p.31(TL): Alamy/Travel Pictures/Pictures Colour Library; p.31(B): Shutterstock/Olivier Le Queinec; p.32(B): Shutterstock/Bruce Rolff; p.33(CL): Shutterstock/Concept Photo.

Video stills by Rob Maidment and Sharp Focus Productions: p.30, 64, 66, 67, 68.

Filming in King's College by kind permission of the Provost and Scholars of King's College, Cambridge.

Illustrations by Vicky Woodgate p.12, 19.